THE OXFORD SHAKESPEARE

General Editor · Stanley Wells

THE OXFORD SHAKESPEARE

The Two Noble Kinsmen

BY WILLIAM SHAKESPEARE
AND JOHN FLETCHER

EDITED BY EUGENE M. WAITH

CLARENDON PRESS · OXFORD
1989

Oxford University Press, Walton Street, Oxford OX2 6DP

Oxford New York Toronto
Delhi Bombay Calcutta Madras Karachi
Petaling Jaya Singapore Hong Kong Tokyo
Nairobi Dar es Salaam Cape Town
Melbourne Auckland

and associated companies in
Berlin Ibadan

Oxford is a trade mark of Oxford University Press

Published in the United States by
Oxford University Press (USA)

© Oxford University Press 1989

British Library Cataloguing in Publication Data
Shakespeare, William, 1564–1616
The two noble kinsmen.—(The Oxford Shakespeare).
I. Title II. Fletcher, John, 1579–1625
III. Waith, Eugene M. (Eugene Mersereau)
822.3′3
ISBN 0–19–812939–4
ISBN 0–19–281498–2 Pbk

Library of Congress Cataloging in Publication Data
Shakespeare, William, 1564–1616
The two noble kinsmen/by William Shakespeare and John Fletcher; edited by
Eugene M. Waith. p.   cm.—(The Oxford Shakespeare)
Includes bibliographical references and index.
I. Fletcher, John, 1579–1625. Two noble kinsmen. II. Waith, Eugene M.
III. Title. IV. Series: Shakespeare, William, 1564–1616. Works. 1982.
822.3′3—dc19   PR2870.A2W35   1989   88–10008
ISBN 0–19–812939–4
ISBN 0–19–281498–2 (pbk.)

Typeset by the University Printing House, Oxford
Printed in Great Britain by
The Alden Press Ltd.
Oxford and London

PREFACE

My acknowledgement of indebtedness must begin with the General Editor, Stanley Wells, whose scrupulous oversight has saved me from many errors, and whose suggestions have been of enormous assistance. William Montgomery generously sent me proofs of his own edition of the play for the Oxford *Complete Works* before it appeared and answered a number of queries. With equal generosity Fredson Bowers, also working on an edition, shared with me his opinions on lineation and the division of certain scenes into prose and poetry. On these and other matters both Cyrus Hoy and Robert K. Turner were also most helpful. Derek Attridge and Edward Weismiller gave me valuable advice on metrics; Gail Kern Paster did some research for me at the Folger Library; and both Nicholas Brooke and Lee Bliss gave me answers to troublesome questions. Godfrey Brown very kindly wrote me at length about the history of the Betley window. I am much indebted to the staff of the Beinecke Rare Book and Manuscript Library for assisting my work, and also to Pamela Jordan of the Yale Drama Library. Finally, I thank Hugh Richmond and Paul Werstine for allowing me to quote from unpublished papers on the subject of this play.

EUGENE M. WAITH

CONTENTS

LIST OF ILLUSTRATIONS

INTRODUCTION

FOR many years *The Two Noble Kinsmen* has existed in an authorial no man's land, where it has shared part of the fate of Wordsworth's Lucy, who 'lived unknown' and whom there were consequently 'none to praise | And very few to love'. Surely one reason why the play has been rarely performed and seldom even read is the uncertainty about its authorship that has prevailed. It is not surprising that, if occasionally praised, it has been loved by very few; but as Wordsworth implies that if more people had trod their way to the springs of Dove, their acquaintance with Lucy might have led to a wider appreciation of her qualities, so I hope that greater familiarity with this play may lead to a recognition of its merits beyond the narrow circle of its editors and of a few admiring critics.

Early Publication and Performances

The play was entered in the Stationers' Register on 8 April 1634 by the printer, John Waterson, as 'a TragiComedy called the two noble kinsmen by Jo: ffletcher & Wm. Shakespeare'.[1] That same year the Quarto (Q) appeared with the title-page shown in Fig. 1,[2] where we are told that the play had been presented by the King's Men at Blackfriars, one of the 'private', or enclosed, London theatres. The first performance probably occurred in 1613 or early 1614. The morris dance in 3.5 had been presented as an antimasque in the *Masque of the Inner Temple and Gray's Inn* by Fletcher's collaborator, Francis Beaumont, on 20 February 1613 at Whitehall during the festivities for the marriage of King James's daughter, Princess Elizabeth, to Frederick, Elector Palatine.[3] And it seems likely that *The Two Noble Kinsmen* is

---

[1] S. Schoenbaum, *William Shakespeare: Records and Images* (New York and London, 1981), p. 226.

[2] Forty-five copies are known to survive. In preparing this edition I have used the facsimile edition of the Huntington Library copy in *Shakespeare's Plays in Quarto*, ed. Michael J. B. Allen and Kenneth Muir (Berkeley, Los Angeles, and London, 1981), pp. 837–81.

[3] Although we have no absolute proof that the masque preceded the play, it is

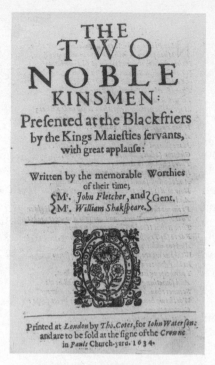

THE
TWO
NOBLE
KINSMEN:
Prefented at the Blackfriers
by the Kings Maiefties fervants,
with great applaufe:

Written by the memorable Worthies
of their time;
Mr. *John Fletcher*, and Gent.
Mr. *William Shakfpeare*.

Printed at *London* by *Tho.Cotes*, for *Iohn Waterfon*:
and are to be fold at the figne of the *Crowne*
in *Pauls* Church-yard. 1 6 3 4.

1. The title-page of the 1634 Quarto.

referred to in Ben Jonson's *Bartholomew Fair*, first performed on 31 October 1614. There the following exchange takes place:

QUARLOUS
. . . Well, my word is out of the *Arcadia*, then: 'Argalus'.
WINWIFE
And mine out of the play, 'Palamon'.

$$(4.3.63-5)^1$$

It has been pointed out that in Samuel Daniel's pastoral tragi-comedy, *The Queen's Arcadia* (1605), there is a character named 'Palaemon' (though none named 'Argalus'), but I think it is most unlikely that Jonson's reference is to that play, which was performed only once, for the Queen and her ladies, by university students at Christ Church, Oxford. It is also worth noting that in Daniel's play 'Palaemon' is always accented on the second

unthinkable that Beaumont would have offered the court an antimasque based on a play that had been publicly performed.

[1] *Bartholomew Fair*, ed. E. M. Waith (New Haven and London, 1963).

syllable. Had Jonson intended a reference to Daniel's character, he would probably have indicated the pronunciation by a different spelling.

A fragmentary record from the King's Office of the Revels seems to show that *The Two Noble Kinsmen* was revived for performance at court in 1619,[1] and since two stage directions in Q (see notes on 4.2.70.1 and 5.3.0.2) include the names of actors who were with the King's Men in 1625–6, there must have been another revival in those years, probably after November 1625, when the theatres reopened after eight months during which the death of King James and an outbreak of the plague had kept them shut. No other seventeenth-century performances are known.

So far the record is fairly straightforward and self-consistent. It does not continue so. On 31 October 1646 Waterson transferred to Humphrey Moseley his rights in three plays by 'Mr fflesher', including 'the Noble kinsman', and by 1653 Moseley was advertising 'The two noble Kinsmen, a Comedy written by Francis Beaumont and John Fletcher, Gent.' With regard to these attributions it is important to recall that in 1646 Moseley was planning a collected edition of what had come to be known as the 'Beaumont and Fletcher' plays although Beaumont's hand is found in only about a quarter of them, while several were written by Fletcher alone and many more by Fletcher with other collaborators. The ignorance or casual disregard of the true authorship of these plays may help to explain the attribution of *The Two Noble Kinsmen* to Fletcher alone in 1646 and to Beaumont and Fletcher later. In the 1646 list only one of the plays (*Monsieur Thomas*) is actually by Fletcher alone; one other (*The Elder Brother*) is by Fletcher and Massinger. When Moseley published *Comedies and Tragedies Written by Francis Beaumont and John Fletcher, Gentlemen* in 1647 the volume contained no plays that had previously been published, so *The Two Noble Kinsmen* waited for its second edition until 1679 when *Fifty Comedies and Tragedies, Written by Francis Beaumont and John Fletcher, Gentlemen* (F) appeared. This part of the publication record attests to Fletcher's, but not to Shakespeare's, authorship. To the continuing discussion of this topic we must now turn.

---

[1] E. K. Chambers, *William Shakespeare: A Study of Facts and Problems*, 2 vols. (Oxford, 1930), ii. 346.

Authorship

The most obvious reason for doubting Shakespeare's collaboration is the fact that *The Two Noble Kinsmen* was not included in any of the seventeenth-century folio editions of his works. Although it is impossible to say why Shakespeare's fellow actors, John Heminges and Henry Condell, the editors of the First Folio (1623), passed over this play, which belonged to the company, it can be pointed out that they omitted *Pericles*, which had already been published as by Shakespeare, and is now generally thought to be, at least in part, his. They also omitted *Sir Thomas More*, of which Shakespeare probably wrote one scene. They seem to have encountered copyright difficulties with *Troilus and Cressida*; its printing was interrupted, and *Timon of Athens* was placed where *Troilus and Cressida* was first intended to go. Finally, however, as Kenneth Muir says in his introduction, they 'obtained a manuscript of the play, so that they could claim not to be simply reprinting the Quarto text'.[1] It is possible that Heminges and Condell could not get the copyright for *The Two Noble Kinsmen*. Sometimes the manuscript of a play was temporarily unavailable, as was the case with Fletcher's *The Wild Goose Chase* when Moseley published the first Beaumont and Fletcher folio (1647). When the second issue of the Shakespeare Third Folio appeared in 1664 *Pericles* was added to the corpus along with six other plays that had been published as Shakespeare's, but in which it is almost certain that he had no hand. If Philip Chetwinde, the publisher of this volume, thought of including *The Two Noble Kinsmen* with these others, he would presumably have found that the copyright was held by the widow of Humphrey Moseley, who apparently transferred it later to the publishers of the second Beaumont and Fletcher folio (1679).[2] There are thus several possible explanations of the exclusion of the play from the Shakespeare folios even if members of Shakespeare's company knew that he was a collaborator.

The use of Shakespeare's name or his initials on the title-pages of plays he did not write[3] has led some commentators to suggest

[1] *Troilus and Cressida* (Oxford, 1982), p. 3.
[2] The point is made by Paul Bertram in *Shakespeare and The Two Noble Kinsmen* (New Brunswick, NJ, 1965), p. 16.
[3] There were six instances before the publication of the First Folio. In the latter half of the century a few more plays were attributed to him in publishers' lists or on title-pages.

that in the case of *The Two Noble Kinsmen* his name was added
to Fletcher's merely to attract more buyers. This explanation is
made unlikely by the reliability of the publisher, John Waterson,
who published several other plays of the King's Men, none of
them falsely attributed.[1] The worst that can be said of him is that
in referring to collaborative plays he sometimes omitted the name
of one collaborator, as in the case of *The Elder Brother* and (in
the 1646 entry in the Stationers' Register) *The Two Noble Kinsmen*.
He never seems to have been guilty of taking Shakespeare's name
in vain, nor can the commercial value of the name in 1634 be
given as a reason for putting it on the quarto title-page. By that
time Fletcher's name was every bit as good, and Waterson put
it first.

None of the evidence reviewed so far presents a compelling
reason to doubt Shakespeare's authorship of part of the play;
certain considerations make it seem probable. If we ask why
Shakespeare, at the height of his career, should have decided to
collaborate with a younger playwright, there is a plausible
answer. Shakespeare's biographers agree in general with the
statement of his first critical editor, Nicholas Rowe:

The latter part of his life was spent, as all men of good sense will wish
theirs may be, in ease, retirement, and the conversation of his friends.
He had the good fortune to gather an estate equal to his occasion, and,
in that, to his wish; and is said to have spent some years before his
death at his native Stratford.[2]

Although evidence that Shakespeare was spending increasing
amounts of time in Stratford is sometimes used to support the
fanciful interpretation of Prospero's renunciation of his magic in
The Tempest—his vow to break his staff and drown his book
(5.1.54, 57)—as Shakespeare's farewell to the stage, there can
be little doubt that he continued to write for the King's Men,
since *Henry VIII* (or *All is True*), a performance of which set fire
to the Globe theatre on 29 June 1613, was probably written
earlier that year.[3] As S. Schoenbaum puts it, 'At most, then, in

---

[1] Among others, John Webster's *The Duchess of Malfi* and Fletcher's *The Elder
Brother* and *Monsieur Thomas*.

[2] 'Some Account of the Life, &c. of Mr. William Shakespear' in *Works* (1709),
p. xxxv.

[3] See the introduction by R. A. Foakes to his edition (reissued with corrections,
London and Cambridge, Mass., 1964), p. xxxiv.

The Tempest he is saying *au revoir* rather than adieu'.[1] It also seems possible that in order to reduce his playwriting obligations he decided to share the work with another playwright, and John Fletcher, the rising star of his company, would have been a suitable choice as a collaborator. With Beaumont, Fletcher had already written such highly successful plays as *Philaster*, *The Maid's Tragedy*, and *A King and No King*. From his point of view collaboration with the leading dramatist of the period would have been most desirable, especially since Beaumont, at about this time, married and moved out of London.

The Two Noble Kinsmen may not be the only play on which Shakespeare and Fletcher collaborated. Since the middle of the nineteenth century many critics have argued that Fletcher's style is detectable in many scenes of *Henry VIII*. The strongest case for Fletcher's participation has been made by Cyrus Hoy, based on his linguistic analysis of all the plays to which Fletcher's name has been attached. In the final instalment of his seven-part study he writes: 'Those who would deny [Fletcher's] presence in the play altogether are wrong to do so, for he is assuredly there. Those who award him ten and one-half of the play's sixteen scenes (the usual ascription) claim too much'.[2] Even R. A. Foakes, the strongest recent defender of Shakespeare's sole authorship, concedes in the second issue of his edition that Hoy's is a 'sane conclusion' (p. xxvii). And there is yet another play which they may have written together, the mysterious *Cardenio*, of which there are tantalizing records but no surviving text. In 1612–13 the King's Men twice performed at court a play called *Cardenno* or *Cardenna*, and on 9 September 1653 Humphrey Moseley registered 'The History of Cardennio, by Mr. Fletcher. & Shakespeare' (Chambers, i. 538–9; ii. 343). It is assumed that the source was the story of Cardenio in *Don Quixote*, which was published in Thomas Shelton's English translation in 1612. Lewis Theobald later wrote a play called *Double Falsehood*, produced in 1727, based on this story, and claimed that it was his adaptation of a Shakespeare play of which he owned manuscript copies. No such manuscripts ever turned up, and Theobald's account has aroused

---

[1] *William Shakespeare: A Documentary Life* (Oxford, 1975), p. 228.

[2] 'The Shares of Fletcher and his Collaborators in the Beaumont and Fletcher Canon' appeared in a series of articles in *Studies in Bibliography*, 8, 9, 11, 12, 13, 14, 15 (1956–62); the comment on *Henry VIII* is in vol. 15, p. 79.

much scepticism, but the records of performance and Moseley's entry in the Stationers' Register make it conceivable that Theobald was telling the truth. If Shakespeare indeed collaborated with Fletcher on *Henry VIII* in 1613, as I believe he did, and possibly on the lost *Cardenio*, it is the more likely that the two playwrights also worked together in that year on *The Two Noble Kinsmen*.

Fletcher's participation is usually, but not universally, accepted today, the conspicuous dissenter from the consensus being Paul Bertram, who believes that Shakespeare wrote the entire play. I return to his argument later. Most of the authorship controversy has focused on the extent to which various scenes of the play correspond with the acknowledged work of Shakespeare, and, among those who deny him a part in the play, on correspondences with the work of other playwrights such as Beaumont or Massinger, both known collaborators of Fletcher's, or Chapman.

It would be inappropriate to recapitulate the full history of the controversy, which can be read in the introduction to Harold Littledale's invaluable edition (pp. 69*–82*),[1] or in Bertram (pp. 197–243), and is summarized in the annotated bibliography by D. V. Erdman and E. G. Fogel in *Evidence for Authorship* (Ithaca, NY, 1966), pp. 486–94. It is useful, however, to have in mind the broad historical outlines and important to understand the grounds for the various conflicting opinions.

Published regularly in collected editions of Beaumont and Fletcher from the seventeeth century to the present time, *The Two Noble Kinsmen* was not included in a collected edition of Shakespeare until Charles Knight placed it among the 'Doubtful Plays' in his *Pictorial Edition* (1839–41). From then on it appeared in some Shakespeare editions but was excluded from others, such as the influential Cambridge and Globe in the nineteenth century or the Pelican and Arden in the twentieth. Sometimes it was placed in a volume of 'Doubtful Plays', as in Knight's *Pictorial* and Henry Tyrrell's edition (n.d., 1853?), or in William Gilmore Simms's *A Supplement to the Plays of William Shakspeare* ('The First American Edition', New York, 1848), or still more damningly in *The Shakespeare Apocrypha*, edited by C. F. Tucker Brooke (Oxford, 1908).

[1] The text appeared in successive publications of the New Shakspere Society, London, 1876; the introduction in 1885.

The differing opinions of Shakespeare's editors on the matter of his participation in *The Two Noble Kinsmen* are revealed by these various tactics. There were also sharp differences of opinion among the editors of Beaumont and Fletcher. Henry Weber, in his 1812 edition of *The Works of Beaumont and Fletcher*, reviewed the arguments of the eighteenth-century editors and, influenced by Charles Lamb's comments, to which we must later return, he not only came out firmly for the title-page attribution, but was the first to attempt a scene-by-scene division between the two collaborators. As a believer in Shakespeare's authorship he was followed by Alexander Dyce in his edition of Beaumont and Fletcher (1843–6). Dyce was a 'convertite', who had said in a 'Memoir' published in the 'Aldine Edition' of *The Poems of Shakespeare* (1832): 'I do not think our poet had any share in its [*The Two Noble Kinsmen*'s] composition: but I must add, that Mr. C. Lamb (a great authority in such matters) inclines to a different opinion' (p. xliii n. 65). By 1846 he had read not only Lamb's comments but also *A Letter on Shakspere's Authorship of The Two Noble Kinsmen* by William Spalding (Edinburgh, 1833), and wrote: 'My own opinion is, that Shakespeare undoubtedly wrote all those portions of *The Two Noble Kinsmen* which are assigned to him by Mr. Spalding'.[1] He left the play out of his first edition of Shakespeare (1857), but when he included it in his second edition in Volume 8 (1866) he became the first editor of Shakespeare to do so without placing it in a group of 'doubtful' plays. By this time the controversy had been joined by many who were not editors and it has continued down to the present day. It has occasionally been enlivened by dramatic conversions such as Dyce's, from disbelief to belief, or Spalding's and F. J. Furnivall's from belief to scepticism.[2]

This brief account of the controversy raises, first of all, the question of why so many connoisseurs of Elizabethan drama denied Shakespeare a part in this play. Some of them found in the non-Fletcherian scenes a degree of indecency of which they believed Shakespeare incapable. Robert Boyle pointed to the First

---

[1] 'Some Account of the Lives and Writings of Beaumont and Fletcher' (issued with the final volume of the *Works*), p. lxxxii.

[2] See Furnivall's 'Forewords' to the New Shakspere Society's edition of Spalding's *Letter* (London, 1876), pp. vii–ix.

Queen's allusions to the pleasures of the marriage bed (1.1.175 ff.) as a passage Shakespeare never would have written.[1] Others thought that the characterization was unlike Shakespeare. Palamon and Arcite were not sufficiently differentiated; Emilia was unworthy of comparison with Shakespearian heroines.[2] Tucker Brooke enthusiastically supported Furnivall, to whom the Emilia of 5.3, unable to decide between Palamon and Arcite, seemed like 'a silly lady's-maid or shop-girl, not knowing her own mind', and hence not a creation of Shakespeare's.[3] Charles Knight persuaded himself that the presence of 'general truths and reflections' in the scenes assigned to Shakespeare was more likely an indication of George Chapman's authorship.[4] One of the more curious arguments against Shakespeare's authorship was that of the famous eighteenth-century editor, George Steevens, who contended that the sheer number of Shakespearian echoes in the play pointed to authorship by an imitator, since Shakespeare would not imitate himself. All of these arguments rest on unusually subjective convictions about what Shakespeare would not have done; in some cases the critic's personal standard of moral or social propriety seems to have been the determining factor.

Less subjective, and indeed in some cases aiming at scientific objectivity, are the arguments that have been made on stylistic grounds for one author or another. Thomas De Quincey made one of the firmest commitments to Shakespeare (and one of the most laudatory comments on the play) in a note to a review in *Blackwood's Magazine* (24 (1828)) of Whateley's *Elements of Rhetoric* (1828). Explaining his omission of Shakespeare from a survey of English rhetoric that he had just given, he wrote:

Shakspeare is no doubt a rhetorician, *majorum gentium*; but he is so much more, that scarcely an instance is to be found of his rhetoric which does not pass by fits into a higher element of eloquence or poetry. The first and the last acts, for instance, of *The Two Noble Kinsmen*, which,

---

[1] 'On Massinger and *The Two Noble Kinsmen*', *The New Shakspere Society's Transactions, 1880–6*, 371–99; p. 383. Boyle believed that Massinger, who 'had a very low ideal of female nature', was the author (p. 391).

[2] See, for example, Henry D. Gray, 'Beaumont and *The Two Noble Kinsmen*', *Philological Quarterly*, 2 (1923), 112–31. Gray thought that the non-Fletcherian scenes were probably either an imitation or a reworking of Shakespeare by Beaumont.

[3] *The Shakespeare Apocrypha*, p. xliii. Furnivall expressed this opinion in his 'Forewords', p. vi.

[4] *Pictorial Edition*, v. 185.

in point of composition, is perhaps the most superb work in the language, and beyond all doubt from the loom of Shakspeare, would have been the most gorgeous rhetoric, had they not happened to be something far better.[1]

He then cited 'the supplications of the widowed queens to Theseus, the invocations of their tutelar divinities by Palamon and Arcite', and 'the death of Arcite' as examples of Shakespeare at his best.

Most identifications based on stylistic evidence take off from the perception of two distinct poetic styles in the play. One of the earliest and most sensitive comments on the two styles is Charles Lamb's in his *Specimens of English Dramatic Poets Who Lived about the Time of Shakspeare* (1808), in which he included much of 1.1, the dialogue of Emilia and Hippolyta from 1.3, and the opening dialogue of Palamon and Arcite in prison in 2.2. Following the last selection he wrote:

This scene bears indubitable marks of Fletcher: the two which precede it give strong countenance to the tradition that Shakspeare had a hand in this play. The same judgment may be formed of the death of Arcite, and some other passages, not here given. They have a luxuriance in them which strongly resembles Shakspeare's manner in those parts of his plays where, the progress of the interest being subordinate, the poet was at leisure for description. I might fetch instances from Troilus and Timon. That Fletcher should have copied Shakspeare's manner through so many entire scenes (which is the theory of Mr. Steevens) is not very probable; that he could have done it with such facility is to me not certain. His ideas moved slow; his versification, though sweet, is tedious, it stops every moment; he lays line upon line, making up one after the other, adding image to image so deliberately that we see where they join: Shakspeare mingles every thing, he runs line into line, embarrasses sentences and metaphors; before one idea has burst its shell, another is hatched and clamorous for disclosure.[2]

Lamb also commented on the differences between Shakespeare's and Fletcher's styles following a selection from a scene (4.1) usually accepted as Fletcher's in *Thierry and Theodoret*. After praising the characterization, he said:

Yet, noble as the whole scene is, it must be confessed that the manner

[1] De Quincey reprinted the review as an essay entitled 'Rhetoric' in his collected works. See *De Quincey's Writings*, vol. xi (Boston, 1853), p. 280.
[2] *The Works of Charles and Mary Lamb*, ed. E. V. Lucas, 7 vols., vol. iv (London, 1904), p. 341.

of it, compared with Shakspeare's finest scenes, is slow and languid. Its motion is circular, not progressive. Each line revolves on itself in a sort of separate orbit. They do not join into one another like a running hand. Every step that we go we are stopped to admire some single object, like walking in beautiful scenery with a guide. This slowness I shall elsewhere have occasion to remark as characteristic of Fletcher. Another striking difference perceivable between Fletcher and Shakspeare, is the fondness of the former for unnatural and violent situations . . . (*Works*, iv. 329)

Spalding, in his scene-by-scene analysis of *The Two Noble Kinsmen*, elaborated on Lamb's distinctions, commenting on Shakespeare's love of metaphor, his pointedness, brevity, and occasional obscurity, and his 'broken' versification, 'full of pauses' and 'sparing of double terminations to his verses'. Fletcher is more diffuse, painting 'illustrative pictures with a careful hand and by repeated touches'; he is 'spirited almost to excess', his versification is 'sweet', and his 'rhythm is of a newer and smoother cast, often keeping the lines distinct and without breaks through whole speeches, abounding in double endings . . .'[1] In the introduction to his Signet edition Clifford Leech seems to have had a very similar distinction in mind when he contrasted the 'complex, "knotted" verse that is close to Shakespeare's in his later years' with 'the open-textured, casual style that Beaumont and Fletcher developed'.[2]

From the first, one of the differences between the two styles was felt to be rhythmical, and several different metrical tests were applied to each scene to determine how many lines were end-stopped, how many contained extra syllables, and how many ended with extra syllables constituting double endings. While both authors admitted extra syllables into their blank verses, Fletcher's lines were more often end-stopped, and he was conspicuously prone to double endings in which the final syllable required almost as heavy an accent as the preceding syllable. The following line from 2.5 of *The Woman's Prize, or The Tamer Tamed* (Fletcher's answer to *The Taming of the Shrew*), written not long before *The Two Noble Kinsmen*, exemplifies emphasis on the final extra syllable:

As good as the wise sailor's wife, and young still.[3]

[1] *Letter on Shakspere's Authorship*, New Shakspere Society edition, pp. 11–38.
[2] Leech, p. 1616.
[3] *The Dramatic Works in the Beaumont and Fletcher Canon*, ed. Fredson Bowers,

Lines with this metrical pattern occur occasionally in the plays of Chapman and Jonson and in Shakespeare's late plays, but much less frequently than in Fletcher's.[1] It therefore seemed significant that the proportions of end-stopped lines, and of lines with extra syllables, double endings, and especially double endings with an emphasized final syllable differed markedly in two sets of scenes in *The Two Noble Kinsmen*. In one set was a rhythm similar to Shakespeare's in his last plays, and in another set a rhythm similar to Fletcher's in plays written wholly by him. The conclusions suggested by this metrical evidence appeared to be confirmed by A. C. Bradley's observation that Shakespeare ended blank verse scenes with a half-line more often than his contemporaries and that in *The Two Noble Kinsmen* a strikingly high proportion of the scenes attributed to Shakespeare ended in this way, whereas very few of those attributed to Fletcher did so.[2] Richard Proudfoot noted an inconsistency in the pronunciation of the name 'Pirithous' which provided a further confirmation of the division between two authors: in the scenes attributed to Shakespeare it is trisyllabic and is accented 'Pìrithòus', while in the scenes attributed to Fletcher it is tetrasyllabic, accented 'Pirìthoùs'.[3]

Bertram, arguing for Shakespeare's authorship of the entire

vol. iv (Cambridge, London, New York, and Melbourne, 1979); all quotations from the 'Beaumont and Fletcher' plays are from volumes of this edition. Charles M. Gayley is one of many who commented on this characteristic of Fletcher's versification (*Francis Beaumont: Dramatist* (London, 1914), p. 243). See also E. H. C. Oliphant, *The Plays of Beaumont and Fletcher* (New Haven, London, and Oxford, 1927) pp. 31–7.

[1] Ants Oras cites Fletcher's use of extra monosyllables, and in particular those that are 'heavily weighted', as a means of determining Fletcher's and Shakespeare's shares in *Henry VIII*; see '"Extra Monosyllables" in *Henry VIII* and the Problem of Authorship', *JEGP*, 52 (1953), 198–213. He provides statistical analyses of *Henry VIII*, *Kinsmen*, late plays by Shakespeare and plays by Fletcher alone. Also see Kenneth Muir's summary of metrical tests in 'Shakespeare's Hand in *The Two Noble Kinsmen*', *Shakespeare as Collaborator* (London, 1960), pp. 98–101. I am indebted to Mary D. Coulter, who discusses the use of extra syllables in the verses of several dramatists of this period in her unpublished Ph.D. dissertation, 'The English Pentameter in Non-Dramatic and Dramatic Verse *c.*1590–1640' (George Washington University, 1982); and to Derek Attridge for his discussion of iambic verse in *The Rhythms of English Poetry* (London and New York, 1982) and for his kindness in answering my queries.

[2] 'Scene-Endings in Shakespeare and in *The Two Noble Kinsmen*', in *A Miscellany* (London, 1929), pp. 218–24.

[3] Introduction to *The Two Noble Kinsmen* (Lincoln, Nebr., 1970), p. xix.

play, sought to discredit metrical evidence of two styles by charging that 'metrical statistics collected from this play have not been based on the original quarto text but on one or another of the various nineteenth-century editions' (p. 22) in which prose has been made into verse, verse sometimes relined, and emendations made which altered the syllabic count. Bertram's complaint about the treatment of the quarto text was well founded, and it is true that some of the metrical tests were made on edited texts, but not all of them were. Littledale refers, for instance, to J. K. Ingram's tests made on 'a literal transcript of the Quarto of 1634' (p. 20*). When Littledale's own count of double endings in comparable scenes such as 1.2 and 2.2 (both of which present Palamon and Arcite in conversation) is checked, using the quarto text, the figures differ only slightly: 32 instead of Littledale's 35 double endings in the 116 lines of 1.2, and 163 instead of 159 double endings in the 281 lines of 2.2—differences easily accounted for by the inevitable slight variations between two readings of certain lines. What stands out in such a comparison is the strikingly larger proportion of double endings in 2.2. It is difficult to believe that one author would vary his versification to this extent in certain scenes of the play, and even more difficult to believe that the variation would correspond closely to the practice of another author. It is only in scenes originally printed as mixed prose and verse and variously treated by succeeding editors that metrical statistics are apt to be invalid.

An important feature of Fletcher's style, which strongly influences what most readers of Fletcher have considered his distinctive rhythm, is his exploitation of some of the showier rhetorical devices, and in particular the patterns of repetition, which appear even more frequently in his verses than in those of his contemporaries, including Shakespeare. In *The Arte of English Poesie* (1589) George Puttenham says that by alliteration (which he calls *parimion*), the most obvious form of repetition, 'ye do . . . notably affect th'ear', and he places the several patterns of *verbal* repetition first among the rhetorical figures which affect both the ear and the mind.[1] Cyrus Hoy discusses Fletcher's use of these patterns in an important article on 'The Language of Fletcherian

[1] *The Arte of English Poesie*, ed. G. D. Willcock and A. Walker (Cambridge, 1936), pp. 174, 198 ff.

Tragicomedy', where he describes and illustrates each of them.[1]
A speech by the frustrated Petruchio of *The Woman's Prize*
contains a fair sample of some of them, reinforced by alliteration,
and also displays the frequent use of end-stopped lines and double
endings discussed above:

> Say, I am made an ass, then;
> I know her aim: may I with reputation
> (Answer me this) with safety of mine honour,
> (After the mighty manage of my first wife,
> Which was indeed a fury to this filly,
> After my twelve strong labours to reclaim her,
> Which would have made Don Hercules horn-mad,
> And hid him in his hide) suffer this Sicely,
> Ere she have warmed my sheets, ere grappled with me,
> This pink, this painted foist, this cockle-boat,
> To hang her fights out, and defie me friends,
> A well-known man of war? if this be equal,
> And I may suffer, say, and I have done.
>
> (2.6.8–20)

A similar rhetoric and rhythm characterize Palamon's speech
when Theseus interrupts the fight in the woods:

> Hold thy word, Theseus;
> We are certainly both traitors, both despisers
> Of thee and of thy goodness. I am Palamon,
> That cannot love thee, he that broke thy prison—
> Think well what that deserves—and this is Arcite:
> A bolder traitor never trod thy ground,
> A falser nev'r seemed friend. This is the man
> Was begged and banished, this is he contemns thee
> And what thou dar'st do, and in this disguise,
> Against thy own edict, follows thy sister,
> That fortunate bright star, the fair Emilia . . .
>
> (3.6.136–46)

Arcite follows him with:

> As I love most, and in that faith will perish,
> As I have brought my life here to confirm it,
> As I have served her truest, worthiest,

---

[1] In *Mirror up to Shakespeare*, ed. J. C. Gray (Toronto, Buffalo, and London, 1984), pp. 99–113. See also Waith, *The Pattern of Tragicomedy in Beaumont and Fletcher* (New Haven and London, 1952), p. 192.

> As I dare kill this cousin that denies it,
> So let me be most traitor, and ye please me.
>
> (ll. 163–7)

Palamon's speech may be compared with one he makes earlier, when he discovers Arcite in the woods. It is also characterized by rhetorical extravagance, and contains one conspicuous example of repetition, yet is noticeably different in the greater number of run-on lines, less alliteration, and a less insistent rhythm:

> Traitor kinsman,
> Thou shouldst perceive my passion if these signs
> Of prisonment were off me, and this hand
> But owner of a sword. By all oaths in one,
> I and the justice of my love would make thee
> A confessed traitor, O thou most perfidious
> That ever gently looked, the void'st of honour
> That ev'r bore gentle token, falsest cousin
> That ever blood made kin! Call'st thou her thine?
> I'll prove it in my shackles, with these hands,
> Void of appointment, that thou liest, and art
> A very thief in love, a chaffy lord,
> Not worth the name of villain.
>
> (3.1.30–42)

Here and elsewhere there is a sufficient overlapping of the two styles so that in listening to the play one is not much aware of differences between them, though the differences appear to me incontestable.[1] Another illustration of them is provided by comparison of the two scenes in which Theseus is begged to change his mind. First the climax of the intercession in the opening scene:

> HIPPOLYTA (*to Theseus*)   Though much unlike
> You should be so transported, as much sorry
> I should be such a suitor, yet I think
> Did I not by th'abstaining of my joy,
> Which breeds a deeper longing, cure their surfeit,
> That craves a present med'cine, I should pluck
> All ladies' scandal on me. ⌈*She kneels*⌉ Therefore, sir,

---

[1] See my 'Shakespeare and Fletcher on Love and Friendship', *Shakespeare Studies*, 18 (1986), 235–49; reprinted in Waith, *Patterns and Perspectives in English Renaissance Drama* (Newark, Del., 1988), pp. 289–303.

As I shall here make trial of my prayers,
Either presuming them to have some force,
Or sentencing for aye their vigour dumb,
Prorogue this business we are going about, and hang
Your shield afore your heart, about that neck
Which is my fee, and which I freely lend
To do these poor queens service.
ALL THE QUEENS (*to Emilia*)   O, help now!
Our cause cries for your knee.
EMILIA (*to Theseus, kneeling*)   If you grant not
My sister her petition in that force,
With that celerity and nature which
She makes it in, from henceforth I'll not dare
To ask you anything, nor be so hardy
Ever to take a husband.

(1.1.186–205)

Then the final pleas to spare the kinsmen when Theseus has
come upon their fight in the woods:

HIPPOLYTA   Sir, by our tie of marriage—
EMILIA
By your own spotless honour—
HIPPOLYTA   By that faith,
That fair hand, and that honest heart you gave me—
EMILIA
By that you would have pity in another,
By your own virtues infinite—
HIPPOLYTA   By valour,
By all the chaste nights I have ever pleased you—
THESEUS
These are strange conjurings.
PIRITHOUS (*kneeling*)   Nay then, I'll in too.
By all our friendship, sir, by all our dangers,
By all you love most, wars and this sweet lady—
EMILIA
By that you would have trembled to deny
A blushing maid—
HIPPOLYTA   By your own eyes, by strength,
In which you swore I went beyond all women,
Almost all men, and yet I yielded, Theseus—
PIRITHOUS
To crown all this, by your most noble soul,
Which cannot want due mercy, I beg first—

HIPPOLYTA
　Next hear my prayers—
EMILIA　　　　　　　　　Last let me entreat, sir—
PIRITHOUS
　For mercy.
HIPPOLYTA　Mercy.
EMILIA　　　　　　　Mercy on these princes.
　　　　　　　　　　　　　(3.6.195–211)

The chorus of pleas in the second passage is as typical of Fletcher's repetitive rhetoric ('he lays line upon line', Lamb said), as Hippolyta's speech in the first passage is typical of what Leech called 'the complex "knotted" verse that is close to Shakespeare's in his later years'.

Vocabulary tests have also been used to determine authorship. A. C. Hart found that with respect to the frequency of words not previously used by Shakespeare the scenes in *The Two Noble Kinsmen* attributed to him corresponded closely to the plays of his last period, whereas in the scenes attributed to Fletcher the frequency was far greater.[1] Another test that has been used successfully on plays of uncertain authorship is based on a writer's linguistic preferences. Fletcher's fondness for *ye* in place of *you*, for example, and for the contraction *'em* has long been noticed. From a careful count of the instances of such preferences Cyrus Hoy has been able to allocate the shares of the various collaborators in the plays published as by Beaumont and Fletcher in the Folio of 1679.[2] In the case of *The Two Noble Kinsmen*, however, the linguistic evidence is not conclusive. The linguistic preferences in the section attributed to Shakespeare, while they accord with his, do not unmistakably point to him, and although all the instances of *ye* in the play occur in the section attributed to Fletcher, there are fewer of them than would be expected. The relative infrequency of this form may be explained by a hypothetical history of the text which will be given later. One can only conclude with Hoy that his statistics support the stylistic evidence of two authors and, without proving the attribution to Shakespeare and Fletcher, accord with it.

The case for Shakespeare's participation in the play has been

---

[1] 'Shakespeare and the Vocabulary of *The Two Noble Kinsmen*', in *Shakespeare and the Homilies* (Oxford, 1934), pp. 242–56.
[2] See p. 6 n. 2; *Kinsmen* is treated in vol. 15, pp. 71–6.

persuasively argued by Marco Mincoff and Kenneth Muir on the basis of imagery characteristic of him,[1] and they have both shown that the characterization, said by some critics to be quite unlike Shakespeare's, is in fact very similar to that in his other late plays. There are many echoes of passages in both Shakespeare and Fletcher,[2] a few of which are mentioned in the notes of this edition, but parallel passages are notoriously fallible indicators of authorship.[3]

The strongest case for dividing the authorship between Fletcher and Shakespeare can be made by comparing parallel scenes such as the two intercessions with Theseus (in 1.1 and 3.6), discussed above, the dialogues between Palamon and Arcite in Thebes (1.2) and in Theseus' prison (2.2), their encounters in the woods (in 3.1, 3.3, and 3.6), and Emilia's soliloquies (in 4.2 and 5.3). The kinsmen are introduced in a scene (1.2) which has no source in Chaucer but serves the important function of establishing the basis of their friendship as a shared ideal of virtuous conduct. The prison scene illustrates this friendship by a series of increasingly extravagant protestations up to the moment when they see Emilia in the garden beneath their window, fall in love with her, and instantly become angry rivals. It is not only the rhetoric and the versification of the second scene which are characteristic of Fletcher but also the theatrical abruptness of the change in their

[1] Marco Mincoff, 'The Authorship of *The Two Noble Kinsmen*', *English Studies*, 33 (1952), 97–115; Kenneth Muir, chapters on *The Two Noble Kinsmen* in *Shakespeare as Collaborator*, pp. 98–147. I am less persuaded by the evidence of 'image-clusters', the closely associated images and ideas described by E. A. Armstrong in *Shakespeare's Imagination* (London, 1946), on which Muir places considerable emphasis. In some cases it is difficult to prove that the association exists, and, as Proudfoot points out (p. xviii), there is nothing to prevent one poet's image-cluster becoming 'the imaginative property of another who knows his work'.

[2] Littledale gives a number of these in the notes and introduction to his edition.

[3] In a paper read to the Shakespeare Association of America during its 1986 meeting in Montreal, Donald K. Hedrick proposed that Nathan Field, who collaborated with Fletcher in the *Four Plays, or Moral Representations, in One* (1612), and with Fletcher and Massinger in *The Honest Man's Fortune* (1613), was the author of the non-Fletcherian parts of *Kinsmen*. His argument, based to a considerable extent on his belief that the rivalry between Palamon and Arcite is a dramatization of the competition between the collaborators, does not seem to me convincing. The linguistic preferences recorded by Hoy for Field writing alone or in collaboration (*Studies in Bibliography*, 12 (1959), 91–108) do not correspond with those in the non-Fletcherian scenes of *Kinsmen*, nor do those scenes resemble Field's dramatic work elsewhere.

relationship. Startling dramatic turns such as this are conspicuous features of the plays Fletcher wrote alone and of those he wrote with collaborators. The careful preparation of the theme of friendship in the earlier scene is equally characteristic of Shakespeare. In the margin of *The Two Noble Kinsmen* in an edition of Beaumont and Fletcher which Lamb had used in assembling his *Specimens* Coleridge wrote:

On comparing the prison scene in this act (II) with the dialogue between the same speakers in the first [act], I can scarcely retain a doubt as to the first act's having been written by Shakespeare: assuredly not by Beaumont or Fletcher.[1]

Palamon's opening speech when he first encounters Arcite in the woods (in 3.1) has been cited above as an example of Shakespearian rhetoric. In *The Knight's Tale* Arcite replies to Palamon's angry denunciation with a boast that Palamon would never leave the wood alive if he were armed, but since Palamon is a 'worthy knight' and wants to settle their rival claims by combat, Arcite will bring him weapons the following day (ll. A 1574–1619). In the play this brief exchange is augmented to a dialogue of over ninety lines in which Arcite's chivalry is presented as a striking contrast to Palamon's hostility. Indeed Arcite is so consistently restrained and gentle in his answers that toward the end of the scene Palamon exclaims:

> O you heavens, dares any
> So noble bear a guilty business? None
> But only Arcite . . .
>
> (ll. 89–91)

Thus the motif of chivalry is given greater importance and the conflict between friendship and love-inspired rivalry is clearly enunciated in Palamon's troubled cry, which has no parallel in the source. Once again the groundwork is laid for the thematic developments of later scenes.

Nor is there anything in *The Knight's Tale* corresponding to the next encounter in the woods (in 3.3), in which Arcite brings food and wine to give Palamon strength for the combat. Here Arcite's chivalrous impulse leads to a surprising reassertion of their

---

[1] *Coleridge's Miscellaneous Criticism*, ed. Thomas M. Raysor (London, 1936), p. 92.

friendship and brief suspension of their rivalry. Arcite courteously fends off some insulting remarks, persuades Palamon to sit down, and bids him 'Drink a good hearty draught, it breeds good blood, man' (l. 17). Soon Palamon is proposing a toast 'to the wenches | We have known in our days!' (ll. 29–30), and they indulge in reminiscences of their amours, in which each makes broad hints about the indiscretions of the other. Suddenly, however, Palamon turns angry again, and the scene ends with threats, as Arcite leaves to get armour.

Not only is this scene very different in tone from the first encounter, but it contains one of the few examples of characterization that cannot be reconciled with information given in another scene. Palamon's jovial references to his affairs with wenches do not square with his later protestations of purity in his prayer to Venus (5.1.95–106). Both R. A. Foakes and Lee Bliss have commented recently on the special concern with sexuality in the plays of Fletcher and his collaborators.[1] So in this respect 3.3 is Fletcherian, as it is also in a conversational tone at which Fletcher shows his adeptness in many plays. Here, as elsewhere, the imitation of familiar speech results in verse that is sometimes so free as to come close to prose, though it also sometimes displays the distinctive rhythm of Fletcher's more formal verse, as in Arcite's offer of a 'hearty draught', with its natural but metrically superfluous final syllable. The pattern of the scene—friendly exchanges suddenly brought to a halt by an outburst of anger—repeats the dramatic effect of the prison scene. One might guess that the achievement of this effect was, in fact, the very *raison d'être* for the scene.

To the third encounter in the woods Arcite brings the promised weapons, and, as in the source, they arm each other with chivalrous courtesy, each helping the other, says Chaucer, 'As friendly as he were his owne brother' (l. A 1652). But again the play enlarges on the hint in Chaucer. The friendly mutual arming leads, on the verge of combat, to a powerful assertion of their friendship and affection. Palamon says: 'Fight bravely, cousin; give me thy noble hand.' To which Arcite replies: 'Here,

---

[1] Foakes, 'Tragicomedy and Comic Form', and Bliss, 'Tragicomic Romance for the King's Men, 1609–1611: Shakespeare, Beaumont, and Fletcher', in *Comedy from Shakespeare to Sheridan: Change and Continuity in the English and European Tradition* (Newark, London, and Toronto, 1986), pp. 82–4, 153–7.

Palamon. This hand shall never more | Come near thee with such friendship' (ll. 101–3). It is a most effective dramatic moment built on the basis provided by Shakespeare in his treatment of the first encounter, but the heightened emotions are as typically Fletcherian as the rhythm of many of the lines or as the rhetoric of the pleas to Theseus, which come in the latter part of the scene.

When Emilia, urged by Theseus to choose one of the two kinsmen, studies the miniature portraits of them, which she carries with her, she first praises in the highest terms each of Arcite's features: 'What an eye, | Of what a fiery sparkle and quick sweetness . . . What a brow | Of what a spacious majesty . . . Palamon | Is but his foil, . . . of an eye as heavy | As if he had lost his mother' (4.2.12–28). Then this rhapsody is interrupted by misgivings and she exclaims:

> O, who can find the bent of woman's fancy?
> I am a fool, my reason is lost in me . . .
>   Palamon, thou art alone
> And only beautiful, and these the eyes,
> These the bright lamps of beauty, that command
> And threaten love, and what young maid dare cross 'em? . . .
>   Lie there, Arcite;
> Thou art a changeling to him, a mere gypsy . . .
>
>   (ll. 33–44)

The shift is as abrupt as when friendship changes to angry rivalry between Palamon and Arcite in prison or in the woods. It is presented in a conspicuously balanced speech, and in verse which, despite a considerable proportion of run-on lines, has several marks of Fletcher's style, including various patterns of repetition.

Neither the glittering rhetorical devices nor the sudden change of heart are to be found in her later soliloquy, as she stands outside the arena where the contest is being fought, and once again compares the pictures of her suitors:

> Arcite is gently visaged, yet his eye
> Is like an engine bent, or a sharp weapon
> In a soft sheath; mercy and manly courage
> Are bedfellows in his visage. Palamon
> Has a most menacing aspect; his brow
> Is graved, and seems to bury what it frowns on;

Yet sometime 'tis not so, but alters to
The quality of his thoughts. Long time his eye
Will dwell upon his object.

(5.3.41–9)

Here the comparison is more thoughtful and more complex.[1] In each of the rivals she finds opposing characteristics: Arcite looks gentle, though his eye is like a weapon—mercy and courage combined; Palamon has a threatening look, but not always—sometimes he appears more meditative. In both of them hard and soft qualities combine. Such a balancing of opposites is characteristic of Shakespeare, as is the serious play on words ('graved . . . seems to bury').

The differences to be found when these comparable scenes are juxtaposed seem to me to confirm the opinions of those who, ever since the time of Lamb, have found two poetic styles in the play and have identified them as the styles of Fletcher and Shakespeare. In each of the scenes I have discussed distinctive characteristics of style accompany equally distinctive characteristics of dramatic treatment. On the basis of these differences most of the scenes of the play can be assigned with some assurance to one or the other collaborator. The exceptions are very short scenes, where the evidence is scanty, and prose scenes, where most of the stylistic criteria I have discussed are inapplicable. In Fletcher's dramatic writing there is relatively little prose, although, as already noted, he sometimes composes a conversational blank verse that closely resembles, and sometimes drifts into, prose. The most likely division of labour is the following:

Shakespeare: 1; 2.1; 3.1–2; 4.3; 5.1, 3–4
Fletcher: 2.2–6; 3.3–6; 4.1–2; 5.2

It is difficult to be sure about the prose scenes (2.1 and 4.3). Two reasons for assuming a change of authorship between 2.1 and 2.2 are that this scene division, given in Q, is technically unnecessary (see note on 2.1.55.1), and that there are some inconsistencies between the two (see note on 2.2.6–55). The Doctor in 4.3 somewhat resembles the Doctor in *Macbeth* and the scene contains two instances of *hath*, a form used seldom by Fletcher but rather often by Shakespeare; in this play it occurs

---

[1] I have also compared these soliloquies in 'Love and Friendship', pp. 243–5.

only once in a scene that is certainly by Fletcher (2.2). These observations, however, do not constitute proof. Another scene containing a good deal of prose is 3.5, the scene of the morris dance, but almost all commentators give it to Fletcher, and I am inclined to agree. It is well to keep in mind that a scene by one collaborator may have been revised or partially rewritten by the other. The first thirty-three lines of Shakespeare's 5.1, for instance, bear some of the signs of Fletcher's style. The prologue and epilogue are probably by Fletcher, though their brevity and conventional nature make it difficult to be certain. The somewhat salacious tone of the prologue, anticipating that of prologues later in the century, seems more like Fletcher than Shakespeare. This tone mingles with the epilogue's conventional fear that the audience may not have been pleased, and here the repeated use of 'ye' also suggests Fletcher's hand. In all these repects the epilogue to *Valentinian* (1614) is remarkably similar, and both end with the humble suggestion that a better play may soon come along. Compare the last seven lines of the epilogue to *The Two Noble Kinsmen* with these from *Valentinian*:

> Then noble friends, as ye would choose a miss
> Only to please the eye a while and kiss,
> Till a good wife be got, so let this play
> Hold ye a while until a better may.

Text

The 1634 Quarto, on which the 1679 Folio is based, provides the only authoritative text, and it is, in the main, a good one. Opinions have differed about the nature of the manuscript given to the printer, but on one point everyone agrees: it had been annotated by the 'bookkeeper', or prompter. Clear evidence that this was the case is found in several places, such as the warning marginal notes at 1.3.58–64 and 1.4.26–7 (see collations and notes at these points), where directions are given to have properties ready for the next scene. Even more telling are the references in two stage directions (4.2.70.1 and 5.3.0.2) to the names of actors in the company in 1625–6 (see above, p. 3). Since the company's bookkeeper at this time was Edward Knight, the annotations are presumably his, and it may be that he transcribed the entire play, as he did *The Honest Man's Fortune*, a manuscript of which survives in his hand and with a licence dated 1625.[1] If the printer's copy was a transcript by Knight the uncharacteristic infrequency of 'ye' in Fletcher's scenes would be understandable, since we know that when he made a copy of Fletcher's *Bonduca* he altered many instances of 'ye' to 'you'.[2] Bertram believed that the prompter's annotations were made on a manuscript in Shakespeare's hand, and offered this theory in support of his contention that Shakespeare was the sole author. As part of the evidence for his belief he cited what he considered to be characteristically Shakespearian spellings and misprints which might have been due to Shakespeare's handwriting (pp. 84, 104–19), but Hoy showed in his review of Bertram's book that the spellings in question were not distinctively Shakespearian and that the misprints represented common errors in reading Elizabethan handwriting (*Modern Philology*, 67 (1969), 83–8). The likelihood that Q was printed from a scribal transcript is greatly increased by the compositorial analysis made by Paul Werstine, who argues persuasively that the type was set by two compositors, as Frederick O. Waller first suggested.[3] From the measurement of spacing before and after certain punctuation marks Werstine finds that one set of pages in Q differs from another in this respect, and concludes that variation of this sort, while not proving, strongly suggests the work of two compositors. His finding in the main confirms the results of Waller's similar investigation. Since Waller did not publish his evidence and Werstine did not see the unpublished dissertation until after he had made his own test, the similarity of their conclusions is the more remarkable. Werstine notes that the two hypothetical compositors also seem to have differed in their treatment of marginal stage directions and their punctuation of speech-heads.

One consequence of assuming that there were two compositors can be seen by returning to Proudfoot's observation that the

[1] Sir Walter Greg noted that the colons in the warning direction at 1.3.58–64 were characteristic of Knight (*The Editorial Problem in Shakespeare*, 2nd edn. (Oxford, 1951), p. 39 n. 2).

[2] See Hoy, 'Shares', *Studies in Bibliography*, 8 (1956), p. 139.

[3] Werstine's analysis is contained in an unpublished essay. Waller made a case for two compositors in his unpublished Ph.D. dissertation, 'A Critical, Old-Spelling Edition of *The Two Noble Kinsmen*', University of Chicago, 1957, and summarized his conclusions in 'Printer's Copy for *The Two Noble Kinsmen*', *Studies in Bibliography*, 11 (1958), 61–84.

name 'Pirithous' is differently pronounced in the sections of the play allotted respectively to Fletcher and Shakespeare (see above, p. 12). He also noted that in Shakespeare's scenes, where it is trisyllabic, it is usually spelled 'Pirithous' or 'Pyrithous', a spelling probably derived from Plutarch, while in Fletcher's scenes, where it is tetrasyllabic, it is usually spelled 'Perithous', probably influenced by Chaucer's 'Perotheus' (Proudfoot, p. xix). The fact that these variant spellings do not correspond exactly with the variant pronunciations is, however, puzzling: the 'Pir' spelling occurs four times in Fletcher's scenes, in either the text or stage directions, and the 'Per' spelling three times in Shakespeare's scenes. Since both compositors set both spellings, it is clear that the variation is not due to their individual spelling preferences, but since they seem to have followed the spellings of the two authors it is hard to understand why, in these few instances, both of them would have changed the spelling. As Werstine says, it is easier to believe that the anomalous spellings were the result of a half-hearted attempt by the transcriber to regularize his copy. Thus the case for a transcript by Knight is strengthened.

The hypothesis of two compositors bears also on the matter of mislineation, which will be discussed in Appendix B. Here it need only be noted that both of them worked on a scene (4.3) which everyone agrees is prose, though it is set mostly as verse. Again it is easier to suppose that the mistake was made by the scribe than that the two compositors shared in it. Finally, Werstine suggests, there are errors in the placement of stage directions on pages set by both compositors which can best be explained by supposing that the directions were marginal annotations of the bookkeeper–scribe, inaccurately moved into the text by the compositors.

It seems reasonable to me to conclude that a transcript of the play prepared by Edward Knight as prompt copy for a revival in 1625–6 was given to Thomas Cotes in 1634 and set in type in his shop by two compositors. The numbering of two scenes in Act 2 as 'Scaena 4' may be due to the sharing of work between the two compositors. The first of these scenes is on a page set by Compositor A on page 31 (E4); the second is on the following page (E4^v), set by Compositor B, possibly working at the same time. By the time he came to the next scene, on page 34 (F1^v), he was apparently aware of his mistake and numbered it correctly

'Scaena 6'. The misnumbering of Scenes 5 and 6 in Act 3 as 6 and 7 cannot be explained in the same way, since Compositor A was responsible for the first error and Compositor B for the second. The possibility remains that the error was in their copy and was made by the scribe. If, as Werstine suggests, a Scene 5 in the manuscript that Knight was copying had been cut, he might have gone on to transcribe the following two scenes without changing their numbering.

Sources

In this section I shall discuss the sources of specific episodes in the play, leaving for the next section the more general influence of literary, social, and intellectual traditions. The playwrights' indebtedness to Chaucer is acknowledged by the Prologue (l. 13) with a frankness unusual in the drama of the period. *The Knight's Tale* of Palamon and Arcite is the principal source for the main plot, and the relationship between the play and this source has been treated in depth by Ann Thompson in *Shakespeare and Chaucer* (Liverpool, 1978) and, most recently, with great sensitivity, by E. Talbot Donaldson in *The Swan at the Well: Shakespeare Reading Chaucer* (New Haven and London, 1985). Fletcher presumably read Chaucer in Thomas Speght's *The Workes of our Antient and Learned English Poet, Geffrey Chaucer*, first published in 1598, and then, revised and enlarged, in 1602.[1] Robert K. Turner's observation that a puzzling term in the description of one of Palamon's knights may be explained by an error that appeared in Speght's second edition (see note at 4.2.104) makes it likely that this was the one Fletcher consulted. When Shakespeare drew on *The Knight's Tale* in *A Midsummer Night's Dream*, he probably used Stow's 1561 printing of Thynne's edition (1532); Donaldson

[1] A cousin of Fletcher's close collaborator, Francis Beaumont—another Francis Beaumont (one of the Beaumonts of Cole Orton), who was later Master of the Charterhouse—was a close friend of Speght's at Cambridge. He wrote a commendatory epistle, claiming to be 'one of them which first procured you to take in hand this work', and praising Chaucer as more original than the writers of classical comedy (sig. a5). Here and elsewhere I quote from the 1602 edition. For this identification of the author of the epistle see T. W. Baldwin, 'The Three Francis Beaumonts', *Modern Language Notes*, 39 (1924), 505–7, and Lady Newdigate-Newdegate, *Gossip from a Muniment Room* (London, 1897), pp. 94, 134.

2. In an illustration to a French translation of Boccaccio's *Teseida*, *c*.1455, by the Master of René of Anjou, Palamon and Arcite peer through their window grille at Emilia in her enclosed garden.

finds no clear indication of which edition he was following for the later play.

Chaucer took the story from Boccaccio's *Teseida*, intended as a vernacular epic in the tradition of Virgil's *Aeneid* and, especially, Statius' *Thebaid*, a Roman epic on the war of the 'seven against Thebes', written in the first century AD, and much more highly regarded in the Renaissance than it is today. 'Moral songs' and 'love lyrics' had been written in vernacular poetry, Boccaccio said, but no 'poems on the theme of warfare', of which the *Teseida* was to be the first.[1] In fact, it is less closely allied to classical epic than to medieval romance, in which the familiar combination of love and war is recalled by Speght's description of Chaucer's version of the story: 'A tale fitting the person of a knight, for that it discourseth of the deeds of arms and love of ladies' (fol. 1). There are occasional suggestions that the collaborators knew Boccaccio's poem or one of the later prose versions of it (see note

---

[1] *The Book of Theseus*, trans. Bernadette Marie McCoy (New York, 1974), xii. 84–5 and Introduction, p. 3.

27

on 4.2.94–116), and they probably knew the *Thebaid*, though there are no direct borrowings from it. For certain details Shakespeare certainly made use of Plutarch's 'Life of Theseus' (see notes on 1.1.48 and 1.2.28). It is possible that the playwrights consulted Lydgate's *Story of Thebes*, which Speght printed with his edition of Chaucer, though there is no proof that they did. They would have found there an account of the widowed queens going to Theseus, waiting in the temple of the 'goddesse Clemence, as my master Chaucer list to endite', and of the burial of their husbands after Theseus has defeated Creon (fol. 374 in the 1602 edition).

Two earlier plays about Palamon and Arcite, both of them lost, are known to have been performed. A *Palamon and Arcite* by Richard Edwards was performed at Christ Church, Oxford, for Queen Elizabeth in two parts on 2 and 4 September 1566, but from a contemporary account it seems to have been totally unlike *The Two Noble Kinsmen*.[1] Another *Palamon and Arsett*, performed in 1594 by the Admiral's Men, is known only from entries in Henslowe's diary.[2]

No source for the sub-plot as a whole is known, but at several points Fletcher was clearly indebted to previous works. His most specific debt was to Beaumont's *Masque of the Inner Temple and Gray's Inn* (1613), from which he took the entertainment offered by the Schoolmaster in 3.5 to Theseus and his hunting-party. The character of the Schoolmaster may have been based in part on the schoolmaster, Rombus, in Sir Philip Sidney's brief entertainment, *The Lady of May* (1579?), to whom Holofernes in *Love's Labour's Lost* also bears at least a generic resemblance. Such pedants have a long dramatic ancestry. Parts of the Schoolmaster's speech presenting his entertainment sound very like Quince acting as prologue to *Pyramus and Thisbe* for Theseus in *A Midsummer Night's Dream* (see note on 3.5.100–32).[3]

It has often been remarked that the Jailer's Daughter, in her mad scenes, is somewhat like Ophelia. She also resembles, in a general way, some of the pathetic heroines of earlier Beaumont-

[1] The account is given in Littledale, pp. 9*–11*.

[2] R. A. Foakes and R. T. Rickert, *Henslowe's Diary* (Cambridge, 1961), pp. 24–5.

[3] For other, more general, connections between the two plays see Glynne Wickham, 'The Two Noble Kinsmen, or A Midsummer Night's Dream, Part II?', *Elizabethan Theatre*, 7 (1980), 167–96.

and-Fletcher plays; at certain moments both her situation and her words come very close to those of Viola in *The Coxcomb* (1609?; see note on 2.4.6–7).[1] When she imagines that she is going to marry Palamon, whom she has let out of prison, even though her father may be hanged for it, her situation is very similar, as Ann Thompson has noted, to that of Mopsa in Book 4 of the *Arcadia* (first printed in 1593; see note on 5.2.77–81).[2]

Occasion

We have seen that the play was performed at Blackfriars sometime between the performance of Beaumont's masque at court on 20 February 1613 and, in all likelihood, the opening performance of *Bartholomew Fair* on 31 October 1614 (see pp. 1–2). Although it is not one of the fourteen plays known to have been given at court for Princess Elizabeth and her newly wedded husband, the Elector Palatine, there are good reasons for thinking the King's Men put it on not long after that event. As Muriel Bradbrook noted, the combination of wedding preparations and mourning made it singularly appropriate for a time when England was still lamenting the death, in November 1612, of Elizabeth's brother Henry, the Prince of Wales, while it celebrated her wedding. Glynne Wickham believes that the play may even have been commissioned for the occasion.[3]

The theory of a connection between the play and the wedding of Elizabeth and the Protestant Elector Palatine is reinforced by an awareness of the revival at Prince Henry's court of the Elizabethan enthusiasm for chivalry, associated, as Sir Roy Strong has shown, with advocacy in the Prince's entourage of a firmly Protestant foreign policy. Not only did the Prince delight in chivalrous sports, but his political and moral views made him, as Strong says, 'the heir to the mantles of two late Elizabethan heroes, Sir Philip Sidney and Robert Devereux, 2nd Earl of Essex,

---

[1] Robert M. Clements, Jr., points to a few other possible borrowings from the same play in his unpublished Ph.D. dissertation, 'A New Look at *The Two Noble Kinsmen*' (University of California, Berkeley, 1974), p. 193.

[2] 'Jailer's Daughters in "The Arcadia" and "The Two Noble Kinsmen"', *Notes and Queries*, NS 26 (1979), 140–1.

[3] M. C. Bradbrook, 'Shakespeare and his Collaborators', in *Shakespeare 1971*, ed. Clifford Leech and J. M. R. Margeson (Toronto, 1972), p. 30; Wickham, 'The Two Noble Kinsmen', pp. 176–9.

as the epitome of militant Protestant chivalry'.[1] He was therefore as much in favour of his sister's Protestant match as he was opposed to his father's thought of a Catholic match for himself. He was also said to be very fond of Elizabeth, asking for her in his dying words. It is not surprising that he was 'the prime mover' in organizing the wedding festivities (Strong, p. 176), and quite probable that his interests were in the minds of those who, after his death, were concerned with carrying them out.[2] Strong suggests that Beaumont may originally have intended to gratify the Prince's taste for chivalry with a device for a combat at the barriers, in which the Olympian Knights who dance the 'Main Masque' in his *Masque of the Inner Temple and Gray's Inn* would have taken part (p. 180). Jonson had already written *Prince Henry's Barriers* for him, with its theme of the revival of British chivalry, and also the masque of *Oberon*, based on Arthurian romance. As Frances Yates showed in *Astraea* (pp. 88–107), romance provided the scenarios for many an Elizabethan chivalric entertainment, such as those at Woodstock in 1575 and Ditchley in 1592 or the annual Accession Day Tilts. Hence the fact that *The Knight's Tale* was a chivalric romance made it a logical choice for anyone planning an entertainment associated with Princess Elizabeth's wedding and aware of her brother's tastes. Whether or not Fletcher and Shakespeare were asked to write a play for this occasion, it is very likely that in writing their play for Blackfriars the occasion was uppermost in their minds and exercised a powerful influence on the nature of the play.

The Play in Performance

The stage history of *The Two Noble Kinsmen* is very brief. After the few performances mentioned at the beginning of this

---

[1] *Henry, Prince of Wales and England's Lost Renaissance* (New York and London, 1986), p. 14. On the subject of Elizabethan chivalry see Frances Yates, *Astraea: The Imperial Theme in the Sixteenth Century* (London and Boston, 1975), pp. 88 ff., and *Shakespeare's Last Plays: A New Approach* (London, 1975), pp. 11–40. See also Arthur B. Ferguson, *The Chivalric Tradition in Renaissance England* (Washington, London, and Toronto, 1986), pp. 66–82, 140–2.

[2] A masque, apparently intended for the celebration of the wedding but never given, explicitly advocated a pro-Protestant policy; see David Norbrook, '"The Masque of Truth": Court Entertainments and International Protestant politics in the Early Stuart Period', *The Seventeenth Century*, I (1986), 81–110; also Strong, pp. 181–2.

introduction the original play was apparently not seen until the twentieth century. Hugh Richmond, who has given the most complete account that I have seen, speculates plausibly that, like certain other plays on the fringe of the Shakespearian canon, it has 'suffered critical disfavor from assumptions of incoherence or inferiority because of the possibility of shared authorship between Shakespeare and some lesser, supposedly incompatible play-wright'.[1] Such suspicions, he believes, may have discouraged production while they emboldened critics to be 'condescending or openly contemptuous'. The negative attitudes of critics and directors have thus tended to reinforce each other.

At the beginning of this long period of neglect Sir William Davenant saw in the play sufficient theatrical potential to warrant writing an adaptation called *The Rivals*, performed with great success by the Duke's Company in 1664, in January 1665, and again in November 1667, with Thomas Betterton as Philander, the character corresponding to Palamon.[2] It was published in 1668.

The adaptation and its reception throw various lights on the original play. The prompter John Downes reported that 'The play, by the excellent performance, lasted uninterruptly nine days with full audience'.[3] Exactly when the premiere took place is uncertain, but Pepys saw the play on 10 September 1664, and though he thought it 'no excellent play', he praised the acting. Both Downes and Pepys make much of the singing and dancing. Downes writes of 'a very fine interlude in it, of vocal and instrumental music, mixed with very diverting dances', and Pepys singles out Winifred Gosnell, who 'comes and sings and dances finely' (*London Stage*, p. 83). She apparently took the part of Celania, who corresponds to the Jailer's Daughter, but from the 1668 quarto we know that Mary ('Moll') Davis later played this part. Her performance is praised by Downes, who says: 'all the women's parts admirably acted; chiefly Celia [i.e. Celania], a shepherdess being mad for love; especially in singing several wild and mad songs—"My

---

[1] Seminar paper first given at the 1985 meeting of the Shakespeare Association of America, p. 1; see also G. Harold Metz, 'The Two Noble Kinsmen on the Twentieth Century Stage', *Theatre History Studies*, 4 (1984), 63–9. In what follows I am much indebted to these two essays.

[2] *The London Stage, 1660–1800*, Part 1: 1660–1700, ed. W. Van Lennep (Carbondale, Ill., 1960), pp. 83, 85, 86, 124.

[3] *Roscius Anglicanus* (1708), p. 24.

lodging it is on the cold ground," etc. She performed that so charmingly that not long after it raised her from her bed on the cold ground to a bed royal' (*Roscius Anglicanus*, pp. 23–4). Charles II probably saw her in the part at the 1667 revival, after which she did indeed become Charles II's mistress, to the chagrin of another of his mistresses, Lady Castlemayne, as Pepys reports.[1] It is worth noting that the success of Celania's role corresponds closely to the success that the Jailer's Daughter has enjoyed in modern productions of *The Two Noble Kinsmen*.

The enthusiasm of Restoration commentators for song and dance even in serious plays is usually dismissed as a sign of frivolity and bad taste, Pepys's praise for the 'divertisement' in Davenant's *Macbeth* being the prime example (*Diary*, 7 January 1666/7),[2] but, as Rose Zimbardo suggests, it was probably due to their concern for the patterning of drama, in which such 'divertisements' provided not only a desirable variety but also significant counterparts to other elements in the design of the play.[3] A somewhat similar point of view may have been common in the early part of the century, for song and dance were often included in serious plays then, too. In the cases of *Macbeth* and *The Two Noble Kinsmen* Davenant merely added to what he found, giving to the witches in *Macbeth* additional songs and dances, and to his Celania more songs than the Jailer's Daughter has. To the morris dance he added 'a hunt in music' and another dance. It is a matter of record that the country dance which served as an antimasque in Beaumont's masque, contrasted with the main masque of the Olympian Knights, was a notable success (see Appendix A), and if, as seems likely, it had been performed by some of the King's Men,[4] they would have been repeating their performance at Blackfriars, where it is reasonable to suppose that the dance delighted the audience as the later version of it did in 1664. In *The Two Noble Kinsmen* it immediately precedes the combat of Palamon and Arcite in the woods, as in the masque

---

[1] *A Biographical Dictionary of Actors . . . in London, 1660–1800*, ed. Philip H. Highfill, Jr., Kalman Burnim, and Edward Langhans, vol. iv (Carbondale, Ill., 1975), p. 222.

[2] *Pepys on the Restoration Stage*, ed. Helen McAfee (New Haven, London, and Oxford, 1916), p. 70.

[3] *A Mirror up to Nature* (Lexington, Ky., 1986), pp. 72–5.

[4] Professional actors were often used in the antimasques of masques performed at court.

it preceded the appearance of the Olympian Knights. Although Davenant's augmentation of the music and dance slightly postpones the combat, he exploits the same contrast. Through his eyes and those of his audience we are better able to understand how this part of the sub-plot of Fletcher and Shakespeare's play may have worked. One further indication of the popularity of the entertainment in the woods in Davenant's play (and hence, perhaps, in its source) is Downes's comment that 'Mr. Price introducing the dancing by a short comical prologue [corresponding to the Schoolmaster's prologue] gained him an universal applause of the town' (p. 23).

Davenant was obviously aware that *The Two Noble Kinsmen*, though described as a tragicomedy, had an ending rather far removed from the general rejoicings which that form seems to promise. To make his version truly tragicomic he made several significant alterations, and in so doing made it more like the tragicomedies in the Beaumont-and-Fletcher corpus than like the late Shakespearian romances. In this connection it is significant that he omits most of Shakespeare's first act (in this respect anticipating one recent production of *The Two Noble Kinsmen*) and totally changes the fifth act.[1] In *The Rivals* Theocles (= Arcite) lives to marry Heraclia (= Emilia), and Philander gets Celania, whom Davenant turns into a suitable match by making her the daughter of the Provost, who is in charge of the prison, but is no mere jailer. Immediate responsibility for the prisoners is given to his man, Cunopes, who thus has one part of the role of the original Jailer.

Other major alterations make possible the happy ending. There is no final combat, though Philander and Theocles ask for it. Arcon (= Theseus) insists that Heraclia choose which is to live and which to die, and subjects her and the kinsmen to various trials in the hope of arriving at a decision. Here Davenant introduces an episode similar to one which appears in some of the oldest and most popular stories of friendship, where one friend is falsely accused of a crime and is defended by the other. Two accusations and two defences make the choice between Davenant's rivals as difficult as ever, but when the Provost arrives with Celania, whose madness has been cured by a cordial,

---

[1] He sometimes follows the text closely, and occasionally anticipates the emendations of later editors of the play, as the collations will show.

Philander is persuaded to accept her love, announcing, 'I lose a rival and preserve a friend'. Both kinsmen are allowed to live. The agonized reflections on divine governance which make the ending of *The Two Noble Kinsmen* memorable have no place in this Fletcherian tragicomedy.

The first known revival of Fletcher and Shakespeare's play was that of the Old Vic in the spring of 1928 with a strong cast, including Eric Portman as Arcite, Ernest Milton as Palamon, Barbara Everest as Emilia, and Jean Forbes-Robertson as the Jailer's Daughter. It was greeted with some of the 'condescending' and even 'contemptuous' reviews to which Richmond refers, though also with praise for the acting and recognition of the effectiveness of certain scenes. A. G. Macdonell in *The London Mercury* (17:102 (April, 1928), 697) is fairly representative in his embarrassment at 'the nobility of character and sentiment' in the conversations between the kinsmen, but he was impressed by Jean Forbes-Robertson's outstanding performance, and commented that the Jailer's Daughter goes mad 'in the most beautiful, touching, Ophelian way'. Ernest Milton played Palamon as a comic character in a red wig. According to Sir Rupert Hart-Davis in an obituary of Milton:

When he made his first entrance he was met by a gale of laughter . . . in a split second he realized that it was useless to play this part straight, as he had rehearsed it, so he gently burlesqued it for the rest of the evening, stealing the show and most of the notices.[1]

The audience evidently shared Macdonell's embarrassment at chivalric nobility and sentiment. Milton's decision to burlesque the part was a desperate one, though in Macdonell's opinion he carried the idea out 'extremely well'.

The Old Vic's production foreshadowed later ones in more than one respect. The problem of how to present the nobility of the kinsmen troubled succeeding directors, while succeeding actresses showed again that the Jailer's Daughter could be a very appealing role. Hugh Richmond calls attention to the importance given to choreography by Andrew Leigh, as shown by the programme note: 'Dance arranged by Ninette de Valois', the well-known foundress of the first English ballet school. She was clearly responsible for the 'Wedding Masque' mentioned in the pro-

---

[1] *The Times*, 5 August 1974.

gramme, and for 'the hunting and maying, the morris dancing and tilting with which this play abounds'. In this emphasis on ritual and spectacle the Old Vic was again followed by others, but in this case was itself following the lead of the King's Men in 1613 and the Duke's Company in 1664.

Between 1928 and 1954 the play apparently lapsed again into the status of closet drama except for a public reading given by the Nottingham Shakespeare Society in 1936. In 1954 and the years following, however, the possibilities of staging it began to be explored more frequently. There were four performances by the Harvard University Dramatic Club in 1954; the next year it was put on by Antioch College (in Yellow Springs, Ohio) at the Antioch Area Festival and by the Birmingham University Theatre Group at the Edinburgh Festival Fringe. As a radio play it was broadcast by the BBC in 1956, and in 1957 Nevill Coghill directed a production at Merton College, Oxford. Outdoor performances were given by the Reading University Drama Society in Stratford-upon-Avon in 1959 and by the Drama Department of Bristol University at the Royal Fort, Bristol, in 1964. Four years later the Interluders of Hereford performed the play at the Stable Court Theatre, Saltram House, Devon; in 1970 there was a modern-dress production by Michael Friend for the British Council in London.[1]

Four professional productions during the seventies merit special comment. In 1973 the play was mounted at the York Theatre Royal as part of the York Festival of the Arts. Hugh Richmond, after noting the mixed reviews it received, concludes that it was nevertheless 'certainly a success', and attributes the success in large part to the transformation of the proscenium-arch theatre by the addition of a large apron stage, extending over the stalls 'with flights of steps to the boxes and the front of the dress circle'. Some spectators were even seated on the stage. Reviewers commented on how this approximation of an Elizabethan stage engaged the audience in the performance. Richmond comments: 'We must recognize the need to approximate to Renaissance conditions of performance if this play is to work well. Its values and interest are not those of the kind associated with the realistic

---

[1] I am indebted for information about several of these performances to Niky Rathbone, the Shakespeare Librarian of the City of Birmingham Public Libraries Department.

tradition behind a proscenium arch : it depends on stylized, highly artificial approaches to its themes.'

One significant omission from the York production was that of the rustics and their morris dance, which to some critics is an irrelevancy. As we have seen, Davenant did not so consider it, nor did the Old Vic in 1928. To the tradition of emphasizing the masque-like features of the play the New Theatre Company returned with their outdoor production in Regent's Park, London, in 1974. For Richmond 'The importance of the dancing remains my most marked impression of the Regent's Park production, which was elaborately choreographed'. The battles were made into 'stick/sword dances in the morris tradition', reminding J. W. Lambert in *The Sunday Times* (4 August 1974) of 'Japanese (or perhaps Archaic Greek) stampers and stave-tappers'. In this case choreography seems to have achieved the effect of stylization that was suggested at York by the abandonment of realistic staging. In their different ways these two productions made similar points about the nature of the play.

In 1979 the Cherub Company gave an experimental and heavily cut performance with an all-male cast at the Edinburgh Festival Fringe and later at the Young Vic Studio in London. The morris dance was again left out, but the various cuts 'helped to illuminate structural patterns in the play' for Gerald Berkowitz in *Shakespeare Quarterly* (31 (1980), 165–6): 'the fact that the real couples in the main plot are the two women and the two men; the contrast between Emilia, who can't love either man who wants her, and the Jailer's Daughter, who switches her love from one man to another without even realizing it; and the ironic parallels between the first and last scenes'. Bare torsos, leather trousers, and 'exaggeratedly phallic codpieces' for the male roles with 'whiteface and painted breasts for the women' emphasized and stylized sexual distinctions. The homosexual overtones in the costuming of the kinsmen 'owed more to Cocteau than to Plato' according to Tony Howard in *Research Opportunities in Renaissance Drama* (22 (1979), 75). Clearly, they raised a question that has concerned several critics and that will be discussed in the next section of this introduction. G. M. Pearce found the actors wooden in some roles, but she praised Anthony Best as the Jailer's Daughter for the sensitivity with which he managed the mad scenes and for conveying 'the sexual language of the young girl naturally and without ridicule' (*Cahiers Élisabéthains*, 17 (1980), 100–1). It is noteworthy that, as Tony Howard said, 'for all the apparent fatuity of the theme, the audience was evidently gripped by Fletcher's compelling narrative line in Acts II and III', and that to Howard himself, despite his reservations, the 'tender ferocity of the arming scene was most striking'.

In the same year the play was presented at the Globe Playhouse of Los Angeles by the Shakespeare Society of America in repertory, and for Joseph H. Stodder and Lillian Wilds 'this seldom-produced work shone with unexpected brilliance among the more familiar and accepted plays of the canon' (*Shakespeare Quarterly*, 31 (1980), 258). Like several previous directors, Walter Scholz emphasized dance and ritual 'with almost uniformly satisfying results', according to the *Shakespeare Quarterly* reviewers. 'The play began with the full cast onstage, dancing, while the prologue was presented. The next scene, depicting the three Queens in black, was a persuasive example of the power that ritual could achieve when blended effectively into the action of the play.' Although they found some of the acting weak, they had nothing but praise for Suzanna Peters as the Jailer's Daughter. The conception of this role was for them 'perhaps the most remarkable achievement of this imaginative production'.

In 1975 Rick Abrams directed the play at the University of Texas at Austin 'in a bold, geometrical style with back projections of an arresting kind', as Richmond reports, and four years later directed another production for Shakespeare Players Incorporated, a regional theatre group in Richmond, Virginia. Richmond himself produced two versions of the play in 1979 at the Berkeley campus of the University of California, one in an outdoor theatre for an invited audience, the other as a two-hour videotape for television, later broadcast on California cable networks.

The production by the Jean Cocteau Repertory Company, New York City, in 1981 won very little praise from Maurice Charney and Arthur Ganz in *Shakespeare Quarterly* (33 (1982), 220), though their dissatisfaction was in part with the play itself. They were pleased, at least, by the Jailer's Daughter, 'very winningly played by Phyllis Deitschel'. In 1985 the Berkeley Shakespeare Festival staged a successful production, described by Jonas Barish[1]

---

[1] In a letter to me, dated 16 Dec. 1985.

as 'a highly creditable, frequently moving performance, with a strong cast that played excellently together as an ensemble. . . . The play demonstrated its effectiveness throughout. The ritual scenes with the three queens and the prayer scenes prior to the final combat all were powerfully effective.' In this performance Barish was especially struck by 'the centrality of the Jailer's Daughter' and spoke of 'the virtuoso performance of Nancy Carlin' in the role. Hugh Richmond, who noted that the part was 'scaled down from daring sexual adventuress to disturbed adolescent, still clutching her doll', felt, nevertheless, that it was she 'who first and best established the audience's amazed rapport with the play's central theme of the comic pathos of humanity's uneasy relationships to the sexual drive'. The play was heavily cut, 'with some loss', as Richmond said, 'to the force, scale and authority of its serious, ritual aspects. Similarly the morris dance was quite perfunctory and marginal in significance compared to the duels.' Much was made of the sword fight in Act 3—too much, according to Barish—and the kinsmen were introduced wrestling together in Act 1, as they lamented the corruption of Thebes. Although this business successfully dramatized the element of male bonding, it to some extent undermined the seriousness of the dialogue. Phyllis Brooks, the reviewer for *Shakespeare Quarterly* (37 (1986), 396–7), commented, not unfavourably, on many moments in the main plot which were greeted with 'big laughs', but even those who found an excess of jocularity in the production thought that it demonstrated the stageworthiness of the play.

In 1986 the Royal Shakespeare Company opened their new Swan Theatre in Stratford-upon-Avon with *The Two Noble Kinsmen*, directed by Barry Kyle. The 450-seat theatre, well described by Keith Brown as 'an elegantly skeletal replica in modern idiom of the Elizabethan open theatre' (*Times Literary Supplement*, 23 May 1986), proved to be an excellent place for the staging of Tudor and Stuart plays, and this play benefited, as it had at York, from the thrust stage and surrounding audience, even though the staging was far from Elizabethan in conception. Barry Kyle and Bob Crowley, the designer, drew the inspiration for this production from Japanese theatre. 'The opening scene', as Nancy Maguire reported (*Shakespeare Bulletin*, 4:4 (July/August 1986), 8–9), 'was like an overly-ornate Kabuki drama: actors frozen in constrained poses and holding shiny gold masques to their faces formed a backdrop, and characters in red and black oriental robes flitted about the lengthy promontory stage. With startlingly surreal effect, roses fell out of Hippolyta's bosom when Theseus, after pursuing and shooting her with bow and arrows, pulled out the arrow.' As this description makes clear, the production not only imposed some Japanese conventions on those of chivalric romance and Tudor–Stuart drama, but also occasionally, though infrequently, added stage business in no way indicated in the text. The suggestion of samurai warriors was presumably intended to facilitate the acceptance by the audience of the bond between Palamon and Arcite, and for some viewers the gamble succeeded. Michael Billington wrote of 'Barry Kyle's enjoyable, ritualistic, Kurusawa-influenced production' (*Manchester Guardian Weekly* (25 May 1986), p. 20), and Keith Brown said: 'By dressing the characters in the Palamon–Arcite story in quasi-Japanese garb and through unpedantic borrowings from Japanese theatrical conventions, we are given an integrating context of associations in which the slightly formalized feel of much of the play can be fully brought out'. To me the Japanese conventions were mainly a distraction—a needless complication added to a seventeenth-century version of a medieval elaboration of Greek legend. Another distraction was the unusual presentation of the prison cell, from the window of which Palamon and Arcite see Emilia, as a cage suspended over the stage. Nancy Maguire commented that 'Kyle and Crowley refuse to let the audience become comfortable with the set', and at times it appeared that the actors were not entirely comfortable with it either. According to the architect of the Swan, Michael Reardon, and the actor who played Palamon, Gerard Murphy, one reason for devising this curious stage machine was to exploit the verticality of the relatively narrow space above the stage and between the surrounding balconies.[1] The idea, though theatrically logical, resulted in some awkward stage business when the kinsmen were taken out of their 'cell' and led away through a trapdoor, but despite what appeared to me the handicaps of the basic conception, the production was continuously engaging, and certain scenes were extraordinarily effective. As all the reviewers agreed, Imogen

---

[1] This explanation was given at a session on 'The Second Swan' during the annual meeting of the Shakespeare Association of America in April 1987.

3. Imogen Stubbs as the Jailer's Daughter climbs the mast of her imaginary ship near the end of Act 4, Scene 1, in the RSC's Swan Theatre production of 1986.

Stubbs as the Jailer's Daughter gave a superb performance. In her mad scenes she made her uninhibited sexuality both amusing and touching, and the staging of 4.1, where she shinned up a pole that she took for the mast of a ship, encouraged by her father and friends, was spectacularly successful (Fig. 3). It should be noted that the Japanese conventions were absent in the sub-plot. In the main plot two scenes stood out for me: the arming of Palamon and Arcite before the combat in the forest was genuinely moving, whatever doubts one might have about the design of the armour, and so was the final scene.

In his director's note in the programme Kyle wrote: 'I felt that what has appeared to be an unfocused play mixing up tragic conflicts with morris dancing, is organic. It's not a mixture, it's a compound. So I've tried to help by cutting about 350 lines, and striking a new balance. The longer scenes are not always saying more, so I've cut. Act One contains a lot of clotted language—I've tried to make it more speakable by editing.'[1] The cutting to which this admirable perception led was originally very judicious, as one can see in the programme/text, though during the run of the play more cuts were apparently made. It will not surprise anyone familiar with the style of Shakespeare's last plays that a large share of the cutting was done in his scenes. The result was indeed a text that was 'more speakable', and another virtue of this production was that the lines were well spoken.

The New Jersey Shakespeare Festival also produced *The Two Noble Kinsmen*, directed by Paul Barry, in 1986. Here samurai warriors were replaced by what appeared to be American Civil War soldiers, and the ladies wore crinolines. The scene was still given as Athens, though all references to Thebes were removed from the text. The extensive cutting was done according to a very different plan from Kyle's at Stratford: the play began with 1.4 as Theseus entered victorious and the prisoners, Palamon and Arcite, were dragged on stage. Aside from this major excision there were only occasional relatively light cuts. The other major alteration of the text consisted in the telescoping and reconceiving of many secondary roles. The Schoolmaster became a Mountebank, who also served as the Doctor, the Jailer's friend, and the speaker of the prologue and epilogue. Pirithous, surprisingly, took the place of the Jailer's second friend in 4.1. Of less significance was the transformation of the countrymen into wrestlers and dancers or the substitution of Nell, one of the country wenches, for the Jailer's brother.

The loss of the first three scenes was a serious one. Not only was the parallel of the two intercessions with Theseus in Acts 1 and 3 destroyed, but the initial emphasis on the triumph of compassion over self-interest was absent, as were the presentation of the idealism of the kinsmen in Thebes and the introduction of the force of friendship in the dialogue of Hippolyta and Emilia. The transformation of the Schoolmaster into a Mountebank and the combination of this role with that of the Doctor robbed the

---

[1] *The Two Noble Kinsmen*: A programme/text, Swan Theatre Plays (London, 1986), p. 5.

speeches made by those characters of most of their appropriate-
ness, however economical these changes may at first have
appeared, and the friendship of Pirithous for the Jailer was hard
to accept.

One simple set served for the entire play. Upstage, slightly to
the left of centre, was a small pavilion, supported on classical
columns. Behind it, against the back wall, a ramp climbed from
stage right to the height of the roof of the pavilion. The chief use
of this space was as the prison for Palamon and Arcite, who were
chained, one by his left wrist to the left side of the stage, the
other by his right wrist to the right side, the chains being, of
necessity, extremely long. Thus rigidly confined, they were obliged
to carry on their long dialogue, in the course of which they see
and fall in love with Emilia. Though possibly a little less exotic
than the suspended cage at Stratford, this roof-top prison was
equally awkward.

The performance was, nevertheless, lively and sometimes
moving. The scenes with the Jailer's Daughter, played by Margaret
Emory, once more proved their effectiveness, and the morris
dance was well done, with several musicians added to the taborer
called for in the text. As at Stratford, one of the best scenes was
that of the arming of Palamon and Arcite in the woods before
their combat.

The fact that the Davenant adaptation and a large proportion
of the productions of this century have proved to be effective
theatrical entertainment is crucial to an assessment of the
dramatic worth of *The Two Noble Kinsmen*. In interpreting the
play we need to pay attention to the success enjoyed by several
actresses in the role of the Jailer's Daughter, to the effectiveness
in various productions of spectacular scenes such as the interrupted wedding procession, the morris dance, the sword-play in
the woods, and the prayers in the last act, and to the fact
that certain scenes in both plots have often been moving. To
incorporate into our understanding of this play what can be
learned from these performances is to grasp its structure more
completely than any but the most imaginative reading can enable
us to do.

Interpretation

If uncertainty about the authorship of *The Two Noble Kinsmen* is one reason for its neglect by directors and its dismissal by some reviewers as inferior or downright silly, surely another is the problem posed for any contemporary spectator or reader by the conventions of chivalric romance. As some awareness of the laws of heroic behaviour in Homer's time is needed for an understanding of Achilles, so an awareness of the ideals of chivalry is a necessary first step in approaching Palamon, Arcite, Emilia, and Theseus. Since medieval feudal society looked to knighthood, as Arthur B. Ferguson points out, to protect the community 'against both aggressors and transgressors', it was natural that bravery, or *prouesse*, was an essential virtue,[1] as it clearly is in *The Two Noble Kinsmen* with its many scenes of combat and even of trial by combat. Boccaccio, it will be remembered, had set out to write a 'poem of warfare'. With bravery were closely associated several other virtues, and all of them were memorably presented in the romances which continued to be immensely popular long after chivalry had ceased to be a political reality. What Ferguson calls the 'Indian summer' of English chivalry was the late fifteenth and the early sixteenth centuries, but, as we have already seen, such chivalric activities as tilting were revived not only at the court of Elizabeth I but also by Prince Henry. No doubt such late descendants of the medieval knight as Sir Philip Sidney were romantic figures; yet they embodied in actuality many of the virtues found in the romances, including Sidney's own *Arcadia*. It should be noted here that a powerful nostalgia for a better time in the past coloured all these later appearances of chivalry in fiction and court life.[2] One consequence for *The Two Noble Kinsmen* is a double removal of the action of the story: an imaginary Greece is endowed with chivalric ideals in a medieval tale which is held up for admiration in a seventeenth-century play.

The anonymous *Ordene de chevalerie* and Ramon Lull's *Libre del ordre de cavayleria*, both of the thirteenth century, prescribe for

---

[1] *The Indian Summer of English Chivalry* (Durham, NC, 1960), p. 104.

[2] Mark Rose discusses the popularity of romance and 'the Elizabethan effort to turn reality into romance' in 'Othello's Occupation: Shakespeare and the Romance of Chivalry', *English Literary Renaissance*, 15 (1985), 293–311, p. 296; he focuses attention on the bearing of chivalric themes on *Othello*.

4. A Tudor combat (possibly a trial by combat) with swords on foot, without barriers but taking place within double fences. A 'judgehouse' stands at the rear; noble spectators may have shared the judges' privileged viewpoint. The crowds indicate how popular an entertainment the tournament continued to be.

the knight a life governed by the loftiest ideals, the striving for which finds a fitting emblem in the motif of the quest, found in so many romances. Although, as Maurice Keen is at pains to demonstrate, the origins of chivalry were secular,[1] it had close ties with Christianity, and many of its ideals were also those of the Church. The very fact of chivalric idealism has a direct bearing on the four principal characters of the play, all of whom are seen at various moments making a conscious effort to behave nobly. In two major scenes (1.1 and 3.6) Theseus is persuaded to reconsider a hasty decision made largely on the basis of self-

[1] *Chivalry* (New Haven and London, 1984), pp. 18–43.

interest; Palamon and Arcite are introduced by Shakespeare through a dialogue (in 1.2) in which they discuss leaving Thebes because of its corruption but decide they must put duty before personal preference, and stay in order to defend their city against an enemy; Emilia's repeated unwillingness to choose between the kinsmen is based on her conviction that to favour either one would be to wrong the other.

One virtue required of the knight was courtesy, which had for the Middle Ages and the Renaissance a far greater significance than adherence to a few rules of polite speech and behaviour. Interpreted as a manifestation of nobility of spirit, it was sometimes said to include all other virtues, and, as Derek Brewer says, had an important religious component.[1] In the context of the chivalric tradition the extraordinary politeness with which Palamon and Arcite (and especially Arcite) curb their mutual resentment can be seen as a key indication of the striving for nobility established by Shakespeare in their first scene.

Another classic knightly virtue was liberality or 'largesse', which might mean anything from bounty to generosity of spirit (Keen, pp. 7–10).[2] When Palamon and his knights give the Jailer their purses for his daughter's wedding the gesture means something more than a charitable impulse. It is another demonstration of their adherence to the code of chivalry.

Since the knight was expected to protect the weak, including damsels in distress (Keen, p. 9), it is not surprising that on the original concept of chivalry was grafted the idea of *Frauendienst* and the ideal love glorified in courtly romances (Keen, p. 14; Ferguson, *Indian Summer*, p. 122). When Hippolyta takes the part of the widowed queens and urges Theseus to arm himself for battle with Creon, it is in order 'To do these poor queens service' (1.1.199). The instant infatuation of Palamon and Arcite with Emilia is made acceptable largely by means of one of the most familiar conventions of courtly romance, love at first sight. Without the 'willing suspension of disbelief' brought by acceptance of this convention the transformation of the kinsmen's lives

[1] *Chaucer in his Time* (London, 1963), pp. 145, 204–37; see also my 'Shakespeare and the Ceremonies of Romance', in *Shakespeare's Craft*, ed. Philip H. Highfill, Jr. (Carbondale and Edwardsville, Ill., 1982), pp. 124–8; repr. in Waith, *Patterns and Perspectives*, pp. 148–66.

[2] See also my *Ideas of Greatness* (London and New York, 1971), pp. 12–15.

and the total commitment of each of them to Emilia are bound to seem absurd, even though instant infatuations of a less exalted sort are not uncommon in the dramatic and non-dramatic fictions of today. In the romances the 'fine amor', exemplified here by love for Emilia, becomes an ideal analogous to the others for which the knight must endlessly strive (Waith, *Ideas of Greatness*, pp. 16–20).

Compassion, or pity, though not listed in the treatises on chivalry as one of the knightly virtues, is implied in the duty to protect the weak and is intimately related to both largesse and courtesy. It is, of course, a Christian virtue as well, and in *The Two Noble Kinsmen* it assumes great importance. When Theseus takes pity on the widowed queens the Third Queen says: 'Thou, being but mortal, makest affections bend | To godlike honours' (1.1.229–30), and Theseus replies:

> As we are men,
> Thus should we do; being sensually subdued,
> We lose our human title.
>
> (ll. 231–3)

Pity, if not godlike, as the Third Queen would have it, is a qualification for true humanity when it takes precedence over desire and self-interest. The second time that Theseus is persuaded to take a higher ethical stance the word 'mercy' is insistently repeated and Theseus moves from 'Say I felt | Compassion' (3.6.212–13) to 'For now I feel compassion' (l. 270). Pity is also a salient feature in Emilia's make-up, as she not only fears to do an injustice by choosing either of the kinsmen but also feels sorrow for whichever one may be defeated in the combat. Staying away from the arena, she exclaims: 'O, better never born | Than minister to such harm!' (5.3.65–6).

Chaucer makes much of pity throughout *The Knight's Tale*, remarking, when Theseus spares Palamon and Arcite in the woods, 'For pitee renneth soone in gentil herte' (l. A 1761), a line he used 'in almost identical form', as Robinson points out, in three other poems.[1] The association with gentility, or innate nobility, makes pity a virtue appropriate for a knight. It is also a prominent feature of the source of one part of Boccaccio's story. In the *Thebaid* Statius tells how the widowed queens sought the

---

[1] See Robinson's note on this line.

aid of Theseus, and how they waited for him in Athens at the Temple of Clemency, to which Statius devotes a lengthy description.[1] Of it J. H. Mozley says: 'One of the best known passages of the *Thebaid* is the description of the altar and grove of Clementia at Athens, in which the poet gives beautiful expression to the old Athenian ideal of humanity, lines that breathe the spirit of a purer religion than any known to the ancient world, and may well have given rise to Dante's belief that Statius was a Christian' (*Statius*, I. xvi). Both Boccaccio and Chaucer mention the temple—'this temple of the goddesse Clemence' (*The Knight's Tale*, l. A 928); in the play, where it is not mentioned, the spectacular staging of the queens' intercession achieves a comparable emphasis.

The treatment of pity in Renaissance poetics is also relevant. This is not to say that Fletcher and Shakespeare wrote their play to accord with any theory or that they were even familiar with the treatises I shall mention, but that the dramatic importance of pity was a concept which, in one form or another, they were likely to have encountered. Vincenzo Maggi, in an effort to explain why the sorrow evoked by 'the spectacle of piteous events' in tragedy is also pleasurable, says this is because 'it is human and natural for men to feel pity'.[2] Giovanni Battista Pigna makes the same point about the pleasure accompanying the sorrow we feel for the victims of disastrous changes of fortune: 'it is a human thing to have pity on the afflicted' (*I romanzi* (1554); Weinberg, pp. 447–80). Antonio Viperano asks whether 'we take joy in the very fact that pity is implanted in man by nature' (*De poetica libri tres* (1579); Weinberg, p. 762). This insistence that pity is 'human and natural', similar to Theseus' comment that without compassion 'We lose our human title', is gradually replaced in the seventeenth century by the idea that Dryden expresses in his Preface to *Troilus and Cressida*, where, somewhat like the Third Queen, he calls pity 'the noblest and most god-like of moral virtues'.[3] Earlier writers seem to exalt pity in a somewhat similar way when they bracket it with wonder (instead of fear) as one

[1] *Statius*, ed. and trans. J. H. Mozley, 2 vols. (London and Cambridge, Mass., 1928), ii. 481–3.

[2] *In Aristotelis librum de poetica communes explanationes* (1550), cited in Bernard Weinberg, *A History of Literary Criticism in the Italian Renaissance* (Chicago, 1961), p. 406.

[3] *Essays of John Dryden*, ed. W. P. Ker, 2 vols. (Oxford, 1926), i. 210.

The two Noble Kinsmen

5. Palamon and Arcite sit chained to a pair of stocks in prison, watched over by the Jailer (from Tonson's edition of Beaumont and Fletcher, vol. 7, published in 1711). Presumably it is Emilia, with her woman or perhaps Hippolyta, who is shown in the background; the picture does not correspond to an exact point in the play. Architecture, garden, and women's dresses are of the eighteenth century, but there may be an attempt to portray Jacobean doublets and ruffs.

of the proper effects of tragedy. Franciscus Portus, for example, says that Sophocles 'arouses the tragic emotions of pity and wonder', using the Latin terms 'misericordia, & admiratio' (*Prolegomena* [1575?]; Weinberg, p. 565). Sidney speaks of tragedy 'stirring the affects of admiration and commiseration'.[1] In the comments of these literary theorists, though their ultimate source is the much discussed Aristotelian theory of the arousal and purgation of pity and fear by tragedy, we find a view of pity analogous to that which is implied in the treatises on chivalry. Thus, in several ways, the emphasis on pity in the play supports the idealism of the principal characters.

[1] *Elizabethan Critical Essays*, ed. G. Gregory Smith, 2 vols. (Oxford, 1904), i. 177.

48

An essential knightly virtue when chivalry was a political reality was loyalty—to the knight's overlord in the first place, and also to his fellow knights; and it receives a corresponding stress in the romances. In some cases two knights further bound themselves to each other by becoming 'sworn brothers', or 'blood brothers' if their mutual oaths were accompanied by the mingling or drinking of blood. Chaucer has Palamon rebuke Arcite for being a 'traitour | To me, that am thy cosyn and thy brother | Ysworn ful depe . . .' (ll. A 1130–2).[1] Fletcher and Shakespeare omit any reference to sworn brotherhood. Instead, they invoke the classical ideal of friendship, which, like ideal love, had been absorbed into the chivalric tradition as it appeared in the romances, and was also, on its own, highly respected in the Renaissance. Friendship, as defined by Aristotle in the *Nichomachaean Ethics* and by Cicero in *Laelius de amicitia* and *De officiis*, is the best of all human relationships. Founded on the virtue of both friends, their mutual respect and shared ideals, it is entered into for its own sake rather than for any material reward or benefit. Laelius says 'that friendship cannot exist except among good men', and later: 'Wherefore it seems to me that friendship springs rather from nature than from need, and from an inclination of the soul joined with a feeling of love rather than from calculation of how much profit the friendship is likely to afford'.[2] In *De officiis* Cicero cites the 'ideally perfect friendship' of Damon and Phintias (or Pythias), one of whom was willing to offer his life to save the other from execution.[3] There must be an absolute reciprocity between them even if there is some difference of age or status. *One Soul in Bodies Twain*, the title Laurens J. Mills took from Nicholas Grimald for a study of this tradition (Bloomington, Ind., 1937), describes the perfect blending of identities envisioned by more than one writer. Montaigne, in his essay 'Of Friendship' as translated by John Florio, says: 'In the amity I speak of, [the friends] intermix and confound themselves one in the other with

[1] See Robinson's note on this line, where he discusses the background of this custom.

[2] *Laelius de amicitia*, iv. 18; viii. 27 in Cicero, *De senectute, De amicitia, De diviniatione*, trans. Wm. A. Falconer (London and New York, 1923), pp. 127, 139. Clements has a good discussion of the friendship tradition in his dissertation (see p. 29 n. 1), pp. 214–72.

[3] Cicero, *De officiis*, trans. Walter Miller (Cambridge, Mass. and London, 1961), III. x, p. 313.

so universal a commixture that they wear out, and can no more find the seam that hath conjoined them together.' And speaking of his friendship with Étienne de la Boétie, he continues: 'If a man urge me to tell wherefore I loved him, I feel it cannot be expressed but by answering: "Because it was he; because it was myself".'[1] Following in the footsteps of his classical predecessors, Montaigne asserts the superiority of friendship to the unequal relationship between parents and children (p. 198), and as for love of women:

To compare the affection toward women unto it, although it proceed from our own free choice, a man cannot, nor may it be placed in this rank. Her fire, I confess it . . . to be more active, more fervent, and more sharp. But it is a rash and wavering fire, waving and diverse. . . . In true friendship it is a general and universal heat . . . (p. 199)

Marriage (as distinguished from philandering) is a constraining covenant, very different from friendship, which is freely entered into for its own sake. Montaigne regrets that friendship cannot be a union of bodies as well as of minds, but considers that women 'could never yet by any example attain unto it' (p. 200). After reading Montaigne's lyrical praise of friendship it is easier to understand why Shakespeare makes a point of the kinsmen's shared disgust with the corruption of Thebes in the introductory scene (1.2), and to see that when Fletcher gives them such extravagant protestations of mutual love in prison (2.2), he is not merely building up to an ironic turn, though no doubt that is one of his aims. Though he may also expect his audience to smile at youthful ardour, their sentiments are well within a tradition which was taken seriously.

Twentieth-century spectators and readers are apt to assume that a relationship between men described in these terms must be homosexual. This is the assumption of both Bradbrook (p. 32) and Wickham (p. 183), and, as we have seen, some contemporary productions have strongly suggested homosexuality. It is most unlikely, however, that Fletcher and Shakespeare intended such suggestions or that audiences at that time would have interpreted the bond between the kinsmen in this way.[2] Montaigne is again

---

[1] *The Essays of Montaigne, Done into English by John Florio, Anno 1603*, with an introduction by George Saintsbury, 3 vols. (1892; repr. New York, 1967), i. 202.

[2] Richmond comments sensibly that 'our preoccupation with homosexuality and lesbianism has unbalanced our reaction to historical same-sex relationships'.

helpful. After regretting that friendship cannot have a physical dimension, he says 'And this other Greek licence is justly abhorred by our customs' (p. 200). Not only is it abhorrent but it was never true friendship, since the love between a man and a boy, as described by Plato, is again an unequal relationship. Only when physical passion has been displaced by spiritual love is friendship possible. 'To conclude', says Montaigne, 'all can be alleged in favour of the Academy is to say that it was a love ending in friendship' (p. 202).[1]

In Renaissance England, as in classical Greece and Rome, a sharp distinction seems to have been made between a man's love of boys and a homosexual relationship between adult males. The former, taken for granted in classical times, was often tolerated in England in situations such as that of tutor and pupil, whereas the latter was a disgraceful and punishable offence. K. J. Dover says that 'the reciprocal desire of partners belonging to the same age-category is virtually unknown in Greek homosexuality', which is, rather, a matter of 'the pursuit of those of lower status by those of higher status'.[2] In England at the time of *The Two Noble Kinsmen*, although King James's susceptibility to handsome young men such as his favourite, Robert Carr, was well known, and had perforce to be accepted, such homosexual attachments were considered abominations, and were constantly scourged by the snarling satirists of the period. It is significant that the word 'homosexuality' did not exist, and that the relationship was discussed in terms of the physical act, the crime of sodomy or buggery, curiously associated with sorcery by some of those who inveighed against it. Even less moralistic writers do not depict unambiguously homosexual relationships between adult males

[1] Gregory Vlastos makes an interestingly related distinction between Plato and Aristotle. In Platonic love a person is loved only in so far as that person presents an image of the Idea. Hence there is an element of utility in the relationship rather than the simple wish for the other person's good that distinguishes Aristotelian friendship. See 'The Individual as an Object of Love in Plato', *Platonic Studies* (Princeton, 1973), 3–34; also John M. Cooper, 'Aristotle on Friendship', *Essays on Aristotle's Ethics*, ed. Amélie O. Rorty (Berkeley, California, 1980), 301–40. For these references I am indebted to Professor Annette C. Baier.

[2] *Greek Homosexuality* (New York, 1980), pp. 16, 84. See also p. 103, where Dover quotes Plutarch: 'Those who enjoy playing the passive role we treat as the lowest of the low'; and see Paul Veyne, 'Homosexuality in Ancient Rome', *Western Sexuality*, ed. Philippe Ariès and André Béjin, trans. Anthony Forster (Oxford, 1985), p. 30; Alan Bray, *Homosexuality in Renaissance England* (London, 1982), pp. 19 ff.

in a favourable light. When Christopher Marlowe, who cannot be accused of orthodoxy, presents the affair of Edward II and Gaveston, he shows considerable sympathy for the King, and distances himself from those characters who view his infatuation most severely, but if his portrayal of these two men is placed side by side with Fletcher and Shakespeare's of Palamon and Arcite or of Theseus and Pirithous the great difference in kind is immediately clear. Edward is the victim of a passion which contributes to his undoing, though it is not the principal cause, and from the first moments of the play we know that Gaveston intends to use it as the means of his self-advancement. The relationship is never spoken of in the terms used by Hippolyta of Theseus and Pirithous (1.3.41–7) or by Palamon and Arcite of themselves in 2.2 and throughout. When Marlowe has Mortimer Senior defend Edward in conversation with Mortimer Junior the terms used and the examples given carry conflicting messages. 'The mightiest kings have had their minions' (1.4.390)[1] might well have suggested to Marlowe's contemporaries the French King Henry III (1574–89), whose favourites, known as '*les mignons du roi*', were as cordially envied and hated as Robert Carr was later to be. The first examples—'Great Alexander lov'd Hephaestion; | The conquering Hercules for Hylas wept' (ll. 391–2)—evoke legendary friendships which hardly fall in the category of relationships between kings and their minions. Achilles and Patroclus, mentioned next, are ideal friends in Homer, but we know from *Troilus and Cressida* that their relationship was sometimes regarded more cynically, and Socrates' love for Alcibiades, though defended by Plutarch as a love of virtue, was undoubtedly perceived by some as homosexual infatuation. Even Mortimer Senior ends his defence by saying that 'riper years' will wean Edward 'from such toys' (l. 400). This is a far cry from the ideal friendship described by Cicero.

As I have already remarked, the bond between Palamon and Arcite in Chaucer is that of sworn brotherhood. They are friends, of course, as they are in Boccaccio, but in neither version of the story is the relationship given the overtones of the classical ideal found in Fletcher and Shakespeare's play. For their portrayal of friendship, however, there were many models in earlier literature

---

[1] Quotations are from the edition by H. B. Charlton and R. D. Waller, revised by F. N. Lees (London, 1955).

and drama. One was near at hand in Sidney's *Arcadia*, where Pyrocles and Musidorus, who are, like Palamon and Arcite, cousins, are also friends in the classical style, as appears clearly in a conversation between them in the third book, at a moment when they are disguised as Dorus and Zelmane (an Amazon). Dorus has just confessed to his cousin his love for Pamela, and is about to propose that he temporarily leave Zelmane in order to further his love affair and also his cousin's love for Philoclea:

And therefore now, said Dorus, my dear cousin, to whom nature began my friendship, education confirmed it, and virtue hath made it eternal, here have I discovered the very foundation whereupon my life is built: be you the judge betwixt me and my fortune.

After Dorus has explained his plan, Pyrocles–Zelmane replies:

If I bare thee this love, virtuous Musidorus, for mine own sake, and that our friendship grew because I, for my part, might rejoice to enjoy such a friend, I should now so thoroughly feel mine own loss that I should call the heavens and earth to witness how cruelly ye rob me of my greatest comfort, measuring the breach of friendship by mine own passion. But because indeed I love thee for thy self, and in my judgement judge of thy worthiness to be loved, I am content to build my pleasure upon thy comfort: and then will I deem my hap in friendship great when I shall see thee, whom I love, happy.[1]

William Craft shows how thoroughly the *Old Arcadia* is pervaded by the Ciceronian ideal, and makes the point that Sidney's interest in it was due in part to the recommendation of his friend Hubert Languet, who wrote to him about applying Cicero's ideas to his own friendships.[2] Craft believes that in the revised *New Arcadia* Sidney intended to show the friends transcending the Ciceronian ideal by means of a yet more self-sacrificial love for the two heroines (pp. 66–7). The passages quoted above are from the 1593 edition, in which the continuation of the incomplete *New Arcadia* is based on the *Old Arcadia*.

John Lyly had also portrayed Ciceronian friendships in fiction (*Euphues* (1578)) and on the stage (notably in *Endymion* (1591)),

---

[1] *The Prose Works of Sir Philip Sidney*, ed. Albert Feuillerat, 4 vols. (Cambridge, 1912), ii. 2–3.
[2] 'Remaking the Heroic Self in the *New Arcadia*', *Studies in English Literature*, 25 (1985), 45–55; see James M. Osborn, *Young Philip Sidney, 1572–1577* (New Haven and London, 1972), pp. 144–5.

and Richard Edwards's *Damon and Pythias* (1565) was still well-enough known in 1614 for Jonson to burlesque it in *Bartholomew Fair*. Much earlier there were several romances, such as *Amis and Amiloun*, in which the friendship of two knights was an important feature.[1]

In many of these stories the friends become rivals in love. A nice balance of opposing values provided by the classical ideal of friendship and the idealized love found in medieval lyrics and romances may have contributed to the popularity of the conflict between love and friendship as a fictional motif. One of the oldest and most widely circulated examples of this *topos* is the story incorporated by Boccaccio in the *Decameron* as the eighth story of the tenth day, the story of Titus and Gisippus, translated by Sir Thomas Elyot in the twelfth chapter of the second book of *The Governor* as an illustration of 'perfect amity'.[2] When Titus falls in love with the fiancée of Gisippus he debates the claims of love and friendship, but, unwilling to betray his friend and unable to stop loving, he falls ill. Gisippus, discovering the cause of Titus' illness, allows him to have the girl. After many years and many turns of the plot, Titus returns this friendly gesture by offering his life to save the life of Gisippus, who has been wrongly accused of murder. Titus claims that he is the murderer, but Gisippus insists on his own guilt. So impressed is the true murderer by this display of innocence and altruism that he exculpates the friends by confessing his crime, and at the end Titus gives his sister in marriage to Gisippus. 'Friendship, then, is a most sacred thing', says Boccaccio, and concludes with four paragraphs in its praise.[3] Here there can be no doubt that friendship is the more highly valued relationship.

This is less certain in Lyly's mythological play *Endymion*. When Eumenides is forced to decide between gratifying his love for Semele and saving his friend Endymion from a magic spell, he embarks on a long euphuistic debate, toward the end of which he reflects, in a classical vein, that 'The love of men to women is a thing common and of course: the friendship of man to man

[1] See Mills, *One Soul in Bodies Twain*, p. 39.
[2] See *The Boke Named the Gouernour*, ed. H. H. S. Croft from the 1st edn. of 1531, 2 vols. (1883; repr. New York, 1967), ii. 132–74; and see 'Love and Friendship', pp. 235 ff., where I discuss the source of the story.
[3] *The Decameron*, trans. G. H. McWilliam (Harmondsworth, Baltimore, and Victoria, Australia, 1972), pp. 793–4.

is infinite and immortal'.[1] He therefore chooses his friend's welfare. In another plot, however, we encounter Endymion's love for Cynthia, which is anything but 'common and of course'. It consists in eternal aspiration and contemplation, and thus resembles the rarified love found in medieval lyrics and romances. Cynthia finally permits Endymion to be her lover in this special sense and Eumenides is also united with Semele. Both love and friendship win.

In Fletcher and Shakespeare's version of the story of Palamon, Arcite, and Emilia it can hardly be said that either wins. Friendship, to be sure, receives much more emphasis than it is given by Boccaccio or Chaucer. As we have already seen, the ideal nature of the kinsmen's friendship is established in the first scenes in which they appear—1.2 by Shakespeare and 2.2 by Fletcher—in dialogues which have no counterpart in the source. In another addition (1.3) Hippolyta and Emilia discuss the friendship of Theseus and Pirithous and Emilia's girlhood friendship with Flavina. It appears that women, *pace* Montaigne, are also capable of such ideal relationships. In the last act, by significantly altering the presentation of Arcite's last moments, Shakespeare further heightens the importance of friendship. In Chaucer's beautiful and touching episode Arcite sends for Emelie and Palamon and says a long farewell to Emelie, 'my lady, that I love most':

> Alas the death, alas mine Emely,
> Alas departing of our company:
> Alas, mine hearts queene, alas my liues wife,
> Mine hearts ladie, ender of my life.
>
> (ll. A 2767, 2773–6)

He praises Palamon and urges Emelie to recognize his cousin's merits if she ever decides to marry again: 'Foryet not Palamon, the gentle man' (l. A 2797). Then he looks at her, and his last words are 'mercy, Emelie!' Shakespeare's version of the scene of Arcite's death begins with Palamon and his three knights being led to the scaffold as losers of the combat. When the dying Arcite is carried in after his fatal accident, Palamon knows that his life has been saved only by the loss of his friend. Their exchange of

---

[1] 3.4.114–16 in *The Complete Works of John Lyly*, ed. G. Warwick Bond, 3 vols. (Oxford, 1902), iii. 50.

words in the presence of all the principal characters is brief but highly charged. Palamon greets Arcite with:

> O miserable end of our alliance!
> The gods are mighty, Arcite. If thy heart,
> Thy worthy, manly heart, be yet unbroken,
> Give me thy last words. I am Palamon,
> One that yet loves thee dying.

To which Arcite replies:

> Take Emilia,
> And with her all the world's joy. Reach thy hand—
> Farewell; I have told my last hour. I was false,
> Yet never treacherous; forgive me, cousin.
> One kiss from fair Emilia; (*they kiss*) 'tis done;
> Take her; I die.
>
> > *He dies*
> > (5.4.86–95)

Palamon asks for and receives the last words.

In the scenes I have just discussed friendship appears to be the greatest boon life can offer and the loss of a friend the greatest catastrophe, but the dramatic power of the play arises from conflict, and the conflicting power of love is not understated. More than one critic has observed that it is often portrayed negatively as a destructive passion, making the kinsmen quarrel and the Jailer's Daughter go mad. When Palamon prays to Venus, his way of flattering her is to recall the grotesque infatuation of an octogenarian for his fourteen-year-old bride (see note on 5.1.107–18). Yet it would be wrong to say that love is invariably seen in an unfavourable light. From first to last the love of Theseus and Hippolyta is presented as a firm bond based on mutual admiration as well as physical attraction (with somewhat too much emphasis on the latter for one nineteenth-century critic (see above, pp. 8–9)). And the kinsmen must be believed when they protest their absolute commitment to 'Queen Emilia, | Fresher than May', in Arcite's words (3.1.4–5), or 'That fortunate bright star, the fair Emilia', as Palamon puts it (3.6.146). This is the language of Elizabethan love-poetry, non-dramatic and dramatic, and it invokes the conventions of romance.

More easily credible for a twentieth-century audience is the love of the Jailer's Daughter for Palamon, and although its hopelessness does indeed unsettle her mind, a spectator is more apt to be struck by the pathos of her situation than by the destructive power of love. Her mad scenes, invariably effective in performance, as has already been noted, make an important contribution to the portrayal of love in the play. While the bawdy double meanings of some of her lines are mainly amusing, they testify to a sexuality freed of inhibition, which is treated in only one other scene, and there quite briefly, when the kinsmen reminisce about their youthful escapades with women (3.3.29–42). The continual harping of the Jailer's Daughter on Palamon's sexual attraction gives a solidity and credibility to her desire, which might otherwise resemble a young girl's crush on a popular entertainer. Her frank overtures to the Wooer, under the delusion that he is Palamon, provide a remarkably affecting moment. The love of the Jailer's Daughter helps to place that of the kinsmen, which is very different from her simple, unaffected desire, and different, too, from the casual lust of their youth, but not to be confused with the endless, unsatisfied longing of an Endymion. Though Arcite in disguise seems content to remain, like a good Petrarchan lover, Emilia's servant, making no effort to approach her, he has told Palamon that he loves her 'as a woman' rather than worshipping her as a goddess (2.2.163–5), and it is clear that both of them, in fact, look forward to a consummation of their love in marriage.

In three scenes of Act 3, in the centre of the play, the thematically central conflict of love and friendship is powerfully dramatized. In the first (3.1), a scene written by Shakespeare, Palamon interrupts Arcite's rhapsodic soliloquy in praise of Emilia with a savage rebuke. Here the conflict is realized not mainly in the spectacle of two friends quarrelling but, more effectively, in the determined courtesy with which Arcite restrains his resentment, offers to bring Palamon food and files to remove his shackles, and continues to address him affectionately until Palamon puts by his rage sufficiently to say 'I do embrace you and your offer' (3.1.93). In the second and third meetings of the kinsmen in the forest Fletcher builds on the tension established by Shakespeare. In Scene 3, Arcite courteously sets out food and drink and proposes that they avoid the subject of Emilia, as for a while they do, teasing each other about 'the wenches | We have known in our days' (3.3.29–30). Then the friendly conviviality is broken with an abruptness characteristic of Fletcher, as Palamon's anger suddenly erupts once more. The conflict is focused with still greater intensity in the episode of arming before the combat in 3.6. Chivalric courtesy barely conceals the underlying affection of two men driven by their rivalry in love toward mortal combat. With dialogue and stage business that come close to encapsulating the main issue of the play, this is one of its most moving and theatrically effective scenes. Palamon says:

> I could wish ye
> As kind a kinsman as you force me find
> A beneficial foe, that my embraces
> Might thank ye, not my blows.
>
> (ll. 20–3)

And, as he carefully adjusts Arcite's armour:

> I would have nothing hurt thee but my sword;
> A bruise would be dishonour.
>
> (ll. 87–8)

About to fight, they pause to say farewell for what they suppose will be the last time. Palamon holds out his hand to Arcite, who takes it, saying:

> Here, Palamon. This hand shall never more
> Come near thee with such friendship.
>
> (ll. 102–3)

Shortly after this, their fight is interrupted by the arrival of Theseus.

By emphasizing the value of friendship as they do, Fletcher and Shakespeare place their heroes in a no-win situation as they begin their fight over Emilia. Victory for either one means killing his friend. When Theseus agrees not to punish them for breaking his laws, and arranges for a less lethal form of combat to determine which kinsman shall have Emilia, he adds the stipulation, not in the source, that the loser and his three assistants shall be executed. Although this additional turn of the screw, by which the no-win situation is perpetuated, may be seen as a step toward melodrama by the playwrights, it may also be seen to present a parallel to the mysterious and seemingly arbitrary decisions of the gods, who determine the final outcome of the story. When

Emilia, who has refused to be responsible for the death of one
kinsman by choosing the other, gets word that Arcite has won
the combat, she speaks as if the gods had not only picked the
winner but had also doomed the loser to the death which, in
fact, Theseus decreed:

> Is this winning?
> O all you heavenly powers, where is your mercy?
> But that your wills have said it must be so,
> And charge me live to comfort this unfriended,
> This miserable prince, that cuts away
> A life more worthy from him than all women,
> I should and would die too.

> (5.3.138–44)

The kinsmen's hopeless dilemma is again almost identified with
the hopelessness of human beings controlled by incomprehensible
divine decrees when Palamon, addressing Arcite's corpse, says:

> O cousin,
> That we should things desire which do cost us
> The loss of our desire! That naught could buy
> Dear love but loss of dear love!

> (5.4.109–12)

and Theseus, in the concluding speech of the play, says:

> The gods my justice
> Take from my hand, and they themselves become
> The executioners. . . .
> O you heavenly charmers,
> What things you make of us! For what we lack
> We laugh, for what we have are sorry; still
> Are children in some kind.

> (ll. 120–2, 131–4)

Unrelieved by any Boethian consolation, it is a much darker
ending than that of *The Knight's Tale*. To some extent, the
hopelessness of the ending is due, as Talbot Donaldson argues,
to human perversity as much as to divine ordinance,[1] for, even
before Theseus orders death for the loser, each of the kinsmen
seems determined on death if he cannot win Emilia; but this
determination is rooted in a chance encounter and an emotional
commitment which neither man can control. The play seems to

---

[1] *The Swan at the Well*, pp. 72–3.

suggest that human beings are as powerless to resolve the conflict between love and friendship as they are to resist the manipulation of their destinies by the gods. In an important essay Philip Edwards, one of the first to see that the design of *The Two Noble Kinsmen* is grounded in an idea, describes that idea as the growth from innocence to experience—from the innocence of youthful friendship to the experience of sexual desire and marriage.[1] Innocence there surely is in Emilia's account of her girlhood friendship and in the kinsmen's exuberant confidence that a lifetime in prison will be made idyllic by their friendship, but the experience which they are forced to confront is something more sinister than the adult world of love and marriage. It is a recognition of the powerlessness of even the best intentioned and most enlightened to control their lives, and the fact that there are circumstances in which the choice of one good means the loss and even the destruction of another.

The dilemmas of Palamon, Arcite, and Emilia strike most of us as extraordinarily contrived and improbable, but it is the terms in which these dilemmas are presented, rather than the basic issues, which make them difficult to take seriously. Sexual rivalry between friends is a fairly common situation in modern fiction and drama, where the friendship is a more familiar form of male bonding than the lofty classical ideal, and the love more a matter of sexual infatuation than the *fine amor* of medieval romance. Such infatuations are often presented as occurring either at first sight or at least very suddenly, and the consequences are likely to be, as in Harold Pinter's *Betrayal*, a clandestine affair between a wife and her husband's best friend. In this play the conflict of love and friendship leads to the break-up of both the marriage and the affair. In the absence of gods to blame, the characters become disillusioned with each other, and the irony of this development is emphasized by presenting the story in reverse chronological order, so that the ending presents the naïve hopes of the couple who are about to become illicit lovers, but who, we know, will not be happy long. In order to respond to the no less serious conflicts of *The Two Noble Kinsmen* it is necessary to accept imaginatively some of the conventions and assumptions that were familiar to audiences in 1613.

[1] 'On the Design of *The Two Noble Kinsmen*', *A Review of English Literature*, 5 (1964), 89–105.

A number of these, as we have seen, were closely associated with chivalric romance. Not only are the ideals to which Theseus, Palamon, Arcite, and Emilia aspire framed in terms of romance, but their characters, like those in most romances, are presented in relatively simple outlines. Much more attention is given to conflicting ideals than to conflicting motives. Palamon and Arcite, like their prototypes in Chaucer, are nearly indistinguishable except in those scenes in Act 3 where it is dramatically advantageous to show one more angry and the other more courteous.

The court masque, which clearly provided a model for some of the spectacular scenes of the play, was governed by another set of conventions which would have helped to shape the response of a seventeenth-century audience. As has already been noted, the Schoolmaster's entertainment for Theseus in 3.5 was borrowed directly from Beaumont's *The Masque of the Inner Temple and Gray's Inn* (see above, pp. 1 and 29, and Appendix A), and just as the morris dance there serves as a foil for the discovery of the Olympian Knights of the main masque, so it serves in the play as a foil for the scene of the arming and aborted combat of Palamon and Arcite. The abrupt contrast of moods is identical. The more general influence of masque conventions is notable in the wedding procession of the first act, the second intercession with Theseus in 3.6, and the prayers of the last act. Ceremonial scenes did not originate with the masque; they are found in the dumb shows of such early plays as *Gorboduc* (1562) and *Jocasta* (1566) and in dramatized romances such as *The Rare Triumphs of Love and Fortune* (1582) and *The Trial of Chivalry* (1601?).[1] The court masque, with the spectacular staging of Inigo Jones, however, gave a new impetus to the popularity of this kind of scene and reinforced the association it had often had with the supermundane and with the display of magnanimity. The spectacular triumph of the main masquers over the forces of evil and disorder was calculated to inspire wonder at the transcendent power of good. This response is eminently appropriate at the conclusion of the two scenes (1.1 and 3.6) in which Theseus is persuaded by kneeling suppliants to show compassion. Wonder

---

[1] See Waith, '*Titus Andronicus* and the Wounds of Civil War', in *Literary Theory and Criticism*, ed. Joseph P. Strelka (Bern and New York, 1984), pp. 1352–7), reprinted in Waith, *Patterns and Perspectives*, pp. 127–37; also Waith, 'Ceremonies', pp. 113–37.

at the superiority and incomprehensible mystery of the gods is a suitable response to the most spectacular scene of all (5.1), in which, one after another, each of the three principal characters, accompanied by a train of followers, prays at an altar for divine assistance and is answered by strange sights and sounds. Though Blackfriars could not duplicate the staging of court entertainments, it had sufficient machinery to suggest those fashionable occasions. Masque-like spectacle, then, was well calculated not only to make the play theatrically effective but also to support the emphasis on wonder characteristic of romance.[1]

The Collaborative Structure

Although a division of labour between the playwrights corresponding to plot and sub-plot might seem to have been the simplest, the evidence reviewed in the section on authorship suggests a different and more interesting scheme of collaboration. If the assignment of scenes given at the end of that section is accepted, Shakespeare, the senior partner, writing the entire first act and the first scene of the second, introduced the characters of both plots, wrote all the scenes of the main plot in the last act, and some scenes of both plots in Acts 3 and 4. The work of the two playwrights is tightly interlaced. One curious result of this arrangement, though it need not have been deliberately so planned, is a number of closely comparable scenes, one written by one collaborator and one by the other, as has been noted in the discussion of their contrasting styles. It is not always Shakespeare who wrote the first of such similar scenes. Although he was responsible for the first intercession with Theseus and the first dialogue between Palamon and Arcite, Fletcher wrote the first two of the several soliloquies of the Jailer's Daughter (in 2.4 and 2.6) and Shakespeare the third (in 3.2); Fletcher also wrote the first of Emilia's debates with herself on the respective merits of the two kinsmen. In comparing some of these scenes I have pointed, in both the section on authorship and elsewhere (in 'Love

---

[1] It is of more than passing interest that the Greek verb *thaomai*, 'to wonder at', is etymologically related to *theaomai*, one meaning of which is 'to view as spectators', and hence to *theatron*, from which 'theatre' is derived. Michael Goldman refers to some other etymological relatives of 'theatre' in *Acting and Action in Shakespearean Tragedy* (Princeton, 1985), pp. 169–70.

and Friendship'), to Fletcher's characteristic way of making the most dramatically out of the inherent tensions in a situation and to Shakespeare's equally characteristic way of combining the exploitation of emotional tension with philosophical reflection. What I have called the 'idea' of the play seems largely to emerge in his scenes. But, after acknowledging that the collaborators at times saw different sorts of potential in their material, and after noting that occasionally their divergent perspectives resulted in minor inconsistencies of characterization, one is bound to be surprised by how close and efficient the collaboration was. Though we have no way of knowing what sort of plan they agreed upon, it seems reasonable to guess that Shakespeare's was the vision that determined the meaning and the predominant tone. The fact that he wrote the exposition and the conclusion strongly supports this supposition. In most of the scenes that Fletcher wrote, several of them crucial with respect to both plot and theme, he adhered closely to their plan. It is he, for example, who did most to establish the Ciceronian basis of the friendship between Palamon and Arcite (in 2.2), and after Shakespeare set the pattern for the strange mixture of hostility and courtesy in their encounters in the forest, Fletcher not only maintained it but made it the basis for the most effective presentation in the entire play of the conflict between love and friendship (in 3.6). Each playwright leads into and also builds upon scenes written by the other. To examine each scene with regard to what follows and what precedes it is to recognize not only the closeness of the collaboration but the soundness of the plan they were following.

The structure of *The Two Noble Kinsmen*, broadly considered, falls into a familiar Elizabethan and Jacobean category of alternating plot and sub-plot. Here the sub-plot of the Jailer's Daughter and the essential complication of the main plot—the conflict between love and friendship—are first introduced in the second act, the first act serving as an extended but essential prologue devoted to the introduction of the characters in the main plot and the establishment of both the atmosphere of chivalric romance and the theme of friendship. It opens and closes with impressive spectacles—Theseus' wedding procession and the 'funeral solemnity' for the dead kings. In the course of this 'prologue' the audience also encounters the first instances of what is to become the prominent pattern of action interrupted—the deferral of

Theseus' wedding and the decision of Palamon and Arcite not to leave Thebes.

From the beginning of Act 2 to the end of the play main plot and sub-plot alternate regularly except in three instances. In the first of these (2.3), following a main-plot scene, Arcite, released from prison, encounters the Countrymen who are to take part in the Schoolmaster's entertainment for Theseus. This episode (it can hardly be called a plot), though firmly attached to the main plot, has its own distinctive character. The scene of the entertainment itself (3.5), bringing characters from both the main plot and the sub-plot on stage, is followed by a crucial scene of the main plot, the interrupted fight in the woods. The third exception to the regular alternation is the sequence of the final two scenes, both of which belong to the main plot, though the second (5.4) also provides the reported happy ending of the story of the Jailer's Daughter.

The important questions are: to what extent and in what ways does such an alternation of plot and sub-plot serve the purposes of the authors? We have already seen that responses to the sub-plot have varied from stern disapproval of the character of the Jailer's Daughter to delight in the performance of her scenes. Many critics would label these scenes with that simplest and hoariest of structural explanations, 'comic relief'. There is certainly some welcome comedy in them, but there is more than that, as has already been suggested in the discussion of the frank sexuality of the mad scenes. As the agent of Palamon's release from prison the Jailer's Daughter is an improvement over the otherwise unknown friend in *The Knight's Tale*, and, most obviously, she is made to be an illuminating counterpart to Emilia. At a time when Emilia thinks she will never fall in love the Jailer's Daughter falls in love instantly. Emilia, persuaded that she must accept one of the eponymous kinsmen, cannot decide which is most admirable; the Jailer's Daughter, comically and pathetically single-minded, is deluded into mistaking the Wooer for the kinsman of her choice. The sequence of ironic contrasts strengthens the portrayal of both women, who contribute more to the total effect of the play than is sometimes granted. Although the world of *The Two Noble Kinsmen* is a man's world, in which the kinsmen themselves are the central characters, Emilia and the Jailer's Daughter are made the agents for most of the pathos inherent in the story. The bewildered reluctance of the one is as affecting as the hopeless love of the other.

The prominence of the pattern of interrupted action can easily be shown by a list of instances: Theseus' wedding procession is interrupted by the mourning queens and the wedding is postponed; Palamon and Arcite give up their plan to leave Thebes when they hear of the imminent attack on the city; Emilia's girlhood friendship has been cut off by Flavina's death; the friendship of Palamon and Arcite suddenly turns to rivalry in love; when the love of the Jailer's Daughter for Palamon is not returned she escapes into mad fantasy; the kinsmen's fight in the woods is stopped by Theseus' arrival, but then his initial decree of death for both of them is altered after the intercession of Hippolyta, Emilia, and Pirithous; Emilia's wish to remain a virgin is overcome by the unexpected discovery of the kinsmen's love, by her pity for them, and by the attraction she begins to feel; finally, Arcite's victory is cancelled by his fatal accident, and Palamon's death is thereby averted.

Interrupted actions and unexpected developments are, as Barbara Mowat says, characteristic of Shakespeare's late romances and, indeed, of romance itself. Paula Berggren speaks of a more sinister 'incompletion' in this play. She calls it 'an interrupted poem, with a beginning that sets out a group of problems that never truly resolve themselves and an ending that is glorious, terrifying, and finally mute in the face of the universe it conjures up'.[1] While unexpected developments in romance most often lead ultimately to the characteristically happy ending, here they support the dark views expressed by the principal characters in the last act—views rather uncharacteristic of romance but well suited to this 'tragicomedy' which borders so closely on tragedy.

It is Theseus who expresses the last, and perhaps the most hopeless of these views, though it is also he whose change of heart in the first scene provides a model of human behaviour. Thus he is given a crucial role as both exemplar of romantic idealism and spokesman for the pessimistic idea which underlies

---

[1] See Mowat, *The Dramaturgy of Shakespeare's Late Romances* (Athens, Ga., 1976), Chapter 4; and Berggren, '"For what we lack,/We laugh": Incompletion and *The Two Noble Kinsmen*', *Modern Language Studies*, 14 (1984), 3–17; pp. 14–15.

the play. As in *The Knight's Tale* he presides over the entire action, which he in part determines and at the end interprets, his structural importance repeatedly emphasized by the ceremonial scenes in which he appears.

EDITORIAL PROCEDURES

THE basis for the text of this edition is the quarto of 1634 (Q). Spelling and punctuation have been modernized in accordance with the principles of the Oxford Shakespeare, described by Stanley Wells in *Modernizing Shakespeare's Spelling* (Oxford, 1979) and *Re-Editing Shakespeare for the Modern Reader* (Oxford, 1984). The aim is to modernize more consistently than has been done in the past, with the result that what some editors would have preserved as distinctive Elizabethan forms of words have been treated here as variant spellings and have been altered. The object of modernization is to remove some of the differences between the experience of the modern reader and that of the reader for whom the text was printed. We cannot make ourselves into Elizabethan readers or spectators, and we should welcome the challenge to participate imaginatively in a period when the language differed somewhat from that spoken today, but the important differences are not those of spelling, and we should not be encouraged to confuse the quaintly archaic with the spirit of the times. Such alterations are not recorded unless they have been disputed or appear to be disputable, in which case they appear in the collations in this form:

travail] Q (travell)

where the spelling of the control text is given in round brackets. In this edition the syllabic form of the past participle is indicated by an accent ('èd') and the non-syllabic form by the absence of that accent. The distinction between the two is based on Q, which normally spells the non-syllabic form without an 'e' (e.g. 'markd' for 'marked'). Except in the case of this distinction, no attempt has been made to mark accentuations required by the metre, but in the notes the reader's attention is called to certain categories of words, such as those ending in '-tion', of which the pronunciation varies. One other convention should be noted: when 'and' means 'if', either by itself or in the phrase 'and if', it is silently changed to 'an' for the sake of clarity.

This text follows Q more closely than most modernized texts in the treatment of one category of words. Contractions such as 'ev'n' and 'nev'r' have not been changed to 'e'en' and 'ne'er', which are not, in any case, common in modern English. The reason for retaining Q's spelling in these cases is the belief that it may have metrical significance. Seventeenth-century dramatists experimented with ways of varying and loosening the rhythm of the blank verse line, frequently adding extra syllables. Ben Jonson indicated one metrical variation by printing an apostrophe 'between two unelided but lightly sounded syllables', which were to be taken as equivalent to one syllable (see Jonson, ix. 50). In a somewhat similar way, words such as 'ev'n' and 'nev'r', which undoubtedly counted as one syllable, may nevertheless have been heard as comprising two lightly sounded syllables. Building on the metrical studies of Edward Weismiller, Mary D. Coulter analyses these developments in her unpublished Ph.D. dissertation, 'The English Pentameter in Non-Dramatic and Dramatic Verse *c.*1590–1640' (George Washington University, 1982). Since verse rhythm is one of the distinctive features of an author's style, it seems wise to retain what may be authorial distinctions in Q between, for example, 'never', 'nev'r', and 'ne'er', all of which occur.

Departures from the original punctuation are noted only when they affect the meaning, as, for example, when a full stop is replaced by a comma, or when the punctuation of the control-text makes it uncertain whether a subordinate clause depends on a main clause preceding or following it. In such cases the modernized punctuation is treated as an emendation, recorded in the collations, and often discussed in the notes.

Speech-prefixes have been silently normalized and are given in full. Significant clarifications of the copy text, such as 'ALL THE QUEENS' for '*All.*', are noted in the collations, but not variant spellings such as 'Perithous' for 'Pirithous'. Q's stage directions are retained and often amplified, marginal directions normally being moved into the text, except when they consist in the bookkeeper's notations of props to be ready or warnings to actors. Such marginal notations are recorded in the collations and discussed in the notes. All alterations of Q's stage directions are recorded in the collations except for directions for a speech to be spoken 'aside' or 'to' another character; all of these are to be understood as editorial; a dash is used to mark the end of an aside. Added stage directions are not bracketed if the specified action is clearly implied in the dialogue, nor are they attributed to a particular edition. Only stage directions which are editorial guesses are bracketed, and if the guess is a previous editor's, the attribution is given.

With the exception of the stage directions noted above (*'aside'* or *'to . . .'*), all emendations (as distinguished from modernization) of the copy text are recorded in the collations in the traditional form:

Pirithous] THEOBALD; Theseus Q

where the lemma, representing the reading of this edition, is followed by the source of the reading, and, after a semicolon, by the rejected reading of the control text. Citations of the early texts in the collations are given *literatim*, and preserve the early use of u, v, i, and j, but not long s or the various ligatures. Rejected emendations in other editions are not recorded unless a strong case can be made for them. When the adopted reading is substantially, but not exactly, that of the edition from which it is taken, this fact is indicated by either *'subs.'* or the exact reading in round brackets following reference to the source:

1.1] F (*Actus Primus. Scoena Prima.*); *Actus Primus.* Q

He dances] BAWCUTT (*subs.*); *not in* Q

The indication *'not in* Q' following attribution to a later edition carries the further information that the reading is not in any intervening edition. If an editor's reading is based on a previous conjecture, not incorporated in an edition, this is indicated as follows:

one] COLMAN (*conj.* Seward); on Q

References to other plays of Shakespeare are keyed to the Oxford *Complete Works*, ed. Stanley Wells and Gary Taylor (1986); those to other plays by Fletcher and his collaborators to *The Dramatic Works in the Beaumont and Fletcher Canon*, General Editor, Fredson Bowers (Cambridge, 1966–). For reasons given in the introduction, quotations from Chaucer are taken from Speght's 1602 edition with line references to the standard edition of F. N. Robinson (Boston and New York, 1933). Quotations in the commentary and introduction from the works of the playwrights' contemporaries are normally taken from modern-spelling editions; when the original editions have been used, spelling and punctuation have been modernized except where reproduction of early documentary evidence (Stationers' Register entries, Henslowe's diary, title-pages) seemed desirable. There appears to be no good reason for treating the texts used to illuminate Fletcher and Shakespeare differently from the text of their play.

In calling attention to the many proverbs quoted or alluded to in the text of the play I frequently give the form of a proverb as it appears in R. W. Dent's *Shakespeare's Proverbial Language*, but do not do so when the form quoted in the play is almost identical; reference to Dent by letter and number follows:

'To go (swim, run) with the stream' (Dent S930)

Words are normally defined only when they first appear. All words that are glossed are listed in the index.

Abbreviations and References

Place of publication is London unless otherwise noted.

EDITIONS OF FLETCHER AND SHAKESPEARE

Q	*The Two Noble Kinsmen* (1634)
F	*Fifty Comedies and Tragedies. Written by Francis Beaumont and John Fletcher, Gentlemen.* (1679)
1750	*The Works of Mr. Francis Beaumont, and Mr. John Fletcher,* ed. Thomas Seward, Lewis Theobald, and J. Sympson, 10 vols. (1750), vol. 10. Readings from this edition are attributed to Seward, the principal editor, except when he credits one or more of his collaborators. '1750' means that the three editors concur.
Bawcutt	*The Two Noble Kinsmen,* ed. N. W. Bawcutt, New Penguin Shakespeare (Harmondsworth, 1977)
Brooke	*The Shakespeare Apocrypha,* ed. C. F. Tucker Brooke (Oxford, 1908)
Colman	*The Dramatick Works of Beaumont and Fletcher,* ed. George Colman, 10 vols. (1778), vol. 10
Dyce	*The Works of Beaumont and Fletcher,* ed. Alexander Dyce, 11 vols. (1843–6), vol. 11 (1846)
Dyce 1866	*The Works of William Shakespeare,* ed. Alexander Dyce, 2nd edn., 9 vols. (1864–7); vol. 8 (1866)

Kittredge	*The Complete Works of Shakespeare*, ed. G. L. Kittredge (Boston, 1936)
Knight	*The Pictorial Edition of the Works of Shakspere*, ed. Charles Knight, 8 vols. (1839–41), *Doubtful Plays* (n.d.)
Leech	*The Two Noble Kinsmen*, ed. Clifford Leech, The Complete Signet Classic Shakespeare (New York, 1972)
Littledale	*The Two Noble Kinsmen*, ed. Harold Littledale for the New Shakspere Society, revised text and notes (1876), general introduction (1885)
Oxford	William Shakespeare, *The Complete Works*, General Editors, Stanley Wells and Gary Taylor (Oxford, 1966). *The Two Noble Kinsmen* was edited by William Montgomery; textual notes are to be found in *William Shakespeare: A Textual Companion* (Oxford, 1987), esp. pp. 625–36.
Proudfoot	*The Two Noble Kinsmen*, ed. G. R. Proudfoot, Regents Renaissance Drama Series (Lincoln, Nebr., 1970)
Proudfoot 2	Typescript of projected edition of *The Two Noble Kinsmen* for *The Shakespeare Apocrypha*
Riverside	*The Riverside Shakespeare*, Textual Editor, G. B. Evans (Boston, 1974)
Seward	See 1750 above.
Skeat	*The Two Noble Kinsmen*, ed. W. W. Skeat, Pitt Press Series (Cambridge, 1875)
Sympson	See 1750 above.
Theobald	See 1750 above.
Tonson	*The Works of Mr. Francis Beaumont, and Mr. John Fletcher*, printed for Jacob Tonson, 7 vols. (1711), vol. 7
Weber	*The Works of Beaumont and Fletcher*, ed. Henry Weber, 14 vols. (Edinburgh, 1812), vol. 13

OTHER WORKS

Babb	Lawrence Babb, *The Elizabethan Malady* (East Lansing, Mich., 1951)
Bertram	Paul Bertram, *Shakespeare and The Two Noble Kinsmen* (New Brunswick, NJ, 1965)
Bowers	*The Dramatic Works in the Beaumont and Fletcher Canon*, General Editor, Fredson Bowers (Cambridge, 1966–)
Bradbrook	M. C. Bradbrook, 'Shakespeare and his Collaborators',

	Shakespeare 1971, ed. Clifford Leech and J. M. R. Margeson (Toronto, 1972), pp. 21–36
Chambers	E. K. Chambers, *William Shakespeare: A Study of Facts and Problems*, 2 vols. (Oxford, 1930)
Chappell	William Chappell, *Popular Music of the Olden Time* (1859)
Child	Francis J. Child, *The English and Scottish Popular Ballads*, 5 vols. (1884–98; repr. New York, 1965)
Davenant	Sir William Davenant, *The Rivals* (1668)
Dent	R. W. Dent, *Shakespeare's Proverbial Language: an Index* (Berkeley, Calif., 1981)
Donaldson	E. Talbot Donaldson, *The Swan at the Well: Shakespeare Reading Chaucer* (New Haven and London, 1985)
Douce	Francis Douce, *Illustrations of Shakespeare, and of Ancient Manners*, new edn. (1839; repr. New York, 1968)
Downes	John Downes, *Roscius Anglicanus* (1708; repr. Los Angeles, 1969)
Ferguson, *Indian Summer*	Arthur B. Ferguson, *The Indian Summer of English Chivalry* (Durham, NC, 1960)
Freehafer	John Freehafer, 'A Textual Crux in *The Two Noble Kinsmen*', *English Language Notes*, 7 (1969–70), 254–7
Habicht	Werner Habicht, 'Tree Properties and Tree Scenes in Elizabethan Theater', *Renaissance Drama*, NS 4 (1971), 69–92
Heath	Benjamin Heath, MS notes on 1750 edition of Beaumont and Fletcher, quoted by Dyce
Hoy, 'Shares'	'The Shares of Fletcher and his Collaborators in the Beaumont and Fletcher Canon', *Studies in Bibliography*, 8, 9, 11, 12, 13, 14, 15 (1956–62)
Ingleby	C. M. Ingleby, quoted by Littledale
Ingram	J. K. Ingram, quoted by Littledale
JEGP	*Journal of English and Germanic Philology*
Jonson	*Ben Jonson*, ed. C. H. Herford and Percy and Evelyn Simpson, 11 vols. (Oxford, 1925–52)
Jonson, *Complete Masques*	*Ben Jonson: The Complete Masques*, ed. Stephen Orgel (New Haven and London, 1969)
Keen	Maurice Keen, *Chivalry* (New Haven and London, 1984)
London Stage	*The London Stage, 1660–1800*, Part 1: 1660–1700, ed. W. Van Lennep (Carbondale, Ill., 1960)

Manifold   J. S. Manifold, *The Music of English Drama* (1956)

Mason   John Monck Mason, *Comments on the Plays of Beaumont and Fletcher* (1798)

Nicholson   B. Nicholson, quoted by Littledale

OED   *Oxford English Dictionary*, 12 vols. and supplement (Oxford, 1933)

Onions   C. T. Onions, *A Shakespeare Glossary*, 2nd edn. (1919; repr. Oxford, 1953)

Plutarch, *Lives*   Plutarch, *The Lives of the Noble Grecians and Romans*, trans. Sir Thomas North (1579)

Richmond   Hugh Richmond, 'Performance as Criticism', unpublished paper first given at the 1985 meeting of the Shakespeare Association of America

Robinson   *The Complete Works of Geoffrey Chaucer*, ed. F. N. Robinson (Boston and New York, 1933)

Spalding   William Spalding, *A Letter on Shakspere's Authorship of The Two Noble Kinsmen* (Edinburgh, 1833; repr. by F. J. Furnivall for the New Shakspere Society, Series 8, no. 1 (1876)

Speght   *The Workes of our Antient and Learned English Poet, Geffrey Chaucer*, ed. Thomas Speght, 2nd edn. (1602)

Waith, 'Ceremonies'   E. M. Waith, 'Shakespeare and the Ceremonies of Romance', in *Shakespeare's Craft*, ed. Philip H. Highfill, Jr. (Carbondale and Edwardsville, Ill., 1982), pp. 113–37

Waith, *Ideas of Greatness*   E. M. Waith, *Ideas of Greatness* (London and New York, 1971)

Waith, 'Love and Friendship'   E. M. Waith, 'Shakespeare and Fletcher on Love and Friendship', *Shakespeare Studies*, 18 (1986), 235–50; reprinted in Waith, *Patterns and Perspectives*, pp. 289–303

Waith, *Patterns and Perspectives*   E. M. Waith, *Patterns and Perspectives in English Renaissance Drama* (Newark, Del., 1988)

Werstine   Paul Werstine, 'On the Compositors of *The Two Noble Kinsmen*', unpublished paper

Wickham   Glynne Wickham, '*The Two Noble Kinsmen*, or *A Midsummer Night's Dream, Part II?*', *Elizabethan Theatre*, 7 (1980), 167–96

The Two Noble Kinsmen

THE PERSONS OF THE PLAY

PROLOGUE

THESEUS, Duke of Athens

HIPPOLYTA, Queen of the Amazons, later wife of Theseus

EMILIA, her sister

PIRITHOUS, friend of Theseus

PALAMON ⎱ the two noble kinsmen, cousins, nephews of Creon, the
ARCITE ⎰ King of Thebes

Hymen, god of marriage

A BOY, who sings

ARTESIUS, an Athenian soldier

Three QUEENS, widows of kings killed in the siege of Thebes

VALERIUS, a Theban

A HERALD

A WOMAN, attending Emilia

An Athenian GENTLEMAN

MESSENGERS

Six KNIGHTS, three attending Palamon and three Arcite

A SERVANT

The JAILER in charge of Theseus' prison

The JAILER'S DAUGHTER

The JAILER'S BROTHER

The WOOER of the Jailer's Daughter

Two FRIENDS of the Jailer

A DOCTOR

Six COUNTRYMEN, one dressed as a babion, or baboon

Gerald, a SCHOOLMASTER

NELL, a country wench

Four other country wenches: Friz, Maudline, Luce, and Barbery

Timothy, a TABORER

Nymphs, attendants, maids, executioner, guard

EPILOGUE

The Two Noble Kinsmen

Prologue   *Flourish. Enter Prologue*

PROLOGUE

New plays and maidenheads are near akin,
Much followed both, for both much money gi'en,
If they stand sound and well; and a good play—
Whose modest scenes blush on his marriage day
And shake to lose his honour—is like her
That after holy tie and first night's stir
Yet still is modesty, and still retains
More of the maid to sight than husband's pains.
We pray our play may be so; for I am sure
It has a noble breeder and a pure,   10

Prologue 0.1 *Enter Prologue*] *not in* Q   1 PROLOGUE] *not in* Q

Prologue The actor who spoke these lines (he was also called the 'Prologue') wore a special costume. Gary Taylor, in his edition of *Henry V* (Oxford, 1982, p. 91) cites: 'Do you not see this long black velvet cloak upon my back? Have you not sounded thrice? . . . Nay, have I not all the signs of a Prologue about me?' (Thomas Heywood, *Four Prentices of London* (c.1599), A4). The prologue was probably written by Fletcher (see Introduction, p. 23).

0.1 *Flourish* fanfare of trumpets or cornetts (woodwind instruments); both are used in this play. Here trumpets are more likely, as they were used to signal the beginning of a play ('sounding' three times) and the entrance of a Prologue. Trumpets were commonly used to signal the approach of an important person, but in this play cornetts are sometimes specified for this purpose. As J. S. Manifold says (*The Music in English Drama* (London, 1956), p. 20), 'so many of the flourishes are left unspecified in the printed text, that it is hard to establish the dramatists' intention'. Although both trumpets and cornetts were used in the 'private'

theatres, such as Blackfriars, more use was made of cornetts there than in public theatres, where the louder trumpets were more common. Some of the indications for trumpets in this text may have been added for later performances at the Globe.

2 **followed** sought after

3 **stand** remain

4 **his** its. The possessive form 'its' was introduced early in the 17th century, but 'his' continued to be used as a possessive for 'it'.

5 **shake . . . honour** tremble to lose its virginity

6 **holy tie** marriage
stir (sexual) activity. As a verb, 'stir' often meant 'arouse sexual desire'.

7 **modesty** i.e. all modesty, as one says that a friendly person is 'all friendliness'

7–8 **retains . . . pains** i.e. still looks more like a virgin than like a married woman. The comparison of the play to one who is no longer a virgin has suggested to some commentators that the prologue (and epilogue) were written for a revival, but see note on l. 16.

10 **breeder** begetter, i.e. source

A learnèd, and a poet never went
More famous yet 'twixt Po and silver Trent.
Chaucer, of all admired, the story gives;
There, constant to eternity, it lives.
If we let fall the nobleness of this,
And the first sound this child hear be a hiss,
How will it shake the bones of that good man,
And make him cry from under ground, 'O fan
From me the witless chaff of such a writer
That blasts my bays and my famed works makes lighter   20
Than Robin Hood!' This is the fear we bring;
For, to say truth, it were an endless thing,
And too ambitious, to aspire to him,
Weak as we are, and almost breathless swim
In this deep water. Do but you hold out
Your helping hands, and we shall tack about
And something do to save us: you shall hear
Scenes, though below his art, may yet appear
Worth two hours' travail. To his bones sweet sleep;
Content to you. If this play do not keep   30
A little dull time from us, we perceive
Our losses fall so thick we must needs leave.

                                    Flourish. Exit

26 tack] F; *take* Q   29 travail] Q (*travell*)   32.1 *Exit*] *not in* Q

11–12 **poet . . . famous** i.e. no more famous poet ever existed (literally, 'walked')
12 **'twixt . . . Trent** i.e. between Italy and England, or, more generally, in all Western Europe
13 **of** by
14 **There** i.e. in his works
15 **let fall** debase
16 **first . . . hear** This comparison of the play to a new-born babe implies that it is being performed for the first time and hence that the prologue (and epilogue) were written for that occasion.
20 **blasts my bays** destroys my reputation as a poet
21 **Robin Hood** The hero of folklore and popular, rather than courtly, romance; proverbially, 'Tales of Robin Hood are good for fools' (Dent T53).
25–6 **hold . . . hands** The classic appeal for applause, common in the prologues and epilogues of Roman comedy and imitated

by later playwrights.
26 **tack about** as with a sailing-vessel, turn in the wind (of the clapping hands)
28 **may** i.e. which may
29 **travail** The common Elizabethan spelling 'travell' (see collations) suggests a pun: the (approximately) two hours of the play will be labour for the actors and an imaginative journey for the spectators.
30–1 **keep . . . us** i.e. pass a little time pleasantly
32 **Our losses** May refer to the destruction of the Globe Theatre by fire on 29 June 1613; see Introduction, p. 5.
leave give up acting
1.1 The imagined location is near the temple at Athens in which Theseus and Hippolyta are to be married, but no property was needed. The entire first act is probably by Shakespeare (see Introduction, p. 22).

I.I   *Music. Enter Hymen with a torch burning; a boy*
        in a white robe before, singing and strewing flowers.
        After Hymen a nymph, encompassed in her tresses,
        bearing a wheaten garland. Then Theseus between two
        other nymphs with wheaten chaplets on their heads.
        Then Hippolyta, the bride, led by Pirithous, and
        another holding a garland over her head, her tresses
        likewise hanging. After her, Emilia, holding up her
        train. Artesius and attendants

BOY *(sings during the procession)*
    Roses, their sharp spines being gone,
    Not royal in their smells alone,
        But in their hue;
    Maiden pinks, of odour faint,
    Daisies smell-less, yet most quaint,
        And sweet thyme true;

    Primrose, firstborn child of Ver,
    Merry springtime's harbinger,

I.I] F (*Actus Primus. Scoena Prima.*); *Actus Primus.* Q   0.I *Music*] *on line preceding l.* I *in*
Q   0.6 *Pirithous*] THEOBALD; *Theseus* Q   0.9 *Artesius and attendants*] *not in* Q   I
BOY . . . *procession*] OXFORD; The Song, Q; SONG *by the Boy.* DYCE

0.1–9 **Enter . . . attendants** The spectacular
opening procession suggests the court
masque, of which the influence is apparent in many scenes. Compare the opening
of Ben Jonson's *Hymenaei* (1606), for
which an altar to Juno is set up: '*To this*
altar entered five pages attired in white,
bearing five tapers of virgin wax; behind
them, one representing a bridegroom, his
hair short and bound with particolored rib-
bons and gold twist, his garments purple and
white. On the other hand entered Hymen, the
god of marriage, in a saffron colored robe,
his under vestures white, his socks yellow,
a yellow veil of silk on his left arm, his head
crowned with roses and marjoram, in his
right hand a torch of pine tree' (ll. 38–45)
in *Complete Masques*).
0.1 **Hymen** See preceding note.
0.3 **nymph** i.e. young woman; also see note
on 3.1.8.
   encompassed . . . tresses her hair hanging
   loosely about her—a sign of virginity
0.4 **wheaten garland** A traditional symbol
of fertility.
   Theseus Legendary hero and King of

Athens. In the Middle Ages, when there
were Frankish Dukes of Athens, it was
natural for Boccaccio and Chaucer to
refer to Theseus as a duke; Fletcher and
Shakespeare follow suit.
0.5 **chaplets** garlands
0.6 **Hippolyta** In the early legends of
Theseus, Antiope is the Amazon whom
he brings back to Athens, but Status, in
his *Thebaid*, widely read in the Middle
Ages, shows Theseus returning with Hippolyta as his wife. Plutarch, in his 'Life of
Theseus', mentions both legends. Status
also describes the meeting with the
widows of the kings who had fought
against Thebes.
I **BOY . . . procession** The preceding stage
direction shows that the song is sung by
the Boy.
2–3 **royal . . . hue** The red colour of the rose
suggests the shade of red associated with
royalty and called 'royal purple', which
did not denote the mixture of red and
blue now called purple.
5 **quaint** beautiful in design
7 **Ver** spring (personified)

With her bells dim;
Oxlips, in their cradles growing,   10
Marigolds, on deathbeds blowing,
    Lark's-heels trim;

(*Strewing flowers*) All dear Nature's children sweet
Lie 'fore bride and bridegroom's feet,
    Blessing their sense.
Not an angel of the air,
Bird melodious or bird fair,
    Is absent hence.

The crow, the sland'rous cuckoo, nor
The boding raven, nor chough hoar   20
    Nor chatt'ring pie,
May on our bridehouse perch or sing,
Or with them any discord bring,
    But from it fly.

*Enter three Queens in black, with veils stained,
with imperial crowns. The first Queen falls down at*

9 her bells] Q; hairbells SKEAT   13 *Strewing flowers*] This edition; *Strew | Flowers.* Q, *following
ll. 14, 15*   13–14 children sweet | Lie] F (*subs.*); *children: sweete-|Ly* Q   16 angel] Q (*angle*)
20 chough hoar] SEWARD; *Clough hee* Q

9 **her bells** Skeat's emendation, 'hairbells'
(see collations) is appealing, but is effectively rejected in a long note by Littledale,
who notes that bright blue hairbells could
not be called 'dim'.
    bells flowers (even if not precisely bell-
shaped). Compare 'In a cowslip's bell I
lie' (*Tempest* 5.1.89).
    dim pale. Compare 'pale primrose' (*Cym-
beline* 4.2.222).
10 **Oxlips . . . growing** Spring flowers belonging, like the primrose, to the genus *prim-
ula*. The circles of leaves surrounding the
growing buds probably suggested cradles.
11 **on deathbeds blowing** blossoming on
graves
12 **Lark's-heels** larkspur
    trim neat
13 *Strewing flowers* Q's *Strew | Flowers* (see
collations) is an example of the common
imperative form of stage direction; see
also the note on l. 106.
14 **Lie** The Boy bids the flowers he is strewing
to lie at the feet of Theseus and Hippolyta.
15 **sense** i.e. senses

16 **angel** i.e. bird of good omen
19 **sland'rous** because it seemed to mock
married men with its cry of 'cuckold'
20 **boding** prophetic of evil. Proverbial: 'The
croaking raven bodes misfortune (death)'
(Dent R33).
    chough hoar grey-headed jackdaw. As
Seward said, Q's '*Clough hee*' 'is neither
sense nor rhyme' (see collations); his
emendation has convinced most editors.
21 **pie** magpie
22 **bridehouse** site of a wedding
24.1 *Enter three Queens* The final stage
direction of the act apparently requires
three doors, which the Blackfriars stage
had—upstage right, centre, and left (see
note on 1.5.16.1). The queens presumably enter here, as at 1.4.0.4–5, from
the door opposite to the one used by the
wedding procession.
    stained dyed (black for mourning)
24.2 *imperial* Not 'pertaining to an empire'
but, more generally, 'Of or pertaining to
a sovereign state' (*OED*, A. 2).

*the foot of Theseus; the second falls down at
the foot of Hippolyta; the third before Emilia*

FIRST QUEEN (*to Theseus*)

For pity's sake and true gentility's,
Hear and respect me.

SECOND QUEEN (*to Hippolyta*) For your mother's sake,
And as you wish your womb may thrive with fair ones,
Hear and respect me.

THIRD QUEEN (*to Emilia*)

Now for the love of him whom Jove hath marked
The honour of your bed, and for the sake   30
Of clear virginity, be advocate
For us and our distresses. This good deed
Shall raze you out o'th' book of trespasses
All you are set down there.

THESEUS (*to First Queen*)

Sad lady, rise.

HYPPOLYTA (*to Second Queen*) Stand up.

EMILIA (*to Third Queen*)   No knees to me.
What woman I may stead that is distressed
Does bind me to her.

⌜*The Second and Third Queens rise*⌝

THESEUS (*to First Queen*)

What's your request? Deliver you for all.

FIRST QUEEN

We are three queens whose sovereigns fell before
The wrath of cruel Creon; who endured   ·   40

37.1 *The Second . . . rise*] This edition; *not in* Q

25 **gentility's** nobility's
26 **respect** look at, attend to, show consideration for
29 **marked** destined to be
30 **honour . . . bed** your distinguished bridegroom
31 **clear** pure
33–4 **raze . . . there** erase all your sins from the record (kept in heaven)
36 **stead** help
37.1 *The Second . . . rise* It is impossible to tell exactly when the three queens rise or exactly when any of them again kneel and rise. From Theseus' speech (ll. 54 ff.) it appears that the First Queen ignores his earlier requests that she stand, but

the other queens may rise here. The Third Queen is directed to kneel again at l. 106. The repeated kneelings, like those in *The Trial of Chivalry*, which they resemble (see Waith, 'Shakespeare and the Ceremonies of Romance') comprise a conspicuous feature of the spectacle in this scene and in 3.6. These appeals for mercy are based on the belief, characteristic of chivalric romance, in the nobility of which human beings are capable (see Introduction, pp. 44 ff.).
38 **Deliver** speak
40 **Creon** Brother-in-law of Oedipus and King of Thebes after the death of Eteocles, Oedipus' son, in the war of the 'seven

The beaks of ravens, talons of the kites,
And pecks of crows in the foul fields of Thebes.
He will not suffer us to burn their bones,
To urn their ashes, nor to take th'offence
Of mortal loathsomeness from the blest eye
Of holy Phoebus, but infects the winds
With stench of our slain lords. O pity, Duke!
Thou purger of the earth, draw thy feared sword
That does good turns to th' world; give us the bones
Of our dead kings, that we may chapel them;   50
And of thy boundless goodness take some note
That for our crownèd heads we have no roof
Save this, which is the lion's and the bear's,
And vault to everything.

THESEUS   Pray you, kneel not;
I was transported with your speech and suffered
Your knees to wrong themselves. I have heard the
      fortunes
Of your dead lords, which gives me such lamenting
As wakes my vengeance and revenge for 'em.
King Capaneus was your lord; the day
That he should marry you, at such a season   60
As now it is with me, I met your groom
By Mars's altar; you were that time fair—

41 talons] Q (Tallents)   59 lord;] ~ₐ Q; ~ : TONSON

against Thebes'. He forbade the burial of
those who died in their unsuccessful
attack on the city, among them the
husbands of the three queens.
who i.e. the sovereigns

41-2 kites . . . crows Compare 'Under the
canopy . . . I'th' city of kites and crows'
(*Coriolanus* 4.5.38–42).
42 fields i.e. battlefields
46 Phoebus Apollo, god of the sun
46-7 infects . . . lords Compare 'the dead
carcasses of unburied men | That do cor-
rupt my air' (*Coriolanus* 3.3.126–7).
48 purger of the earth Like Hercules,
Theseus was famed in legend for ridding
the world of monsters and bandits. Plutarch, in his 'Life of Theseus' as translated
by Sir Thomas North, says that, 'pricked
forwards with emulation and envy of

[Hercules'] glory, [Theseus] determined
with himself to do the like, and the
rather, because they were near kinsmen,
being cousins removed by the mother's
side' (*The Lives of the Noble Grecians and
Romans* (1579), p. 4).
50 chapel bury in a chapel (a nonce-word).
See *OED*.
51 of out of
52 our . . . heads i.e. the heads of the three
kings
52-3 no roof . . . bear's Again reminiscent
of the passage of *Coriolanus* cited at ll.
41–2.
53 this i.e. the sky
54 vault roof
59 Capaneus Properly three syllables, but
here four (Càpanèus); he was one of the
'seven against Thebes'.
60 should was about to

84

Not Juno's mantle fairer than your tresses,
Nor in more bounty spread her. Your wheaten wreath
Was then nor threshed nor blasted; Fortune at you
Dimpled her cheek with smiles. Hercules, our kinsman—
Then weaker than your eyes—laid by his club;
He tumbled down upon his Nemean hide
And swore his sinews thawed. O grief and time,
Fearful consumers, you will all devour!   70
FIRST QUEEN   O, I hope some god,
Some god hath put his mercy in your manhood,
Whereto he'll infuse power and press you forth
Our undertaker.
THESEUS   O no knees, none, widow;
Unto the helmeted Bellona use them
And pray for me, your soldier.
    ⌜The First Queen rises⌝
Troubled I am.
    He turns away
SECOND QUEEN   Honoured Hippolyta,
Most dreaded Amazonian, that hast slain
The scythe-tusked boar; that with thy arm, as strong
As it is white, wast near to make the male   80
To thy sex captive, but that this thy lord,
Born to uphold creation in that honour
First nature styled it in, shrunk thee into
The bound thou wast o'erflowing, at once subduing

68 Nemean] 1750; Nenuan Q   77.1 *The First Queen rises*] OXFORD; *not in* Q   78.1 *He*] *not in* Q

63 **Juno's mantle** In Book 14 of the *Iliad* Homer describes the beautiful robe she wears to arouse Jove's desire.
64 **in . . . spread** more luxuriantly enveloped
66 **kinsman** See note on l. 48.
67 **weaker than** i.e. overpowered by
68 **Nemean hide** The hide of the lion of Nemea, which Hercules killed as one of his twelve labours.
69 **thawed** softened (by love)
69–70 **time . . . devour** Proverbial: 'Time devours all things' (Dent T236).
73 **Whereto** into which (in addition)
73–4 **press . . . undertaker** urge you forward as champion of our cause
75 **Bellona** goddess of war
78–9 **that . . . boar** Possibly suggested by

Ovid's description in *Metamorphoses*, Book 8 of the hunt for the Calydonian boar, which Atalanta, not Hippolyta, helped to kill. Chaucer refers to Atalanta hunting the 'wild Bore' in his description of the temple of Diana in *The Knight's Tale* (l. A 2070).
80 **wast . . . make** almost succeeded in making
82–3 **uphold . . . it in** i.e. maintain the pristine order of the created world
84 **bound . . . o'erflowing** i.e. limit which you, as a woman, were exceeding. The orthodox view was that woman's place was one degree below man's in the hierarchy of creation.

Thy force and thy affection; soldieress
That equally canst poise sternness with pity,
Whom now I know hast much more power on him
Than ever he had on thee, who ow'st his strength
And his love too, who is a servant for
The tenor of thy speech; dear glass of ladies,   90
Bid him that we, whom flaming war doth scorch,
Under the shadow of his sword may cool us;
Require him he advance it o'er our heads;
Speak't in a woman's key, like such a woman
As any of us three; weep ere you fail.
Lend us a knee;
But touch the ground for us no longer time
Than a dove's motion when the head's plucked off;
Tell him if he i'th' blood-sized field lay swoll'n,
Showing the sun his teeth, grinning at the moon,   100
What you would do.

HIPPOLYTA   Poor lady, say no more;
I had as lief trace this good action with you
As that whereto I am going, and never yet
Went I so willing way. My lord is taken
Heart-deep with your distress; let him consider.
I'll speak anon.

THIRD QUEEN (*kneeling to Emilia*) O, my petition was
Set down in ice, which by hot grief uncandied
Melts into drops; so sorrow, wanting form,
Is pressed with deeper matter.

---

90 thy] SEWARD; the Q   104 willing,̬] SEWARD; ~, Q   106 *kneeling to Emilia*] This edition;
kneele to Emilia. Q, at end of line

85 **soldieress** (first recorded use in *OED*)
86 **equally** judiciously
   poise balance
88 **ow'st** ownest
89 **servant** i.e. as a lover is the servant of
   the beloved, eager to carry out her wishes
90 **tenor** purport
   glass of mirror or model for
94 **key** tone
99 **blood-sized field** battlefield covered with
   blood
102 **had as lief trace** would as willingly
   pursue
104 **taken** afflicted

106 **anon** soon
   kneeling Q's *kneele* (see collations) is
   another example of the imperative form
   of stage direction (see note on l. 13).
107 **Set . . . ice** coldly made
   uncandied thawed
108 **wanting form** lacking the shape of elo-
   quent expression
109 **pressed . . . matter** forced out (in the
   form of tears) by intensified feeling; with
   perhaps the further suggestion that sorrow has its proper form (tears) pressed
   on it by 'deeper matter'

EMILIA   Pray stand up;
Your grief is written in your cheek.
THIRD QUEEN   O woe,   110
You cannot read it there; there through my tears,
Like wrinkled pebbles in a glassy stream,
You may behold 'em. Lady, lady, alack!
He that will all the treasure know o'th' earth
Must know the centre too; he that will fish
For my least minnow, let him lead his line
To catch one at my heart. O pardon me;
Extremity, that sharpens sundry wits,
Makes me a fool.
            ⌜*She rises*⌝
EMILIA   Pray you say nothing, pray you;
Who cannot feel nor see the rain, being in't,   120
Knows neither wet nor dry. If that you were
The ground-piece of some painter, I would buy you
T'instruct me 'gainst a capital grief, indeed
Such heart-pierced demonstration; but alas,
Being a natural sister of our sex,
Your sorrow beats so ardently upon me
That it shall make a counter-reflect 'gainst
My brother's heart and warm it to some pity,
Though it were made of stone. Pray have good comfort.

112 pebbles] F; peobles Q   glassy] 1750; glasse Q   113 'em.] ~ˌ Q; ~ ! COLMAN   119
She rises] LEECH; *not in* Q   123 grief,] PROUDFOOT; ~ˌ Q

111 **there; there** The first 'there' refers to
her cheek, the second (accompanied by
a gesture) to her eyes.
111–13 **through . . . 'em** you may see my
sorrows (the plural has been substituted
for the singular 'sorrow' or 'grief') dis-
torted by my tears as pebbles are when
seen through water
115 **know . . . too** dig deep
116 **lead** put a lead weight on (to sink into
the heart)
line i.e. fishing-line. The metaphor is
prepared for by the comparison in ll.
111–12 of tears to 'a glassy stream'.
118 **Extremity** extreme suffering. Compare
the proverbial 'Calamity (Extremity) is the
touchstone of a brave mind' (Dent C15a).
sundry wits some minds
119 **Makes me a fool** makes me speak ex-
travagantly

121–2 **If . . . painter** i.e. if you were merely
depicted in a painting
122 **ground-piece** An otherwise unrecorded
term, perhaps meaning an example to
be copied as a teaching aid; see *OED*,
ground, *v*. 5: 'To instruct (a person) in
the fundamental or elementary principles
of any branch of study'.
123 **'gainst** in anticipation of
capital deadly
indeed with the sense of 'specifically'
124 **such . . . demonstration** i.e. such heart-
break as you display
125 **natural . . . sex** i.e. an actual woman
rather than a painting
126 **ardently** burningly, like sunlight
127 **make a counter-reflect** be reflected from
me (as from a mirror)
128–9 **warm . . . stone** Compare the proverbial 'A heart of stone would melt'

THESEUS
　　Forward to th' temple; leave not out a jot　　　　　　130
　　O'th' sacred ceremony.
FIRST QUEEN　　　　　　　　　O, this celebration
　　Will longer last and be more costly than
　　Your suppliants' war. Remember that your fame
　　Knolls in the ear o'th' world; what you do quickly
　　Is not done rashly; your first thought is more
　　Than others' laboured meditance, your premeditating
　　More than their actions. But, O Jove, your actions,
　　Soon as they move, as ospreys do the fish,
　　Subdue before they touch. Think, dear Duke, think
　　What beds our slain kings have.
SECOND QUEEN　　　　　　　　　What griefs our beds,　　140
　　That our dear lords have none.
THIRD QUEEN　　　　　　　　　None fit for th' dead.
　　Those that with cords, knives, drams, precipitance,
　　Weary of this world's light, have to themselves
　　Been death's most horrid agents, human grace
　　Affords them dust and shadow.
FIRST QUEEN　　　　　　　　　But our lords
　　Lie blist'ring fore the visitating sun,
　　And were good kings when living.
THESEUS
　　It is true, and I will give you comfort
　　To give your dead lords graves;
　　The which to do must make some work with Creon.　　150

---

132 longer] 1750; long Q　　138 move] F; mooves Q　　142 drams,] 1750; ~ˌ Q

(Bartlett Jere Whiting, *Proverbs, Sentences, and Proverbial Phrases* . . . (Cambridge, Mass., 1968) H277).

130 **temple** In *The Knight's Tale* Theseus encounters the queens near the 'temple of the goddesse Clemence' (l. A 928), where they have awaited his return. In Shakespeare's version of the incident the temple referred to here is apparently the place where Theseus and Hippolyta are to be married.
134 **Knolls** rings, tolls
136 **laboured meditance** laborious thought

(the only instance of 'meditance' cited in *OED*)
138 **as ospreys . . . fish** Ospreys were thought to have a power which caused fish to roll over and allow themselves to be caught. Compare *Coriolanus* 4.7.34–5.
142 **drams** poisons
　　precipitance suicidal leaps
144 **horrid** horrifying
146 **visitating** making an official visit to inspect
147 **And** i.e. unlike the suicides mentioned above
149 **To give** by giving

88

FIRST QUEEN
　And that work presents itself to th' doing.
　Now 'twill take form; the heats are gone tomorrow.
　Then, bootless toil must recompense itself
　With its own sweat; now, he's secure,
　Not dreams we stand before your puissance,
　Rinsing our holy begging in our eyes
　To make petition clear.
SECOND QUEEN　　　　　　　Now you may take him,
　Drunk with his victory.
THIRD QUEEN　　　　　　　And his army full
　Of bread and sloth.
THESEUS　　　　　　　Artesius, that best knowest
　How to draw out, fit to this enterprise,　　　　　160
　The prim'st for this proceeding, and the number
　To carry such a business, forth and levy
　Our worthiest instruments, whilst we dispatch
　This grand act of our life, this daring deed
　Of fate in wedlock.
FIRST QUEEN (*to the other Queens*) Dowagers, take hands;
　Let us be widows to our woes; delay
　Commends us to a famishing hope.
ALL THE QUEENS　　　　　　　Farewell.
SECOND QUEEN

　We come unseasonably; but when could grief
　Cull forth, as unpanged judgement can, fitt'st time
　For best solicitation?

---

156 Rinsing] Q (Wrinching)　159 Artesius] SEWARD; *Artesuis* Q　167 ALL THE QUEENS] Q
(*All.*)

151 **presents . . . doing** needs to be done now
152 **Now . . . tomorrow** Like molten metal,
　it can be shaped now, but not when it
　cools.
153 **bootless** futile
154 **he's secure** i.e. he feels secure
155 **puissance** trisyllabic (pùissànce); power
157 **petition** our supplication, or our act of
　supplicating
　clear clean, pure
159 **Artesius** This is the only occasion on
　which this character is named. Q's '*Arte-
　suis*' (see collations) seems improbable,
　and Seward's correction has been ac-

cepted by all editors.
160 **draw out** choose
161 **prim'st** best
162 **carry** carry out
164-5 **daring . . . fate** act which challenges
　fate
165 **Dowagers** widows
166 **Let . . . woes** we may as well recognize
　the death of our complaints (since Theseus
　neglects them)
167 **Commends . . . hope** is starving our hope
169 **Cull forth** select
　unpanged untroubled by pain

THESEUS   Why, good ladies,   170
This is a service, whereto I am going,
Greater than any was; it more imports me
Than all the actions that I have foregone,
Or futurely can cope.
FIRST QUEEN   The more proclaiming
Our suit shall be neglected, when her arms
Able to lock Jove from a synod shall
By warranting moonlight corslet thee; O, when
Her twinning cherries shall their sweetness fall
Upon thy tasteful lips, what wilt thou think
Of rotten kings or blubbered queens? What care   180
For what thou feel'st not, what thou feel'st being able
To make Mars spurn his drum? O, if thou couch
But one night with her, every hour in't will
Take hostage of thee for a hundred, and
Thou shalt remember nothing more than what
That banquet bids thee to.
HIPPOLYTA (*to Theseus*)   Though much unlike
You should be so transported, as much sorry
I should be such a suitor, yet I think
Did I not by th'abstaining of my joy,
Which breeds a deeper longing, cure their surfeit,   190
That craves a present med'cine, I should pluck

---

172 was] Q; War THEOBALD   178 twinning] THEOBALD; twyning Q

172 **was** Theobald's emendation (see collations) is tempting and has been widely
accepted, but 'was' makes excellent sense:
for Theseus to say that his wedding is
greater than any service he has performed
fits precisely with his next statement, that
it means more to him than all that he has
done or will do.
  more imports me means more to me
173 **foregone** previously performed
174 **cope** achieve
  The more proclaiming making all the
  more clear that
175-6 **her arms | Able** the arms of her (Hip-
  polyta) who is able
176 **lock** keep
  synod meeting
177 **warranting** sanctioning
  corslet encircle like a corslet, a tight-fitting
  piece of defensive armour

178 **twinning cherries** i.e. cherry lips
  fall let fall
179 **tasteful** having the capacity to taste. The
  OED gives the first instance of the word
  in this sense as 1647.
180 **blubbered** tear-stained. The word was
  not pejorative as in today's usage.
184 **Take . . . hundred** make you spend a
  hundred more hours with her
186 **bids** invites
186-8 **Though . . . suitor** Although it is
  unlikely that you would be so carried
  away, and much as I dislike to beg you
  (to postpone our wedding)
189 **of** from
190 **surfeit** excess (of grief, which makes
  them sick)
191 **present** immediate
191-2 **pluck . . . me** seem to all ladies to
  behave scandalously

All ladies' scandal on me. ⌜*She kneels*⌝ Therefore, sir,
As I shall here make trial of my prayers,
Either presuming them to have some force,
Or sentencing for aye their vigour dumb,
Prorogue this business we are going about, and hang
Your shield afore your heart, about that neck
Which is my fee, and which I freely lend
To do these poor queens service.

ALL THE QUEENS (*to Emilia*)   O, help now!
Our cause cries for your knee.

EMILIA (*to Theseus, kneeling*)   If you grant not   200
My sister her petition in that force,
With that celerity and nature which
She makes it in, from henceforth I'll not dare
To ask you anything, nor be so hardy
Ever to take a husband.

THESEUS   Pray stand up.
    ⌜*Hippolyta and Emilia rise*⌝
I am entreating of myself to do
That which you kneel to have me. Pirithous,
Lead on the bride; get you and pray the gods
For success and return; omit not anything
In the pretended celebration. Queens,   210
Follow your soldier. (*To Artesius*) As before, hence you,
And at the banks of Aulis meet us with
The forces you can raise, where we shall find

---

192 *She kneels*] not in Q   199 ALL THE QUEENS] Q (*All Queens.*)   now!] COLMAN; ~ ₍ Q; ~,
TONSON   200 *kneeling*] not in Q   205.1 *Hippolyta . . . rise*] DYCE; not in Q   211 soldier. As
before,] WEBER (*subs.*, *conj.* Mason); Soldier (as before₍) Q   212 Aulis] THEOBALD; Anly Q

192 *She kneels* Editors place this clearly
  required stage direction at various points.
195 **sentencing . . . dumb** concluding that
  they will always be as ineffectual as if
  they had not been uttered
196 **Prorogue** defer
198 **fee** property
201 **in that force** with the same vigour
202–3 **With . . . in** i.e. with the same speed
  and spontaneity that she shows in making
  it
207 **Pirithous** Here, and in all of Shakespeare's scenes, apparently trisyllabic
  (Pìrithòus); see Introduction, p. 12.

208 **get you** i.e. get you hence, go
210 **pretended** intended
212 **banks** shores. For 'banks' in this sense
  see 1 *Henry IV*, 3.1.62.
  Aulis Q's '*Anly*' (see collations) probably
  resulted from misreading 'u' as 'n' and 'is'
  as 'y', both easy mistakes with Elizabethan
  handwriting. Aulis was famous as the
  port where the Greek fleet assembled to
  sail for Troy, but was prevented from
  doing so by Artemis until Agamemnon
  sacrificed his daughter Iphigenia.

The moiety of a number for a business
More bigger looked.   ⌈*Exit Artesius*⌉
(*To Hippolyta*)   Since that our theme is haste,
I stamp this kiss upon thy current lip;
Sweet, keep it as my token. Set you forward,
For I will see you gone.
      ⌈*The marriage procession moves towards the temple*⌉
(*To Emilia*) Farewell, my beauteous sister. Pirithous,
Keep the feast full; bate not an hour on't.

PIRITHOUS   Sir,   220
I'll follow you at heels; the feast's solemnity
Shall want till your return.

THESEUS   Cousin, I charge you,
Budge not from Athens. We shall be returning
Ere you can end this feast, of which I pray you
Make no abatement. Once more, farewell all.
                  ⌈*The procession goes out*⌉

FIRST QUEEN
Thus dost thou still make good the tongue o'th' world.

SECOND QUEEN
And earn'st a deity equal with Mars.

THIRD QUEEN If not above him, for
Thou, being but mortal, makest affections bend
To godlike honours; they themselves, some say,   230
Groan under such a mast'ry.

215 *Exit Artesius*] WEBER; *not in* Q 218.1 *The marriage . . . moves*] BAWCUTT; *Exeunt* Q 225.1
The procession goes out] BAWCUTT; *not in* Q

214–15 **The moiety . . . looked** a part of a
    force intended for a larger enterprise (than
    the campaign against Thebes; apparently
    Theseus was preparing for another 'busi-
    ness')
215 *Exit Artesius* See note at l. 218.1.
    our . . . haste i.e. we are in a hurry
217 **current** genuine, like a coin (supporting
    the implied metaphor in 'stamp' and 'to-
    ken'), with a play on 'currant', i.e. red.
    In Elizabethan English either spelling co-
    uld be used for either meaning.
218.1 *The marriage . . . temple* It seems likely
    that Q's *Exeunt* (see collations) directs the
    wedding party to start moving toward
    one of the stage doors as Theseus begins
    his farewells. Some editors direct Artesius
    to exit at this point, assuming
    that Theseus' last words are addressed to

him. More likely, they are part of his
farewell to Hippolyta, followed immediately by those to Emilia and Pirithous.
By the time he has finished his speech at
l. 225 the last of the procession is leaving.
220 **full** fully
    bate . . . on't do not shorten it by a single
    hour
221 **solemnity** ceremonial dignity
222 **want** be lacking
    Cousin A courteous form of address;
    Pirithous was not a blood relation.
225 **abatement** curtailment
226 **tongue o'th' world** what the world says
    of you
229 **affections bend** passions subordinate
    themselves
231 **Groan . . . mast'ry** suffer their passions
    to master them

THESEUS   As we are men,
  Thus should we do; being sensually subdued,
  We lose our human title. Good cheer, ladies!
  Now turn we towards your comforts.   *Flourish. Exeunt*

1.2   *Enter Palamon and Arcite*
ARCITE
  Dear Palamon, dearer in love than blood,
  And our prime cousin, yet unhardened in
  The crimes of nature, let us leave the city
  Thebes, and the temptings in't, before we further
  Sully our gloss of youth;
  And here to keep in abstinence we shame
  As in incontinence; for not to swim
  I'th' aid o'th' current were almost to sink,
  At least to frustrate striving; and to follow
  The common stream, 'twould bring us to an eddy   10
  Where we should turn or drown; if labour through,
  Our gain but life and weakness.
PALAMON   Your advice
  Is cried up with example: what strange ruins,
  Since first we went to school, may we perceive
  Walking in Thebes? Scars and bare weeds
  The gain o'th' martialist, who did propound
  To his bold ends honour and golden ingots,
  Which though he won, he had not, and now flirted

---

234 *Flourish*] *placed as in* DYCE; *following l. 233 in* Q
  1.2] Q (Scaena 2.)

232 **sensually subdued** subdued by the senses
233 **human title** claim to humanity
  1.2 The location is Thebes.
  1 **dearer . . . blood** In the first line of their
    dialogue Shakespeare establishes the
    overriding importance of their friendship.
  2 **prime** chief, favourite
  3 **crimes of nature** vices to which human
    beings are prone
  5 **Sully . . . of** mar the lustre of our
  6-7 **to keep . . . incontinence** by remain-
    ing continent we incur as much shame
    as incontinence would bring us else-
    where
  7-8 **to swim . . . current** Proverbial: 'To

go (swim, run) with the stream' (Dent
S930).
  9 **frustrate striving** make our efforts useless
    (since our ideals are not respected)
  11 **turn** revolve indefinitely
  11-12 **if labour . . . weakness** if we managed
    to swim out of the whirlpool, we would
    achieve only survival in a weakened
    condition
  13 **cried up with** supported by
    ruins i.e. ruined men
  15 **bare weeds** ragged clothes
  16 **martialist** soldier
  16-17 **propound | To** propose as a reward
    for
  18 **flirted** jeered at

By peace for whom he fought; who then shall offer
To Mars's so scorned altar? I do bleed   20
When such I meet, and wish great Juno would
Resume her ancient fit of jealousy
To get the soldier work, that peace might purge
For her repletion, and retain anew
Her charitable heart, now hard and harsher
Than strife or war could be.

ARCITE   Are you not out?
Meet you no ruin but the soldier in
The cranks and turns of Thebes? You did begin
As if you met decays of many kinds.
Perceive you none that do arouse your pity   30
But th'unconsidered soldier?

PALAMON   Yes, I pity
Decays where'er I find them, but such most
That, sweating in an honourable toil,
Are paid with ice to cool 'em.

ARCITE   'Tis not this
I did begin to speak of; this is virtue
Of no respect in Thebes. I spake of Thebes,
How dangerous, if we will keep our honours,
It is for our residing, where every evil
Hath a good colour; where every seeming good's
A certain evil; where not to be ev'n jump   40
As they are here, were to be strangers, and
Such things to be, mere monsters.

PALAMON   'Tis in our power
(Unless we fear that apes can tutor's) to

41 are here,] DYCE 1866 (_conj._ Mason); are, here Q   42 be,] LITTLEDALE (_conj._ Nicholson);
∼∧ Q

21 **Juno . . . jealousy** Jupiter's affair with
Alcmene in Thebes set Juno against the
city. In _The Knight's Tale_ Arcite, lamenting his fate in the forest, complains of
her inveterate hatred (ll. A 1543–9).
24 **For her repletion** to cure the diseases
caused by her excesses
retain take into service
26 **out** mistaken
28 **cranks** winding streets. There is probably
a reminiscence here of 'the turnings
and cranks of the labyrinth' in North's
translation of Plutarch's 'Life of Theseus'

(_Lives_, p. 9).
37 **will** wish to
39 **colour** appearance
40 **ev'n jump** just exactly
41 **they are here** i.e. Thebans. Placing the
comma after 'here', following Mason's
conjecture (see collations), clarifies the
reference of 'they' to those who live here
(in Thebes).
42 **Such things** people like the Thebans
mere utter, nothing but
43 **apes** i.e. people who merely imitate others
tutor's tutor us. Palamon means 'Unless

Be masters of our manners. What need I
Affect another's gait, which is not catching
Where there is faith? or to be fond upon
Another's way of speech, when by mine own
I may be reasonably conceived—saved too,
Speaking it truly? Why am I bound
By any generous bond to follow him   50
Follows his tailor, haply so long until
The followed make pursuit? Or let me know
Why mine own barber is unblessed, with him
My poor chin too, for 'tis not scissored just
To such a favourite's glass? What canon is there
That does command my rapier from my hip
To dangle't in my hand, or to go tip-toe
Before the street be foul? Either I am
The fore-horse in the team, or I am none
That draw i'th' sequent trace. These poor slight sores   60
Need not a plantain; that which rips my bosom
Almost to th' heart's—

ARCITE   Our uncle Creon.

PALAMON   He,
A most unbounded tyrant, whose successes
Makes heaven unfeared and villainy assured
Beyond its power there's nothing; almost puts
Faith in a fever, and deifies alone

65 power there's nothing;] SEWARD; power: there's nothing, Q

we are afraid that we might learn from
people we despise'.

45 **Affect** imitate
catching (*a*) attractive; (*b*) infectious
46 **faith** self-reliance
fond upon infatuated with
48 **conceived** understood
saved (presumably from punishment or from damnation)
49 **Speaking it truly** if I speak the truth
50 **generous bond** obligation of honour for a man of noble birth
follow imitate
51 **Follows** i.e. who follows
51–2 **haply . . . pursuit** perhaps until the tailor starts suing the follower (for an unpaid bill)
53 **unblessed** out of favour

54 **for** because
54–5 **just | To** exactly according to
55 **glass** i.e. image in his mirror
canon law
58 **foul** dirty. It would be highly affected to tip-toe on a clean street.
60 **draw . . . trace** pull in the following line (of horses). Palamon does not want to follow (i.e. imitate) anyone.
61 **plantain** herb used for treating wounds
63 **unbounded** uncontrolled
64 **Makes** In Elizabethan English the third person singular form is often used for the plural.
assured i.e. assured that
65 **nothing** i.e. no superior power to control it
66 **Faith** religious belief

Voluble chance; who only attributes
The faculties of other instruments
To his own nerves and act; commands men service,
And what they win in't, boot and glory; one   70
That fears not to do harm; good, dares not. Let
The blood of mine that's sib to him be sucked
From me with leeches; let them break and fall
Off me with that corruption.
ARCITE   Clear-spirited cousin,
Let's leave his court, that we may nothing share
Of his loud infamy; for our milk
Will relish of the pasture, and we must
Be vile or disobedient, not his kinsmen
In blood unless in quality.
PALAMON   Nothing truer.
I think the echoes of his shames have deafed   80
The ears of heav'nly justice: widows' cries
Descend again into their throats, and have not
Due audience of the gods.
       Enter Valerius
                              Valerius.
VALERIUS
The King calls for you; yet be leaden-footed
Till his great rage be off him. Phoebus, when
He broke his whipstock and exclaimed against
The horses of the sun, but whispered to
The loudness of his fury.

70 glory; one] LITTLEDALE (*conj.* Ingram); glory‸ on; Q (*corr.*); glory‸ on‸ Q (*uncorr.*)   83
Enter Valerius] *at end of l. 82 in* Q

67 **Voluble chance** inconstant fortune
67-9 **only . . . act** attributes the powers (and
  achievements) of his agents to his own
  strength (*nerves* meant sinews) and performance alone
67 **attributes** (pronounced àttribùtes)
69-70 **commands . . . glory** demands service
  (in war) of men and also whatever profit
  ('boot') and glory they win
71 **good, dares not** i.e. dares not do good
72 **sib** related
73 **break** burst (from sucking blood)
74 **Clear-spirited** noble-spirited
76 **loud** resounding, i.e. notorious
76-7 **our milk . . . pasture** as milk acquires

the flavour of what the cow eats, we may
  be contaminated by Thebes
79 **quality** character
83 **Due audience of** proper attention from
84 **be leaden-footed** delay
85 **Phoebus** The god of the sun, whose son,
  Phaethon, was killed in a disastrous
  attempt to drive the chariot of the sun.
  As Ovid tells the story in Book 2 of the
  Metamorphoses, Phoebus took out his
  grief and anger on the horses that drew
  the chariot.
86 **whipstock** whiphandle
87 **but whispered to** only whispered, compared to

PALAMON   Small winds shake him;
  But what's the matter?

VALERIUS
  Theseus, who where he threats appals, hath sent   90
  Deadly defiance to him and pronounces
  Ruin to Thebes, who is at hand to seal
  The promise of his wrath.

ARCITE   Let him approach.
  But that we fear the gods in him, he brings not
  A jot of terror to us. Yet what man
  Thirds his own worth—the case is each of ours—
  When that his action's dregged with mind assured
  'Tis bad he goes about.

PALAMON   Leave that unreasoned.
  Our services stand now for Thebes, not Creon.
  Yet to be neutral to him were dishonour,   100
  Rebellious to oppose; therefore we must
  With him stand to the mercy of our fate,
  Who hath bounded our last minute.

ARCITE   So we must.
  Is't said this war's afoot, or it shall be
  On fail of some condition?

VALERIUS   'Tis in motion;
  The intelligence of state came in the instant
  With the defier.

PALAMON   Let's to the King, who, were he
  A quarter carrier of that honour which
  His enemy come in, the blood we venture
  Should be as for our health, which were not spent,   110

92 **who** i.e. Theseus
92–3 **seal . . . wrath** carry out what his angry words threatened
94 **But** except
   gods in him gods he may represent
95 **what man** any man whatever
96 **Thirds** reduces to a third
97 **his action . . . assured** what he is doing is hindered by the consciousness that
   dregged rendered 'turbid as with dregs' (*OED*, whose earliest 17th-century instance is dated 1627–47)
98 **Leave that unreasoned** never mind about that

100 **Yet to be** to continue to be
101 **Rebellious** i.e. treasonable
103 **bounded . . . minute** established the limits of what we can do and the time of our deaths
105 **On fail of** if Thebes fails to meet
106 **intelligence of state** official notice (of the attack)
107 **defier** i.e. Theseus' herald
108–9 **A quarter . . . in** a fourth as honourable as Theseus
110 **as for our health** like a therapeutic bloodletting
   spent wasted

Rather laid out for purchase. But alas,
Our hands advanced before our hearts, what will
The fall o'th' stroke do damage?

ARCITE   Let th'event,
That never-erring arbitrator, tell us
When we know all ourselves, and let us follow
The becking of our chance.   *Exeunt*

1.3   *Enter Pirithous, Hippolyta, Emilia*

PIRITHOUS
No further.

HIPPOLYTA   Sir, farewell. Repeat my wishes
To our great lord, of whose success I dare not
Make any timorous question; yet I wish him
Excess and overflow of power, an't might be
To dure ill-dealing fortune. Speed to him;
Store never hurts good governors.

PIRITHOUS   Though I know
His ocean needs not my poor drops, yet they
Must yield their tribute there. (*To Emilia*) My precious
    maid,
Those best affections that the heavens infuse
In their best-tempered pieces keep enthroned   10
In your dear heart.

EMILIA   Thanks, sir. Remember me
To our all-royal brother, for whose speed
The great Bellona I'll solicit; and
Since in our terrene state petitions are not
Without gifts understood, I'll offer to her

1.3] Q (Scaena 3.)

111 **laid . . . purchase** invested for profit
112 **Our . . . hearts** if our hands are engaged
    further than our hearts
112–13 **what . . . do damage** what damage
    . . . do
113–14 **event . . . arbitrator** Compare the
    proverbial 'The end tries all' (Dent
    E116.1).
113 **event** outcome
115 **When . . . ourselves** when we will know
    what has happened (instead of guessing
    now)
116 **becking** beckoning

1.3 The location is the outskirts of Athens,
    where Hippolyta and Emilia have come
    with Pirithous to see him on his way to
    Thebes.
4 **an** if
    might be i.e. were possible
5 **dure** endure
    Speed success
6 **Store** abundance
    governors managers
9 **affections** inclinations
10 **best-tempered pieces** best-made works
14 **terrene** earthly

What I shall be advised she likes. Our hearts
Are in his army, in his tent.
HIPPOLYTA   In's bosom.
We have been soldiers, and we cannot weep
When our friends don their helms, or put to sea,
Or tell of babes broached on the lance, or women   20
That have sod their infants in—and after ate them—
The brine they wept at killing 'em; then if
You stay to see of us such spinsters, we
Should hold you here for ever.
PIRITHOUS   Peace be to you
As I pursue this war, which shall be then
Beyond further requiring.   *Exit Pirithous*
EMILIA   How his longing
Follows his friend! Since his depart, his sports,
Though craving seriousness and skill, passed slightly
His careless execution, where nor gain
Made him regard, or loss consider, but   30
Playing one business in his hand, another
Directing in his head, his mind nurse equal
To these so diff'ring twins. Have you observed him
Since our great lord departed?

---

31 one] WEBER (*conj.* Mason, *anticipated by* Heath); ore Q

18-22 **We . . . 'em** Hippolyta's boast of her
ability, as a soldier, to take the horrors
of war in her stride, is reminiscent of
Volumnia's assertion: 'The breasts of
Hecuba | When she did suckle Hector
looked not lovelier | Than Hector's fore-
head when it spit forth blood' (*Coriolanus*
1.3.42-4).
20-2 **women . . . killing 'em** In *Christ's Tears
over Jerusalem* Thomas Nashe tells the
story of Miriam, who, during the siege
of Jerusalem, kills, cooks, and eats her
only son, to whose dead body she says:
'For sauce to thy flesh have I infused my
tears' (*Works*, ed. Ronald B. McKerrow,
5 vols. (Oxford, 1958), ii. 71-7).
19 **helms** helmets
20 **broached** impaled
21 **sod** boiled
23 **stay** wait
spinsters spinners; i.e. women who know
only such domestic activities
25 **As** while

25-6 **which . . . requiring** i.e. once the war
has been won, peace will no longer need
to be prayed for
27 **friend** The friendship of Theseus and
Pirithous was famous.
his depart the departure of Theseus
28-9 **passed slightly . . . execution** 'were
given only slight and careless attention'
(Leech)
31 **one** Although it is possible to make
sense of Q's 'ore' (= o'er; see collations),
Heath, in his MS notes to the 1750
edition of Beaumont and Fletcher, was
surely right to suggest 'one' as the correct
reading, since 'one' is followed by 'another'. Weber, who had not seen these
notes, followed Mason, who independ-
ently arrived at the same emendation.
32-3 **nurse equal | To** impartially concerned
with
33 **twins** i.e. his sports and his desire to be
with Theseus

HIPPOLYTA   With much labour;
  And I did love him for't. They two have cabined
  In many as dangerous as poor a corner,
  Peril and want contending; they have skiffed
  Torrents whose roaring tyranny and power
  I'th' least of these was dreadful, and they have
  Fought out together, where death's self was lodged;   40
  Yet fate hath brought them off. Their knot of love,
  Tied, weaved, entangled, with so true, so long,
  And with a finger of so deep a cunning,
  May be outworn, never undone. I think
  Theseus cannot be umpire to himself,
  Cleaving his conscience into twain, and doing
  Each side like justice, which he loves best.
EMILIA   Doubtless
  There is a best, and reason has no manners
  To say it is not you. I was acquainted
  Once with a time when I enjoyed a playfellow;   50
  You were at wars when she the grave enriched,
  Who made too proud the bed; took leave o'th' moon—
  Which then looked pale at parting—when our count
  Was each eleven.
HIPPOLYTA   'Twas Flavina.
EMILIA   Yes.
  You talk of Pirithous' and Theseus' love;
  Theirs has more ground, is more maturely seasoned,
  More buckled with strong judgement, and their needs
  The one of th'other may be said to water

54 eleven] F; a eleven Q   Flavina] SEWARD; *Flauia* Q   58–64] Q *prints marginal direction*:
2. Hearses rea-|dy with Pala-|mon: and Arci-|te: the 3. | Queenes. | Theseus: and | his Lordes
| ready.

34 **labour** diligence
35 **cabined** shared a soldier's tent ('cabin')
37 **Peril . . . contending** i.e. when it was a
   question whether danger or the lack of
   necessities was harder to bear
   skiffed crossed in a small boat
39 **I'th' least of these** at their mildest
40 **where . . . lodged** Theseus and Pirithous
   went to the underworld, where they
   were captured by Hades but rescued by
   Hercules.
41 **brought them off** rescued them
43 **so . . . cunning** such great skill

44 **outworn** worn out (by death)
47 **like** equal
   which Pirithous or Hippolyta
52 **took . . . moon** died (and thus ceased to
   be a devotee of Diana, the goddess of the
   moon and of chastity)
53 **count** age
56 **more ground** a firmer basis
57 **More buckled** better held together
58–64 The marginal stage direction in Q
   (see collations) is one of the indications
   that it was printed from prompt copy.

Their intertangled roots of love; but I
And she I sigh and spoke of were things innocent,   60
Loved for we did, and like the elements
That know not what nor why, yet do effect
Rare issues by their operance, our souls
Did so to one another; what she liked
Was then of me approved, what not, condemned,
No more arraignment; the flower that I would pluck
And put between my breasts—O then but beginning
To swell about the blossom—she would long
Till she had such another, and commit it
To the like innocent cradle, where, phoenix-like,   70
They died in perfume; on my head no toy
But was her pattern; her affections—pretty,
Though happily her careless wear—I followed
For my most serious decking; had mine ear
Stol'n some new air, or at adventure hummed one
From musical coinage, why, it was a note
Whereon her spirits would sojourn—rather dwell on—
And sing it in her slumbers. This rehearsal—

65 not,] COLMAN; ~ ∧ Q   73 happily her careless wear] COLMAN (*conj.* Sympson); happely,
her careles, were Q   75 one] COLMAN (*conj.* Seward); on Q   76 musical] F; misicall Q

61 **for** just because
   elements i.e. the four elements (earth,
   water, fire, and air) of which the universe
   was thought to be made
62–3 **effect | Rare issues** produce remarkable
   results (i.e. all the varied substances that
   exist)
63 **operance** operation
66 **arraignment** formal accusation
70–1 **phoenix-like ... perfume** The phoenix,
   a legendary bird, was said to burn itself
   to ashes in a fire made of aromatic wood,
   and then to rise again from its ashes.
71 **toy** ornament
72 **But was her pattern** that was not her
   model (for imitation)
72–3 **her affections ... followed** Uncertainty
   about the correct reading and punctuation (see collations, l. 73), combined
   with a condensation and puzzling syntax
   reminiscent of Shakespeare's style in
   Troilus, makes the interpretation of these
   lines unusually problematic; though
   'were' can be defended, 'wear' makes
   better sense—the pretty things she wore

happily (or 'haply', by chance), even
   when dressing casually.
72 **affections** things she affected, or fancied
   (in dressing herself)
74 **serious decking** carefully chosen clothes
75 **air** tune
   at adventure at random
76 **coinage** improvisation
78–80 **This ... bastard** Another problematic
   passage (see collations, l. 79, and note,
   ll. 72–3); the sense seems to be: 'This
   account, which happy innocence knows
   well to be an imperfect representation,
   or illegitimate descendant, of a love long
   ago'. This reading takes 'import ment',
   which usually means 'significance', in
   the sense of the French *emportement*,
   'passion'. Lamb's emendation makes
   sense of the incomprehensible 'fury-innocent', though, as the Oxford editor says,
   it is difficult to explain how an initial e
   could have been read as an f. His ingeni-
   ous emendation is based on the assumption of the easier misreading of 'sely' (a
   common spelling of 'seely') as 'fury',

Which seely innocence wots well, comes in
Like old importment's bastard—has this end,   80
That the true love 'tween maid and maid may be
More than in sex dividual.
HIPPOLYTA   You're out of breath,
And this high-speeded pace is but to say
That you shall never—like the maid Flavina—
Love any that's called man.
EMILIA
I am sure I shall not.
HIPPOLYTA   Now alack, weak sister,
I must no more believe thee in this point—
Though in't I know thou dost believe thyself—
Than I will trust a sickly appetite,
That loathes even as it longs; but sure, my sister,   90
If I were ripe for your persuasion, you
Have said enough to shake me from the arm
Of the all-noble Theseus, for whose fortunes
I will now in and kneel, with great assurance
That we, more than his Pirithous, possess
The high throne in his heart.
EMILIA   I am not
Against your faith, yet I continue mine.   *Exeunt*

1.4   *Cornetts. A battle struck within; then a retreat.*
        Flourish. Then enter ⌈from one door⌉ Theseus,

79 seely innocence] OXFORD; fury-innocent Q; ev'ry innocent LAMB; surely Innocence
SYMPSON   82 dividual] SEWARD *and* SYMPSON; individuall Q   out] F; ont Q
    1.4] Q (Scaena 4.)   0.1 Cornetts] *on line preceding* Scaena 4 *in* Q   within] Q (within)   0.2
from one door] This edition; *not in* Q

confusion of long s with f, e with u, and
l with r being fairly common. If the
manuscript read 'innocenc', the final c
could have been taken for a t.

78 **rehearsal** account (of our friendship)
79 **seely** happy
82 **in sex dividual** between persons of different sex. Q's 'sex individuall' (see collations) clearly requires the emendation.
83 **high-speeded pace** i.e. rapid flow of words
91 **ripe . . . persuasion** ready to be persuaded
by you
1.4 The location is outside Thebes.
  0.1 *Cornetts* See note on Prologue, l. 0.1;

here cornetts, called for most frequently
in the indoor private theatres, are specified as part of the sound of battle.
Presumably they are again used for the
flourish that precedes the triumphal entrance of Theseus, since, both off the
stage and on, they played for processions
(Manifold, p. 48).
    struck within fought off-stage (i.e. sounds
of battle are produced)
0.2–5 *from . . . door* The wording of the
stage direction implies that as Theseus
enters on one side, the queens, who are
to meet him, enter from the opposite side.
Some editors delay the entrance of the

victor, ⌈*followed by the Herald and attendants bearing*
Palamon and Arcite on two hearses. From the opposite
door⌉ *the three queens meet him and fall on their*
faces before him

FIRST QUEEN
To thee no star be dark.
SECOND QUEEN   Both heaven and earth
Friend thee for ever.
THIRD QUEEN   All the good that may
Be wished upon thy head, I cry amen to't.
THESEUS
Th'impartial gods, who from the mounted heavens
View us their mortal herd, behold who err,
And in their time chastise. Go and find out
The bones of your dead lords, and honour them
With treble ceremony; rather than a gap
Should be in their dear rights, we would supply't.
But those we will depute, which shall invest   10
You in your dignities, and even each thing
Our haste does leave imperfect. So adieu,
And heaven's good eyes look on you.
                    The Queens rise and exeunt
(*To the attendants, pointing to Palamon and Arcite*)
                              What are those?

HERALD
Men of great quality, as may be judged

0.3–5 *followed . . . door*] This edition; *not in* Q   13 *The Queens . . . exeunt*] This edition; *Exeunt*
Queenes (following those) *in* Q   *To . . . Arcite*] *not in* Q

attendants with Palamon and Arcite (for
which Q gives no direction) until l. 13,
just before Theseus asks about them,
but they would add to the spectacle of
Theseus' triumphal entry, and he need
not turn to look at them until the departure of the queens.

0.4 *hearses* biers
 1 **dark** obscured, and hence unfavourable
4–6 **gods . . . chastise** Compare the proverbial 'God stays long but strikes at last'
(Dent G224).
 4 **mounted** high
 9 **dear** valued (by both you and me)
   rights The word may be heard in the

theatre as 'rites', which is equally appropriate, whether or not a play on words
was intentional.
10 **invest** literally, 'clothe'. The proper
funeral ceremonies will metaphorically
provide a clothing of dignity for the
queens and their dead husbands.
11 **even** complete (*v.*)
14–16 **Men . . . King** Compare 'But by her
coat armours, and by her gere | The
heraulds knew hem best in speciall | As
tho that weren of the blood riall | Of
Thebes, and of sistren two yborne' (*The
Knight's Tale*, ll. A 1016–18).
14 **quality** rank

By their appointment. Some of Thebes have told's
They are sisters' children, nephews to the King.
THESEUS
By th' helm of Mars, I saw them in the war,
Like to a pair of lions, smeared with prey,
Make lanes in troops aghast. I fixed my note
Constantly on them, for they were a mark   20
Worth a god's view. What prisoner was't that told me
When I enquired their names?
HERALD   Wi' leave, they're called
Arcite and Palamon.
THESEUS   'Tis right; those, those.
They are not dead?
HERALD
Nor in a state of life; had they been taken
When their last hurts were given, 'twas possible
They might have been recovered. Yet they breathe
And have the name of men.
THESEUS   Then like men use 'em.
The very lees of such, millions of rates,
Exceed the wine of others. All our surgeons   30
Convent in their behoof; our richest balms,
Rather than niggard, waste; their lives concern us
Much more than Thebes is worth. Rather than have 'em
Freed of this plight, and in their morning state,
Sound and at liberty, I would 'em dead;
But forty-thousandfold we had rather have 'em

---

18 smeared] Q (*corr.*); succard Q (*uncorr.*)   22 Wi' leave] DYCE; We leave Q; We learn DYCE
1866 (*conj.* Heath); We 'lieve LITTLEDALE (*conj.*)   26–7 Q *prints marginal direction*: 3. Hearses
rea-|dy.

15 **appointment** arms and armour
    told's told us
19 **Make lanes in** cut their way through
    note attention
20 **mark** notable sight
22 **Wi' leave** with permission. The herald is
    deferentially polite.
23 **Arcite** Two syllables, normally accented
    on the first; the 'c' is pronounced as 's'.
24–5 **They . . . life** Compare 'Not fully quicke,
    ne fully dead they were' (*The Knight's
    Tale*, l. A 1015).
26–7 Q's marginal direction (see collations)

prepares for the entrance in the next
scene of the three queens with the bodies
of their husbands.
27 **recovered** resuscitated
28 **men** i.e. not corpses
29 **lees** dregs
    rates times
31 **Convent** summon
    in their behoof for their benefit
32 **niggard** spend grudgingly
34 **their morning state** as they were this
    morning (before they were wounded)
35 **would** i.e. would wish

Prisoners to us than death. Bear 'em speedily
From our kind air, to them unkind, and minister
What man to man may do—for our sake more,
Since I have known frights, fury, friends' behests, 40
Love's provocations, zeal, a mistress' task,
Desire of liberty, a fever, madness,
Hath set a mark which nature could not reach to
Without some imposition, sickness in will
O'er-wrestling strength in reason. For our love
And great Apollo's mercy, all our best
Their best skill tender. Lead into the city,
Where, having bound things scattered, we will post
To Athens fore our army.   *Flourish. Exeunt*

1.5   *Music. Enter the Queens with attendants bearing the
         hearses of their knights in a funeral solemnity, etc.*

THE THREE QUEENS (*sing*)
      Urns and odours bring away;
      Vapours, sighs darken the day;
         Our dole more deadly looks than dying;
      Balms and gums and heavy cheers,

---

39 do —] LEECH; ~∧ Q; ~; SEWARD   40 friends'] WEBER; friends, Q   41 Love's] WEBER;
Loves, Q   45 O'er-wrestling] LEECH (*conj.* Bertram); Or wrastling Q   49 fore] SEWARD; for
Q   *Flourish*] *at end of l. 48 in* Q
   1.5] Q (Scaena 5.)   0.1 *Music*] *on line preceding* Scaena 5 *in* Q   *attendants bearing*] BAWCUTT
(*subs.*); *not in* Q   0.2 *etc.*] Q (*&c.*)   1 THE THREE . . . *sing*] This edition; *not in* Q

---

38 **unkind** Fresh air was thought to be
   harmful to open wounds.
39–45 **for . . . reason** Theseus urges them
   to do even more, since he has seen how
   men under various kinds of extreme
   emotional pressure have attempted
   things that they could not naturally
   accomplish, a perverse determination
   overcoming rationality. (He apparently
   guesses that Palamon and Arcite acted
   against their better judgement in fighting
   for Creon.)
41 **zeal** religious enthusiasm
43 **set a mark** fixed a goal
44 **imposition** compulsion
46 **Apollo** the god of healing
46–7 **all . . . tender** let all our best surgeons
   apply their greatest skill
48 **bound things scattered** re-established
   order. Compare 'O, let me teach you how
   to knit again | This scattered corn into

one mutual sheaf' (*Titus* 5.3.69–70).
1.5 The location is again outside Thebes. It
   is noteworthy that the act begins and
   ends ceremonially. As the first ceremony
   stresses the effort to behave nobly, the
   funeral ceremony dramatizes the inevitable end of all efforts. Both the idealism
   of the first and the pessimism of the
   second run through the whole play.
0.2 **knights** i.e. husbands
   etc. The acting company is left free to
   enhance in any way the spectacle of the
   funeral procession.
1 THE THREE . . . *sing* Although there is no
   indication of who is to sing the following
   song, the words suggest that it is sung
   by the queens.
   away on our way
3 **dole** mourning
4 **gums** aromatic resins for incense
   heavy cheers sorrowful faces

Sacred vials filled with tears,
And clamours through the wild air flying.

Come all sad and solemn shows
That are quick-eyed pleasure's foes;
We convent naught else but woes,
We convent naught else but woes.   10

THIRD QUEEN
This funeral path brings to your household's grave;
Joy seize on you again; peace sleep with him!
SECOND QUEEN
And this to yours.
FIRST QUEEN   Yours this way. Heavens lend
A thousand differing ways to one sure end.
THIRD QUEEN
This world's a city full of straying streets,
And death's the market-place, where each one meets.
                                    Exeunt severally

2.1   *Enter Jailer and Wooer*
JAILER I may depart with little while I live; something I
    may cast to you, not much. Alas, the prison I keep,
    though it be for great ones, yet they seldom come;
    before one salmon you shall take a number of minnows.
    I am given out to be better lined than it can appear to

---

10 We convent . . . woes.] BAWCUTT; *We convent, &c.* Q, *at end of l. 9*
    2.1] Q (*Actus Secundus*. Scaena 1.)

---

9 **convent** convene; i.e. summon or bring
    together
11 **brings** leads
13 **this** i.e. this path
15–16 **This . . . meets** Compare 'This world
    is but a throughfare full of wo, | And we
    been pilgrimes passing to and fro: | Death
    is an end of euery worlds sore' (*The
    Knight's Tale*, ll. A 2847–9); also compare
    'As into a great city, or into the main
    sea, so unto death there are many ways.
    It is as the center, wherein all the lines
    do meet; a town of mart, wherein many
    ways from contrary coasts do end' (T.
    Tuke, *Discourse of Death* (1613), sig. C3;
    see Dent W176).
16.1 *severally* i.e. each queen leaves by a

different door with the body of her husband and part of the funeral procession.
2.1 The location is a garden outside a
    prison in Athens, the windows of which
    are represented by the windows of the
    stage gallery. A property tree may have
    been used (see 2.2.238). The scene is
    probably by Shakespeare (see note on
    l. 55.1 and Introduction, p. 22).
1 **depart with** give away
2 **cast to** confer upon (as dowry)
4 **before . . . minnows** Although this sounds
    proverbial, no such proverb is listed in
    the standard collections.
4 **take** catch
5 **given out** reputed
    better lined richer

me report is a true speaker. I would I were really that
I am delivered to be. Marry, what I have—be it what it
will—I will assure upon my daughter at the day of my
death.

WOOER Sir, I demand no more than your own offer, and   10
I will estate your daughter in what I have promised.

JAILER Well, we will talk more of this when the solemnity
is past. But have you a full promise of her? When that
shall be seen, I tender my consent.

WOOER I have, sir.

Enter Jailer's Daughter with rushes

Here she comes.

JAILER (*to Daughter*) Your friend and I have chanced to
name you here, upon the old business; but no more of
that now. So soon as the court hurry is over we will
have an end of it. I'th' mean time look tenderly to the   20
two prisoners. I can tell you they are princes.

JAILER'S DAUGHTER These strewings are for their chamber.
'Tis pity they are in prison, and 'twere pity they should
be out. I do think they have patience to make any
adversity ashamed; the prison itself is proud of 'em, and
they have all the world in their chamber.

JAILER They are famed to be a pair of absolute men.

JAILER'S DAUGHTER By my troth, I think fame but stammers
'em; they stand a grece above the reach of report.

JAILER I heard them reported in the battle to be the only   30
doers.

JAILER'S DAUGHTER Nay, most likely, for they are noble

15.1 *Enter . . . Daughter*] *placed here in* This edition; *after* her? (*l. 13*) *in* Q   *Jailer's*] *not in* Q
with rushes] OXFORD; *not in* Q   19 that, now.] COLMAN; that. | Now, Q

6 **report** rumour
  that what
7 **delivered** reported
  Marry to be sure (originally an oath by
  the Virgin Mary)
8 **assure upon** leave to
11 **estate** endow
12 **solemnity** i.e. the wedding of Theseus
  and Hippolyta
13 **of** from
15.1 **with rushes** Though these words are
  not in the Q stage direction (see collations), it is clear from l. 22 that the
  Jailer's Daughter has rushes, commonly

used as a floor covering in Elizabethan
houses.
20 **tenderly to** carefully after
22 **strewings** i.e. the rushes, which were
  periodically renewed
24–6 **they . . . chamber** in that their friendship (see their dialogue in the next scene)
  is everything to them
27 **absolute** complete, perfect
28 **stammers** imperfectly describes
29 **grece** step
30–1 **only doers** best fighters
32–3 **noble suff'rers** i.e. their patience in
  adversity matches their prowess in battle

suff'rers. I marvel how they would have looked had
they been victors, that with such a constant nobility
enforce a freedom out of bondage, making misery their
mirth and affliction a toy to jest at.

JAILER Do they so?

JAILER'S DAUGHTER It seems to me they have no more
sense of their captivity than I of ruling Athens. They
eat well, look merrily, discourse of many things, but   40
nothing of their own restraint and disasters. Yet sometime a divided sigh, martyred as 'twere i'th' deliverance,
will break from one of them; when the other presently
gives it so sweet a rebuke that I could wish myself a
sigh to be so chid, or at least a sigher to be comforted.

WOOER I never saw 'em.

JAILER The Duke himself came privately in the night, and
so did they; what the reason of it is, I know not.

Enter Palamon and Arcite above in shackles
Look, yonder they are. That's Arcite looks out.

JAILER'S DAUGHTER No, sir, no, that's Palamon. Arcite is   50
the lower of the twain; you may perceive a part of him.

JAILER Go to, leave your pointing. They would not make
us their object. Out of their sight!

JAILER'S DAUGHTER It is a holiday to look on them. Lord,
the diff'rence of men!

Exeunt Jailer, Wooer, and Daughter

48.1 *Enter . . . above*] placed as in WEBER; *after* night, (*l. 47*) *in* Q   *in shackles*] not in Q   55.1
Jailer . . . Daughter] not in Q

36 **toy** trifle
41 **restraint** captivity
42 **divided** incompletely uttered
43 **presently** at once
47 **privately** secretly (accompanying the
prisoners)
48.1 *above* on the upper stage, or gallery
51 **lower** shorter
52 **Go to** a remonstrance similar to 'Come,
come'
52–3 **would . . . object** do not wish to see us
54–5 **Lord . . . men!** how some men excel
others! Compare Goneril, 'O, the difference of man and man!' (*Tragedy of Lear*,
4.2.27).
55.1 *Exeunt . . . Daughter* Q's *Exeunt* (see
collations), taken literally, requires Palamon and Arcite to leave when the others
do, re-entering immediately at the open-

ing of 2.2, and some editors direct them
to do so. Much depends on the staging
of the two scenes, which may best be
considered as presenting a continuous
action in which the two kinsmen appear
on the upper stage at the end of 2.1
and remain there through 2.2. Although
lengthy scenes on the upper stage are
comparatively rare, they are not unknown. A marginal stage direction in
Jonson's *The Devil is an Ass*, performed
in the same theatre three years after
Kinsmen, reads: 'This Scene [2.6] is acted
at two windows, as out of two contiguous
buildings.' Hence, there is no need for
Palamon and Arcite to go out at l.
55.1. Exits and entrances are not always
carefully indicated even in texts printed

⌈2.2⌉

PALAMON
  How do you, noble cousin?
ARCITE   How do you, sir?
PALAMON
  Why, strong enough to laugh at misery
  And bear the chance of war; yet we are prisoners
  I fear for ever, cousin.
ARCITE   I believe it,
  And to that destiny have patiently
  Laid up my hour to come.
PALAMON   O cousin Arcite,
  Where is Thebes now? Where is our noble country?
  Where are our friends and kindreds? Never more
  Must we behold those comforts, never see
  The hardy youths strive for the games of honour,   10
  Hung with the painted favours of their ladies,
  Like tall ships under sail; then start amongst 'em

2.2] Q (Scaena 2.). Q *adds: Enter Palamon, and Arcite in prison.* WEBER *was the first to drop this direction.*

from prompt copy. In this instance the general *Exeunt* may be due to the division of labour between the collaborators: Shakespeare probably wrote the first scene, while Fletcher almost certainly wrote the second. Shakespeare need not have known exactly how Fletcher would begin his part.

2.2 Although, if Palamon and Arcite do not leave the stage, a new scene would not normally begin here, Q's Scene 1 and Scene 2 are structurally complete scenes and probably not written by the same author (see preceding note). It therefore seems appropriate to retain Q's division, while, for reasons given in the preceding note, omitting Q's direction '*Enter Palamon and Arcite in prison*' (see collations). This is one of the few places in the play where the joining of the work of the collaborators is somewhat rough (see note on ll. 6–55).

3 **chance of war** That 'The chance of war is uncertain' is proverbial (Dent C223).

6 **Laid . . . come** consigned the remainder of my life

6–55 Critics have observed that these laments accord poorly with the description we have just heard of the kinsmen's good spirits and avoidance of any comment on their imprisonment. This may be one of the minor inconsistencies, less apparent in performance than in reading, which point to collaboration (see Introduction, p. 20). Fletcher seems to be showing how they arrived at the 'constant nobility' observed by the Jailer's Daughter, and demonstrated in ll. 55–115. In *The Rivals* Davenant introduces Celania, the character corresponding to the Jailer's Daughter, in a scene of the first act similar to Fletcher's 2.2, and containing much of the original dialogue. Celania and her maid come to a window where they can see and overhear the kinsmen just as they are beginning to cheer themselves up. Celania then comments on their good humour and the sweetness of their discourse, like the Jailer's Daughter in *Kinsmen* 2.1.

11 **painted favours** brightly coloured scarves or gloves

And, as an east wind, leave 'em all behind us,
Like lazy clouds, whilst Palamon and Arcite,
Even in the wagging of a wanton leg,
Outstripped the people's praises, won the garlands
Ere they have time to wish 'em ours. O never
Shall we two exercise, like twins of honour,
Our arms again, and feel our fiery horses
Like proud seas under us. Our good swords, now—   20
Better the red-eyed god of war nev'r wore—
Ravished our sides, like age must run to rust
And deck the temples of those gods that hate us;
These hands shall never draw 'em out like lightning
To blast whole armies more.

ARCITE   No, Palamon,
Those hopes are prisoners with us; here we are
And here the graces of our youths must wither
Like a too-timely spring; here age must find us,
And—which is heaviest, Palamon—unmarried.
The sweet embraces of a loving wife,   30
Loaden with kisses, armed with thousand cupids,
Shall never clasp our necks; no issue know us;
No figures of ourselves shall we ev'r see
To glad our age, and, like young eagles, teach 'em
Boldly to gaze against bright arms, and say
'Remember what your fathers were, and conquer!'
The fair-eyed maids shall weep our banishments
And in their songs curse ever-blinded Fortune
Till she for shame see what a wrong she has done
To youth and nature. This is all our world;   40
We shall know nothing here but one another;
Hear nothing but the clock that tells our woes.

20 us.] SEWARD (us;); ~, Q   21 wore] SEWARD; were Q   22 Ravished] SEWARD; Bravishd
Q

15 Even . . . leg i.e. effortlessly, without even   33 figures images, copies
   trying   34–5 like . . . gaze Compare the proverbial
   wanton sportive, carefree   'Only the eagle can gaze at the sun' (Dent
22 Ravished torn from   E3).
28 Like . . . spring i.e. like plants that   38 ever-blinded Fortune The goddess For-
   blossom prematurely in a too-early spring   tune is often said to be blind since she
29 heaviest hardest to bear   disregards merit.
32 issue children   42 tells counts

The vine shall grow, but we shall never see it;
Summer shall come, and with her all delights,
But dead-cold winter must inhabit here still.

PALAMON
  'Tis too true, Arcite. To our Theban hounds
That shook the agèd forest with their echoes
No more now must we hallow; no more shake
Our pointed javelins, whilst the angry swine
Flies like a Parthian quiver from our rages,   50
Struck with our well-steeled darts. All valiant uses—
The food and nourishment of noble minds—
In us two here shall perish; we shall die—
Which is the curse of honour—lastly,
Children of grief and ignorance.

ARCITE   Yet, cousin,
Even from the bottom of these miseries,
From all that fortune can inflict upon us,
I see two comforts rising, two mere blessings,
If the gods please, to hold here a brave patience,
And the enjoying of our griefs together.   60
Whilst Palamon is with me, let me perish
If I think this our prison.

PALAMON   Certainly,
'Tis a main goodness, cousin, that our fortunes
Were twinned together. 'Tis most true, two souls
Put in two noble bodies, let 'em suffer
The gall of hazard, so they grow together,
Will never sink; they must not, say they could.
A willing man dies sleeping and all's done.

64 twinned] Q (twyn'd). *See note on this word.*

48 **hallow** shout. Here and elsewhere this
older word, accented on the first syllable,
is metrically preferable to the modern
halloo, accented on the second syllable.
49 **swine** wild boar
50 **Parthian quiver** It was proverbial that
'The Parthians fight flying away' (Dent
P80).
51 **uses** occupations
54 **lastly** in the end
55 **Children . . . ignorance** sad and unknown
58 **mere** pure
63 **main goodness** major asset
64 **twinned** Compare 'We were as twinned

lambs' (*Winter's Tale*, 1.2.69), where the
word is spelt *twyn'd* as it is here in Q (see
collations). It is possible that the intended
meaning was *twined*, which could be
identically spelt, and makes good sense,
but when *twined* occurs at 4.2.104 it is
spelt *twind*.
66 **gall of hazard** bitter blows of chance
    so provided that
67 **sink** succumb to misfortune
    say i.e. even if
68 **willing man** a man who stoically accepts
his fate
    sleeping i.e. peacefully

ARCITE
    Shall we make worthy uses of this place
    That all men hate so much?
PALAMON   How, gentle cousin?   70
ARCITE
    Let's think this prison holy sanctuary,
    To keep us from corruption of worse men.
    We are young and yet desire the ways of honour,
    That liberty and common conversation,
    The poison of pure spirits, might, like women,
    Woo us to wander from. What worthy blessing
    Can be but our imaginations
    May make it ours? And here being thus together,
    We are an endless mine to one another;
    We are one another's wife, ever begetting   80
    New births of love; we are father, friends, acquaintance;
    We are in one another, families;
    I am your heir, and you are mine; this place
    Is our inheritance; no hard oppressor
    Dare take this from us; here, with a little patience,
    We shall live long and loving. No surfeits seek us;
    The hand of war hurts none here, nor the seas
    Swallow their youth. Were we at liberty,
    A wife might part us lawfully, or business;
    Quarrels consume us; envy of ill men   90
    Crave our acquaintance. I might sicken, cousin,
    Where you should never know it, and so perish
    Without your noble hand to close mine eyes,
    Or prayers to the gods. A thousand chances,
    Were we from hence, would sever us.
PALAMON   You have made me—
    I thank you, cousin Arcite—almost wanton

---

72 **To keep . . . men** Here Fletcher clearly
builds on Shakespeare's portrayal of the
kinsmen in 1.2 as repelled by the corruption of Thebes.
74 **common conversation** indiscriminate
contact with people
75 **women** i.e. temptresses
77 **imaginations** Here, and wherever the
metre requires it, the suffix '-tion' is
disyllabic; a number of other suffixes are

similarly variable, e.g. '-cient', '-cious',
etc.
79 **mine** resource
81 **acquaintance** i.e. acquaintances
86 **surfeits** excesses (leading to disease)
90–1 **envy . . . acquaintance** either (*a*) we
might suffer from coming to know the
malice of evil men, or (*b*) we might come
to envy them.
96 **wanton** unrestrainedly delighted

With my captivity. What a misery
It is to live abroad, and everywhere!
'Tis like a beast, methinks. I find the court here—
I am sure, a more content; and all those pleasures   100
That woo the wills of men to vanity
I see through now, and am sufficient
To tell the world 'tis but a gaudy shadow
That old Time as he passes by, takes with him.
What had we been, old in the court of Creon,
Where sin is justice, lust and ignorance
The virtues of the great ones? Cousin Arcite,
Had not the loving gods found this place for us,
We had died as they do, ill old men, unwept,
And had their epitaphs, the people's curses.   110
Shall I say more?
ARCITE   I would hear you still.
PALAMON   Ye shall.
Is there record of any two that loved
Better than we do, Arcite?
ARCITE   Sure there cannot.
PALAMON
I do not think it possible our friendship
Should ever leave us.
ARCITE   Till our deaths it cannot.
        Enter Emilia and her Woman below
And after death our spirits shall be led
To those that love eternally.
        Palamon sees Emilia and says nothing
                          Speak on, sir.
EMILIA
This garden has a world of pleasures in't.
What flower is this?

115.1 *below*] *not in* Q   117 *Palamon . . . nothing*] *not in* Q   118 This . . . in't] *ascribed to*
Emilia by SEWARD; *printed as the last line of Arcite's speech in* Q

98 **abroad** at large
99 **court** i.e. everything the court could offer
100 **more** greater
105 **What . . . old** What would we have
    been like (if we had grown) old?
109 **ill** wicked
111 **still** 'now as formerly' (*OED*, 4a), i.e.
    'Keep talking'

112 **record** pronounced 'recòrd'
115.1 *Enter . . . below* It is clear that Emilia
    and her woman enter on the main stage,
    which represents the garden beneath the
    prison windows.
117 **those . . . eternally** the spirits of lovers
    in Elysium

WOMAN   'Tis called narcissus, madam.

EMILIA

That was a fair boy, certain, but a fool   120
To love himself. Were there not maids enough?

ARCITE (*to Palamon*)
Pray, forward.

PALAMON   Yes.

EMILIA (*to her Woman*) Or were they all hard-hearted?

WOMAN

They could not be to one so fair.

EMILIA   Thou wouldst not.

WOMAN

I think I should not, madam.

EMILIA   That's a good wench;
But take heed to your kindness, though.

WOMAN   Why, madam?

EMILIA

Men are mad things.

ARCITE (*to Palamon*)   Will ye go forward, cousin?

EMILIA (*to her Woman*)
Canst not thou work such flowers in silk, wench?

WOMAN   Yes.

EMILIA

I'll have a gown full of 'em, and of these;
This is a pretty colour; will't not do
Rarely upon a skirt, wench?

WOMAN   Dainty, madam.   130

ARCITE (*to Palamon*)
Cousin, cousin, how do you, sir? Why, Palamon!

PALAMON

Never till now I was in prison, Arcite.

ARCITE

Why, what's the matter, man?

PALAMON (*pointing to Emilia*)   Behold and wonder!
By heaven, she is a goddess.

---

133 *pointing to Emilia*] not in Q

119–20 **narcissus . . . boy** Ovid tells the story
of the boy Narcissus, who fell in love
with his reflection in a pool and, after
his death, was transformed into a flower
(*Metamorphoses*, iii. 339–510). The story

is referred to later (4.2.32).
122 **forward** go on with what you were
saying
127 **work** embroider
130 **rarely** finely

ARCITE   Ha!
PALAMON   Do reverence;
  She is a goddess, Arcite.
EMILIA (*to her Woman*)   Of all flowers
  Methinks a rose is best.
WOMAN   Why, gentle madam?
EMILIA
  It is the very emblem of a maid;
  For when the west wind courts her gently,
  How modestly she blows, and paints the sun
  With her chaste blushes! When the north comes   140
     near her,
  Rude and impatient, then, like chastity,
  She locks her beauties in her bud again,
  And leaves him to base briers.
WOMAN   Yet, good madam,
  Sometimes her modesty will blow so far
  She falls for't; a maid,
  If she have any honour, would be loath
  To take example by her.
EMILIA   Thou art wanton.
ARCITE (*to Palamon*)
  She is wondrous fair.
PALAMON   She is all the beauty extant.
EMILIA (*to her Woman*)
  The sun grows high; let's walk in. Keep these flowers;
  We'll see how near art can come near their colours.   150
  I am wondrous merry-hearted, I could laugh now.
WOMAN
  I could lie down, I am sure.
EMILIA   And take one with you?
WOMAN
  That's as we bargain, madam.

139 **blows** blooms
  paints the sun colours the sunlight
140 **north** i.e. north wind
143 **leaves . . . briers** i.e. repels him by leaving only her thorns exposed
145 **for't** because of it
150 **We'll . . . colours** The repetition of 'near' is troublesome and may, as the Oxford editor suggests, be a mistake due to 'compositorial eyeskip', but his substitution of 'how close' is dubious. The sense would seem to be: 'if art can come near' or 'how near art can come to', neither of which is metrically satisfactory.
151–2 **laugh . . . down** 'Laugh and lay (or lie) down' was the name of a card game, but also a proverbial expression (Dent L92) with sexual overtones.
152 **one** someone

EMILIA   Well, agree then.
                        Exeunt Emilia and her Woman
PALAMON
  What think you of this beauty?
ARCITE   'Tis a rare one.
PALAMON
  Is't but a rare one?
ARCITE   Yes, a matchless beauty.
PALAMON
  Might not a man well lose himself and love her?
ARCITE
  I cannot tell what you have done; I have,
  Beshrew mine eyes for't! Now I feel my shackles.
PALAMON
  You love her, then?
ARCITE   Who would not?
PALAMON   And desire her?
ARCITE Before my liberty.   160
PALAMON
  I saw her first.
ARCITE   That's nothing.
PALAMON   But it shall be.
ARCITE
  I saw her too.
PALAMON   Yes, but you must not love her.
ARCITE
  I will not, as you do, to worship her
  As she is heavenly and a blessèd goddess.
  I love her as a woman, to enjoy her;
  So both may love.
PALAMON
  You shall not love at all.
ARCITE   Not love at all?
  Who shall deny me?

153.1 *her*] *not in* Q

153 **agree** i.e. make your bargain
158 **Beshrew** curse (a mild oath)
163–5 **I . . . enjoy her** based on *The Knight's
  Tale*, ll. A 1156–9: 'Thou wist it nat

or now | Whether she be woman or
goddesse: | Thine is affection of holinesse,
| And mine is loue, as to a creature'.

PALAMON
I, that first saw her; I, that took possession
First with mine eye of all those beauties   170
In her revealed to mankind. If thou lov'st her
Or entertain'st a hope to blast my wishes,
Thou art a traitor, Arcite, and a fellow
False as thy title to her. Friendship, blood,
And all the ties between us I disclaim
If thou once think upon her.
ARCITE   Yes, I love her,
And if the lives of all my name lay on it,
I must do so. I love her with my soul;
If that will lose ye, farewell, Palamon.
I say again I love, and, in loving her, maintain   180
I am as worthy and as free a lover,
And have as just a title to her beauty
As any Palamon, or any living
That is a man's son.
PALAMON   Have I called thee friend?
ARCITE
Yes, and have found me so; why are you moved thus?
Let me deal coldly with you. Am not I
Part of your blood, part of your soul? You have told me
That I was Palamon, and you were Arcite.
PALAMON   Yes.
ARCITE
Am not I liable to those affections,
Those joys, griefs, angers, fears, my friend shall suffer?   190
PALAMON
Ye may be.
ARCITE   Why then would you deal so cunningly,
So strangely, so unlike a noble kinsman,

187 your blood] F; you blood Q

171 **thou** Up to this point the kinsmen
have addressed each other with the more
formal and polite second person plural;
the singular form here expresses Palamon's anger and contempt. Arcite continues to use the plural form until l. 219.
173 **fellow** The word was sometimes used
contemptuously, as it is here.

174 **blood** kinship
177 **name** family
     lay depended
181 **free** honourable, noble
185 **moved** i.e. angered
186 **coldly** calmly
189 **affections** emotions

To love alone? Speak truly, do you think me
Unworthy of her sight?
PALAMON   No, but unjust
If thou pursue that sight.
ARCITE   Because another
First sees the enemy, shall I stand still
And let mine honour down, and never charge?
PALAMON
Yes, if he be but one.
ARCITE   But say that one
Had rather combat me?
PALAMON   Let that one say so,
And use thy freedom; else if thou pursuest her,   200
Be as that cursèd man that hates his country,
A branded villain.
ARCITE   You are mad.
PALAMON   I must be,
Till thou art worthy, Arcite—it concerns me;
And in this madness if I hazard thee
And take thy life, I deal but truly.
ARCITE   Fie, sir,
You play the child extremely. I will love her,
I must, I ought to do so, and I dare,
And all this justly.
PALAMON   O that now, that now
Thy false self and thy friend had but this fortune
To be one hour at liberty, and grasp   210
Our good swords in our hands, I would quickly teach
   thee
What 'twere to filch affection from another.
Thou art baser in it than a cutpurse.
Put but thy head out of this window more,
And, as I have a soul, I'll nail thy life to't.
ARCITE
Thou dar'st not, fool, thou canst not, thou art feeble.
Put my head out? I'll throw my body out

202 be,] TONSON; ~. Q

197 **let . . . down** fail to act honourably   204 **hazard** risk
203 **concerns** matters to   215 **to't** i.e. to the window frame

And leap the garden, when I see her next,
   Enter Jailer above
And pitch between her arms to anger thee.
PALAMON
  No more; the keeper's coming. I shall live   220
  To knock thy brains out with my shackles.
ARCITE   Do.
JAILER
  By your leave, gentlemen.
PALAMON   Now, honest keeper?
JAILER
  Lord Arcite, you must presently to th' Duke;
  The cause I know not yet.
ARCITE   I am ready, keeper.
JAILER
  Prince Palamon, I must a while bereave you
  Of your fair cousin's company.
                  Exeunt Arcite and Jailer
PALAMON   And me too,
  Even when you please, of life. Why is he sent for?
  It may be he shall marry her; he's goodly,
  And like enough the Duke hath taken notice
  Both of his blood and body. But his falsehood!   230
  Why should a friend be treacherous? If that
  Get him a wife so noble and so fair,
  Let honest men ne'er love again. Once more
  I would but see this fair one. Blessèd garden,
  And fruit and flowers more blessèd that still blossom
  As her bright eyes shine on ye! Would I were,
  For all the fortune of my life hereafter,
  Yon little tree, yon blooming apricot.
  How I would spread and fling my wanton arms
  In at her window! I would bring her fruit   240
  Fit for the gods to feed on; youth and pleasure
  Still as she tasted should be doubled on her,

218.1 *Jailer*] *Keeper* Q (*and so, or 'Keep.', throughout the scene*)   *above*] *not in* Q

218 **leap** leap into
218.1, 244.1 The stage directions here, as
  often in dramatic texts of this period,
  allow the entering character time to cross
  the stage to where he is perceived by

those on-stage.
219 **pitch** throw myself
228 **goodly** good-looking
230 **blood** good parentage
242 **Still as** whenever

And, if she be not heavenly, I would make her
So near the gods in nature they should fear her;
    Enter Jailer
And then I am sure she would love me. How
    now, keeper?
Where's Arcite?

JAILER   Banished. Prince Pirithous
Obtained his liberty; but never more,
Upon his oath and life, must he set foot
Upon this kingdom.

PALAMON   He's a blessèd man.
He shall see Thebes again, and call to arms   250
The bold young men that, when he bids 'em charge,
Fall on like fire. Arcite shall have a fortune,
If he dare make himself a worthy lover,
Yet in the field to strike a battle for her;
And if he lose her then, he's a cold coward.
How bravely may he bear himself to win her
If he be noble Arcite—thousand ways!
Were I at liberty, I would do things
Of such a virtuous greatness that this lady,
This blushing virgin, should take manhood to her   260
And seek to ravish me.

JAILER   My lord, for you
I have this charge too.

PALAMON   To discharge my life.

JAILER
No, but from this place to remove your lordship;
The windows are too open.

PALAMON   Devils take 'em
That are so envious to me! Prithee kill me.

JAILER
And hang for't afterward.

PALAMON   By this good light,
Had I a sword I would kill thee.

JAILER   Why, my lord?

---

246 **Pirithous** Here, and in all Fletcher's
   scenes, tetrasyllabic (Pirìthoùs).
252 **fortune** chance
262 **charge** order

discharge Palamon plays on another
meaning of 'charge': load a gun.
265 **envious** 'full of ill-will' (*OED*, 2)

PALAMON
Thou bring'st such pelting scurvy news continually,
Thou art not worthy life. I will not go.
JAILER
Indeed you must, my lord.
PALAMON   May I see the garden?   270
JAILER
No.
PALAMON Then I am resolved, I will not go.
JAILER
I must constrain you then; and for you are dangerous,
I'll clap more irons on you.
PALAMON   Do, good keeper.
I'll shake 'em so, ye shall not sleep;
I'll make ye a new morris. Must I go?
JAILER
There is no remedy.
PALAMON   Farewell, kind window;
May rude wind never hurt thee. O my lady,
If ever thou hast felt what sorrow was,
Dream how I suffer. Come, now bury me.
                              Exeunt Palamon and Jailer

2.3   *Enter Arcite*
ARCITE
Banished the kingdom? 'Tis a benefit,
A mercy I must thank 'em for, but banished
The free enjoying of that face I die for,
O 'twas a studied punishment, a death
Beyond imagination—such a vengeance
That, were I old and wicked, all my sins
Could never pluck upon me. Palamon,
Thou hast the start now; thou shalt stay and see

268 **pelting** paltry
272 **for** because
275 **morris** Palamon fancifully compares the
     sound he will make with his chains to
     the tinkling of the little bells worn by
     morris dancers.

2.3 The location is the country outside
    Athens. This scene and the remainder of
    the act are by Fletcher.
3 **die** i.e. would die
4 **studied** calculated, deliberate
5 **imagination** what can be imagined

Her bright eyes break each morning 'gainst thy window
And let in life into thee; thou shalt feed   10
Upon the sweetness of a noble beauty
That nature nev'r exceeded, nor nev'r shall.
Good gods, what happiness has Palamon!
Twenty to one, he'll come to speak to her,
And if she be as gentle as she's fair,
I know she's his; he has a tongue will tame
Tempests and make the wild rocks wanton. Come
     what can come,
The worst is death. I will not leave the kingdom.
I know mine own is but a heap of ruins,
And no redress there; if I go, he has her.   20
I am resolved another shape shall make me
Or end my fortunes. Either way I am happy;
I'll see her, and be near her or no more.   *He retires*
          Enter four Countrymen and one with a garland
          before them

FIRST COUNTRYMAN My masters, I'll be there, that's certain.

SECOND COUNTRYMAN And I'll be there.

THIRD COUNTRYMAN And I.

FOURTH COUNTRYMAN Why then, have with ye, boys; 'tis
but a chiding. Let the plough play today; I'll tickle't out
of the jades' tails tomorrow.

FIRST COUNTRYMAN I am sure to have my wife as jealous   30
as a turkey; but that's all one—I'll go through, let her
mumble.

---

23 *He retires*] not in Q   23.1 *Countrymen*] This edition; *Country people* Q   *garland*] Q (*corr.*:
garlond); *Garlon* Q (*uncorr.*)

9 **break** in the sense that day 'breaks'

17 Some editors avoid the irregularity of this six-foot line by placing 'Tempests' at the end of l. 16, but to do so is to alter the rhythm. Occasional hexameters are found in this play (as at 2.5.43) and in many blank-verse plays.
wanton See note on 2.2.96.
Come . . . come whatever may happen. 'Come (hap) what come (hap) may' (Dent C529) was proverbial.

19 **mine own** my own kingdom (Thebes)

21 **another shape** a disguise

23 **no more** i.e. be no more, die

27 **have with ye** I'll go along with you

27–8 **'tis but a chiding** I'll only be scolded (for not working)

28–9 **I'll . . . tails** I'll whip the horses (to make up for lost time)

30–1 **jealous as a turkey** The turkey, introduced into England in the 16th century, is depicted in an emblem book (Arnold Freitag, *Mythologia Ethica* (1579), p. 237), tail spread, jealously defending its territory against an intruder (see Henry Green, *Shakespeare and the Emblem Writers* (London, 1869), pp. 356–8).

31 **that's all one** that doesn't matter

32 **mumble** mutter, i.e. grumble

SECOND COUNTRYMAN Clap her aboard tomorrow night, and stow her, and all's made up again.

THIRD COUNTRYMAN Ay, do but put a fescue in her fist, and you shall see her take a new lesson out and be a good wench. Do we all hold against the maying?

FOURTH COUNTRYMAN Hold? What should ail us?

THIRD COUNTRYMAN Arcas will be there.

SECOND COUNTRYMAN And Sennois and Rycas, and three   40
better lads nev'r danced under green tree; and ye know what wenches, ha! But will the dainty dominie, the schoolmaster, keep touch, do you think? For he does all, ye know.

THIRD COUNTRYMAN He'll eat a hornbook e'er he fail. Go to, the matter's too far driven between him and the tanner's daughter to let slip now; and she must see the Duke, and she must dance too.

FOURTH COUNTRYMAN Shall we be lusty?

SECOND COUNTRYMAN All the boys in Athens blow wind   50
i'th' breech on's. ⌈*He dances*⌉ And here I'll be and there I'll be, for our town, and here again and there again. Ha, boys, hey for the weavers!

FIRST COUNTRYMAN This must be done i'th' woods.

FOURTH COUNTRYMAN O, pardon me.

SECOND COUNTRYMAN By any means, our thing of learning

---

41 ye] SEWARD; yet Q   51 *He dances*] BAWCUTT (*subs.*); *not in* Q

33 **Clap her aboard** board her
34 **stow her** fill up her hold. The sexual double meanings in this passage are obvious.
35 **fescue** a small pointer used in the schoolroom
36 **take . . . out** learn a new lesson
37 **hold against** still intend to take part in **maying** celebration of May Day
38 **ail us** keep us from going ahead
42 **dainty dominie** fussy schoolmaster
43 **keep touch** keep his promise
43–4 **he does all** i.e. everything depends on him
45 **hornbook** 'A leaf of paper containing the alphabet (often, also, the ten digits, some elements of spelling, and the Lord's Prayer) protected by a thin plate of translucent horn, and mounted on a tablet of wood with a handle' (*OED*); it was used in teaching children.

46 **matter's . . . driven** arrangement (or understanding) is too firm
47 **tanner's daughter** Presumably one of the five country wenches who appear in 3.5.
49 **lusty** lively
50–1 **blow . . . on's** 'pant behind us in the race' (Bawcutt); i.e. cannot compete with us
51 *He dances* The rest of the speech seems to call for this action.
53 **hey** hurrah **weavers** He is apparently one, and seems to suggest that he dances in their honour.
55 **O, pardon me** A polite expression of disagreement.
56 **By any means** certainly (he supports the First Countryman) **thing of learning** A mildly sarcastic reference to the schoolmaster.

says so; where he himself will edify the Duke most
parlously in our behalfs. He's excellent i'th' woods;
bring him to th' plains, his learning makes no cry.

THIRD COUNTRYMAN We'll see the sports, then every man 60
to's tackle. And, sweet companions, let's rehearse, by
any means, before the ladies see us, and do sweetly,
and God knows what may come on't.

FOURTH COUNTRYMAN Content; the sports once ended, we'll
perform. Away, boys, and hold!

ARCITE (*coming forward*) By your leaves, honest friends;
pray you, whither go you?

FOURTH COUNTRYMAN Whither? Why, what a question's
that?

ARCITE Yes, 'tis a question to me that know not. 70

THIRD COUNTRYMAN To the games, my friend.

SECOND COUNTRYMAN (*to Arcite*)
Where were you bred, you know it not?

ARCITE   Not far, sir.
Are there such games today?

FIRST COUNTRYMAN   Yes, marry, are there,
And such as you never saw. The Duke himself
Will be in person there.

ARCITE   What pastimes are they?

SECOND COUNTRYMAN
Wrestling and running. (*To his companions*) 'Tis a pretty
fellow.

THIRD COUNTRYMAN (*to Arcite*)
Thou wilt not go along?

ARCITE   Not yet, sir.

FOURTH COUNTRYMAN   Well, sir,
Take your own time. Come, boys.

FIRST COUNTRYMAN   My mind misgives me,

---

57 says] SEWARD; sees Q   66 *coming forward*] *not in* Q

58 **parlously** cunningly, cleverly
59 **plains** open country
    makes no cry is silent (the expression
    was used of hunting dogs); i.e. has no
    effect
60 **sports** athletic contests described in l. 76
60–1 **every . . . tackle** The proverbial 'To

stand to one's tackling' (Dent T7) meant
'to be ready for action'.
    tackle equipment for the morris dance
65 **hold** i.e. hold to your word
78–9 **My . . . hip** I fear this fellow may be a
formidable wrestler

This fellow has a vengeance trick o'th' hip;
Mark how his body's made for't.
SECOND COUNTRYMAN   I'll be hanged, though,   80
If he dare venture. Hang him, plum porridge!
He wrestle? He roast eggs! Come, let's be gone, lads.
                                   Exeunt all but Arcite

ARCITE
This is an offered opportunity
I durst not wish for. Well I could have wrestled,
The best men called it excellent; and run
Swifter than wind upon a field of corn,
Curling the wealthy ears, never flew. I'll venture,
And in some poor disguise be there. Who knows
Whether my brows may not be girt with garlands,
And happiness prefer me to a place   90
Where I may ever dwell in sight of her?   *Exit Arcite*

2.4   *Enter Jailer's Daughter alone*
JAILER'S DAUGHTER
Why should I love this gentleman? 'Tis odds
He never will affect me. I am base,
My father the mean keeper of his prison,
And he a prince. To marry him is hopeless,
To be his whore is witless. Out upon't,
What pushes are we wenches driven to

82.1 *Exeunt . . . Arcite*] This edition; *Exeunt* 4. (*following* Lads.) *in* Q
    2.4] Q (Scaena 4.)

81 **plum porridge** literally a concoction of
    stewed fruits often eaten at Christmas,
    but here an expression of contempt
82 **He roast eggs!** Clearly contemptuous, but
    the exact meaning is uncertain—perhaps
    that he would be a better cook than a
    wrestler, or that he couldn't even cook
    an egg.
83 **offered opportunity** opportunity which
    offers itself
84 **durst not** would not have dared to
    could have wrestled knew how to wrestle
86 **corn** grain
87 **wealthy** rich, abundant
    never i.e. ever. The negative was some-
    times used as an intensifier.
90 **happiness prefer** good luck promote
2.4 The location is indefinite—probably near

the prison.
1 **'Tis odds** the chances are
2 **affect** love
   base of a low class
3 **mean** lowly
6–7 **What . . . us** In writing the scenes for
   the Jailer's Daughter in this act and the
   next Fletcher and Shakespeare may have
   had in mind the situation of Viola in
   The Coxcomb, a play on which Fletcher
   collaborated with Beaumont. Compare
   'these women, when they are once thirteen, God speed the plough' (*The Coxcomb*, 1.3.5–6 in Bowers, i; also see
   Introduction, p. 29, and notes on 2.6.20–
   1, 3.2.1, and 3.4.1).
6 **pushes** efforts

When fifteen once has found us! First I saw him;
I, seeing, thought he was a goodly man;
He has as much to please a woman in him—
If he please to bestow it so—as ever   10
These eyes yet looked on. Next I pitied him,
And so would any young wench, o' my conscience,
That ever dreamed, or vowed her maidenhead
To a young handsome man. Then I loved him,
Extremely loved him, infinitely loved him,
And yet he had a cousin, fair as he too.
But in my heart was Palamon, and there,
Lord, what a coil he keeps! To hear him
Sing in an evening, what a heaven it is!
And yet his songs are sad ones. Fairer spoken   20
Was never gentleman. When I come in
To bring him water in a morning, first
He bows his noble body, then salutes me thus:
'Fair, gentle maid, good morrow; may thy goodness
Get thee a happy husband.' Once he kissed me;
I loved my lips the better ten days after.
Would he would do so ev'ry day. He grieves much,
And me as much to see his misery.
What should I do to make him know I love him?
For I would fain enjoy him. Say I ventured   30
To set him free? What says the law then? (*She snaps
her fingers*) Thus much
For law or kindred! I will do it,
And this night or tomorrow he shall love me.   *Exit*

2.5   *A short flourish of cornetts, and shouts within.
Enter Theseus, Hippolyta, Pirithous, Emilia, Arcite
(disguised) with a garland, ⌈and Countrymen⌉*

31 *She ... fingers*] *not in* Q
   2.5] Scaena 4. Q   0.1 *A ... within*] Q *prints in margin*   A] This edition; This Q   0.3
disguised] *not in* Q   *and Countrymen*] WEBER; *&c.* Q; *and attendants* PROUDFOOT

7 **fifteen** i.e. the age of fifteen
14–15 **loved him ... loved him** A striking
    example of the patterns of repetition
    characteristic of Fletcher's rhetoric (see
    Cyrus Hoy, 'The Language of Fletcherian
    Tragicomedy', Gray, pp. 99–113).
18 **coil he keeps** disturbance he makes

23 **salutes** greets
30 **would fain** would gladly, i.e. wish I might
2.5 The location is near a stadium in Athens.
    Arcite has put on 'some poor disguise'
    (2.3.88), and is probably accompanied
    by some of the Countrymen, though
    Q's direction (see collations) leaves this

THESEUS (*to Arcite*)
  You have done worthily; I have not seen,
  Since Hercules, a man of tougher sinews.
  Whate'er you are, you run the best and wrestle
  That these times can allow.
ARCITE   I am proud to please you.
THESEUS
  What country bred you?
ARCITE   This; but far off, prince.
THESEUS
  Are you a gentleman?
ARCITE   My father said so,
  And to those gentle uses gave me life.
THESEUS
  Are you his heir?
ARCITE   His youngest, sir.
THESEUS   Your father
  Sure is a happy sire, then. What proves you?
ARCITE
  A little of all noble qualities.   10
  I could have kept a hawk and well have hallowed
  To a deep cry of dogs; I dare not praise
  My feat in horsemanship, yet they that knew me
  Would say it was my best piece; last, and greatest,
  I would be thought a soldier.
THESEUS   You are perfect.
PIRITHOUS
  Upon my soul, a proper man.
EMILIA   He is so.
PIRITHOUS (*to Hippolyta*)
  How do you like him, lady?
HIPPOLYTA   I admire him.

uncertain. For the misnumbering of the
scene in Q see collations and Introduction, p. 25.
3 **run the best and wrestle** are the best
  runner and wrestler
4 **allow** admit of, i.e. show
7 **to . . . life** bred me to gentlemanly pursuits
9 **sire** disyllabic here
  proves you shows you to be (a gentleman)
10 **qualities** accomplishments

11 **could have** See note on 2.3.84.
  kept a hawk Hawking (falconry) was an
  aristocratic sport.
12 **deep cry** loud barking (when they are on
  the scent)
13 **feat** skill
14 **Would** used to
  my best piece what I was best at
16 **proper** handsome
17 **admire** marvel at

I have not seen so young a man, so noble—
If he say true—of his sort.
EMILIA   Believe,
His mother was a wondrous handsome woman;   20
His face, methinks, goes that way.
HIPPOLYTA   But his body
And fiery mind illustrate a brave father.
PIRITHOUS
Mark how his virtue, like a hidden sun,
Breaks through his baser garments.
HIPPOLYTA   He's well got, sure.
THESEUS
What made you seek this place, sir?
ARCITE   Noble Theseus,
To purchase name, and do my ablest service
To such a well-found wonder as thy worth;
For only in thy court, of all the world,
Dwells fair-eyed honour.
PIRITHOUS   All his words are worthy.
THESEUS (*to Arcite*)
Sir, we are much indebted to your travel,   30
Nor shall you lose your wish. Pirithous,
Dispose of this fair gentleman.
PIRITHOUS   Thanks, Theseus.
(*To Arcite*) Whate'er you are, you're mine, and I
        shall give you
To a most noble service, to this lady,
This bright young virgin; pray observe her goodness.
You have honoured her fair birthday with your virtues,
And as your due you're hers. Kiss her fair hand, sir.
ARCITE
Sir, you're a noble giver. (*To Emilia*) Dearest beauty,
Thus let me seal my vowed faith.
        He kisses her hand

28 For] F; Fo Q   39 *He . . . hand*] not in Q

19 **sort** social rank
    Believe you may be sure
21 **goes that way** shows that
22 **illustrate** (accented 'illùstrate') make evi-
    dent that he had
23 **virtue** in the sense of Latin '*virtus*', manli-
    ness

24 **got** begotten, i.e. born
26 **purchase name** acquire fame
27 **well-found** well-attested
30 **travel** (*a*) journey (to the court) and (*b*)
    effort (in the games)
32 **Dispose of** find a situation for
35 **observe** respect, pay homage to

When your servant,

Your most unworthy creature, but offends you,   40
Command him die, he shall.
EMILIA   That were too cruel.
  If you deserve well, sir, I shall soon see't.
  You're mine, and somewhat better than your rank
      I'll use you.
PIRITHOUS
  I'll see you furnished, and because you say
  You are a horseman, I must needs entreat you
  This afternoon to ride, but 'tis a rough one.
ARCITE
  I like him better, prince; I shall not then
  Freeze in my saddle.
THESEUS (*to Hippolyta*) Sweet, you must be ready—
  And you, Emilia, and you, friend, and all,
  Tomorrow by the sun, to do observance   50
  To flow'ry May in Dian's wood. Wait well, sir,
  Upon your mistress. Emily, I hope
  He shall not go afoot.
EMILIA   That were a shame, sir,
  While I have horses. (*To Arcite*) Take your choice;
      and what
  You want at any time, let me but know it.
  If you serve faithfully, I dare assure you
  You'll find a loving mistress.
ARCITE   If I do not,
  Let me find that my father ever hated,
  Disgrace and blows.
THESEUS   Go lead the way; you have won it.
  It shall be so: you shall receive all dues   60

---

43 A six-foot line.
  use treat
44 **furnished** provided with what you need
46 **one** i.e. the horse
50 **by the sun** by sunrise
50–1 **to . . . May** The celebration of May
  Day was an important seasonal festival
  in medieval and Renaissance Europe; the
  hunt and the morris dance in Act 3 are
  parts of this celebration. In 3.1 and in

Dream 4.1.102 ff. Shakespeare borrows
from *The Knight's Tale* (ll. A 1673 ff.),
as Fletcher does here, the depiction of
Theseus and Hippolyta celebrating May
Day with a hunt.
55 **want** need
58 **that** that which
59 **won it** i.e. the honour of leading the way
  back to the city

Fit for the honour you have won, 'twere wrong else.
Sister, beshrew my heart, you have a servant
That, if I were a woman, would be master;
But you are wise.

EMILIA　　　　　I hope too wise for that, sir.

Flourish. Exeunt

2.6　*Enter Jailer's Daughter alone*

JAILER'S DAUGHTER
　Let all the dukes and all the devils roar;
　He is at liberty. I have ventured for him,
　And out I have brought him. To a little wood
　A mile hence I have sent him, where a cedar,
　Higher than all the rest, spreads like a plane,
　Fast by a brook, and there he shall keep close
　Till I provide him files and food, for yet
　His iron bracelets are not off. O love,
　What a stout-hearted child thou art! My father
　Durst better have endured cold iron than done it.　　　10
　I love him beyond love and beyond reason,
　Or wit, or safety. I have made him know it;
　I care not, I am desperate. If the law
　Find me and then condemn me for't, some wenches,
　Some honest-hearted maids, will sing my dirge,
　And tell to memory my death was noble,
　Dying almost a martyr. That way he takes
　I purpose is my way too. Sure, he cannot
　Be so unmanly as to leave me here.
　If he do, maids will not so easily　　　20
　Trust men again. And yet he has not thanked me
　For what I have done; no, not so much as kissed me,
　And that, methinks, is not so well; nor scarcely

64.1 *Flourish*] *after* are wise *in* Q　*Exeunt*] Exeunt omnes. Q
　2.6] Q (Scaena 6.)　3 him.] PROUDFOOT;　∼∧ Q　12 it;] COLMAN (*subs.*); ∼∧ Q　15
dirge,] TONSON; ∼. Q

2.6 The location is near the prison.
2 **ventured** risked myself
5 **plane** plane tree
6 **Fast by** close to
　keep close stay hidden
8 **bracelets** i.e. handcuffs
8–9 **love . . . child** i.e. Cupid
10 **Durst . . . it** would have risked death (by

stabbing) rather than have done what I
have done
20–1 **If . . . again** Compare 'if he deceive me
thus, | A woman will not easily trust a
man' (*The Coxcomb*, 1.6.12–13), where
Viola has gone to meet the man she loves
but does not find him at the appointed
place.

Could I persuade him to become a free man,
He made such scruples of the wrong he did
To me and to my father. Yet I hope,
When he considers more, this love of mine
Will take more root within him. Let him do
What he will with me, so he use me kindly,
For use me so he shall, or I'll proclaim him,   30
And to his face, no man. I'll presently
Provide him necessaries and pack my clothes up,
And where there is a path of ground I'll venture,
So he be with me. By him, like a shadow
I'll ever dwell. Within this hour the hubbub
Will be all o'er the prison; I am then
Kissing the man they look for! Farewell, father;
Get many more such prisoners, and such daughters,
And shortly you may keep yourself. Now to him.   *Exit*

3.1   *Cornetts in sundry places. Noise and hallowing*
           as people a-maying. Enter Arcite alone

ARCITE
The Duke has lost Hippolyta; each took

---

33 path] Q; patch LITTLEDALE (*conj.* Ingleby)   39 *Exit*] COLMAN; *not in* Q
   3.1] Q (*Actus Tertius.* Scaena 1.)   0.1–2 *Cornetts . . . a-maying*] Q *prints in margin between*
2.6 *and* 3.1

29 **kindly** affectionately and naturally (as a
   man should use a woman)
31 **no man** i.e. impotent
33 **path of ground** i.e. path on the ground
   through the woods. The emendation
   'patch' (see collations) is tempting, since
   'of ground' in this sense is unusual,
   but 'path' better conveys the Daughter's
   intention of going to Palamon through
   the woods. It is not necessary to emend.
38 **Get** She plays on two meanings: (*a*)
   acquire, and (*b*) beget.
39 **you . . . yourself** (because there will
   be no one else to keep when all your
   prisoners have escaped)
3.1 The location is a forest near Athens. A
   property tree may have been placed on
   the stage to suggest the forest. As Werner
   Habicht says, 'the tree may be said to
   have been one of the essential properties
   on the Elizabethan public stage' ('Tree
   Properties and Tree Scenes in Elizab-

ethan Theater', *Renaissance Drama*, N.S.,
4 (1971), 69–92; p. 92), and hence
surely available also at Blackfriars. The
property used here may have been made
in such a way as to include the 'bush'
mentioned at l. 30. This scene and 3.2
are by Shakespeare.

0.1 *in sundry places* i.e. in various places
off-stage
0.2 *a-maying* The celebration of May Day,
mentioned at 2.3.37, traditionally took
the form of various May games, some
involving Robin Hood and Maid Marian
or the Lord and Lady of May. According
to Henry Bourne, 'the juvenile part of
both sexes are wont to rise a little after
midnight and walk to some neighbouring
wood, accompanied with music and the
blowing of horns, where they break down
branches from the trees, and adorn themselves with nosegays and crowns of
[*see over for n.* 0.2 *cont. and n.* 1

A several laund. This is a solemn rite
They owe bloomed May, and the Athenians pay it
To th' heart of ceremony. O Queen Emilia,
Fresher than May, sweeter
Than her gold buttons on the boughs, or all
Th'enamelled knacks o'th' mead or garden—yea,
We challenge too the bank of any nymph
That makes the stream seem flowers; thou, O jewel
O'th' wood, o'th' world, hast likewise blessed a pace   10
With thy sole presence. In thy rumination
That I, poor man, might eftsoons come between
And chop on some cold thought! Thrice blessèd chance
To drop on such a mistress, expectation
Most guiltless on't. Tell me, O Lady Fortune,
Next after Emily my sovereign, how far
I may be proud. She takes strong note of me,
Hath made me near her, and this beauteous morn,
The prim'st of all the year, presents me with
A brace of horses; two such steeds might well   20
Be by a pair of kings backed, in a field

---

2 laund] Q (land)   11 presence.] SEWARD (*subs.*); ~, Q   13 thought!] SEWARD; ~, Q

flowers; . . . The after-part of the day is chiefly spent in dancing round a tall pole, which is called a Maypole' (*Antiquitates Vulgares* (Newcastle, 1725), pp. 200–1). In this play the Duke's hunting party and the dance presented by the Schoolmaster in 3.5 are parts of the May celebration.
Enter Arcite Arcite's observation of the May Day rites is taken directly from *The Knight's Tale*, ll. A 1497 ff.
1 **took** went to
2 **several** separate, different
laund (or *land*; see collations) opening in the woods, glade. Compare 'And to the land he rideth him full right . . . And when the duke was comen into the laund' (*The Knight's Tale*, ll. A 1691, 1696). On the errata sheet in Speght's 1602 edition 'land' in l. A 1691 is corrected to 'launde'.
4 **To . . . ceremony** most ceremoniously

6 **buttons** buds
7 **enamelled knacks** brightly-coloured ornaments (i.e. flowers)
mead meadow
8 **nymph** A nymph was a lesser divinity in the form of a beautiful maiden who acted as the guardian spirit of a stream or lake.
9 **makes . . . flowers** (since they are reflected in the water)
10 **pace** passage through the woods
12 **eftsoons** from time to time
come between i.e. enter into (her thoughts)
13 **chop on** seize upon (a hunting term)
cold chaste
14 **drop on** happen upon
14–15 **expectation . . . on't** never having expected to
17 **takes . . . me** observes me closely
19 **prim'st** best
21 **backed** mounted
field battlefield

That their crowns' titles tried. Alas, alas,
Poor cousin Palamon, poor prisoner, thou
So little dream'st upon my fortune that
Thou think'st thyself the happier thing, to be
So near Emilia; me thou deem'st at Thebes,
And therein wretched, although free; but if
Thou knew'st my mistress breathed on me, and that
I eared her language, lived in her eye, O coz,
What passion would enclose thee!

Enter Palamon as out of a bush, with his shackles;
he bends his fist at Arcite

PALAMON   Traitor kinsman,   30
Thou shouldst perceive my passion if these signs
Of prisonment were off me, and this hand
But owner of a sword. By all oaths in one,
I and the justice of my love would make thee
A confessed traitor, O thou most perfidious
That ever gently looked, the void'st of honour
That ev'r bore gentle token, falsest cousin
That ever blood made kin! Call'st thou her thine?
I'll prove it in my shackles, with these hands,
Void of appointment, that thou liest, and art   40
A very thief in love, a chaffy lord,
Not worth the name of villain. Had I a sword,
And these house-clogs away—
ARCITE   Dear cousin Palamon—

---

30 he] *not in* Q   36 looked,] LEECH; ~∧ Q; ~! SEWARD   void'st] SEWARD; voydes Q
honour] SEWARD; ~. Q   38 kin!] SEWARD; ~, Q   42 Not] DAVENANT; Nor Q

22 **That ... tried** where their claims to the
throne were being tried by combat
29 **eared** listened to
30 **passion** anger
enclose thee take possession of your mind
bends shakes
33–8 **By ... thine** The punctuation of these
lines in Q (see collations) is, by common
consent, unsatisfactory. I have emended
it, in the main following Seward, but no
punctuation is entirely satisfactory, since
the passage resists clear-cut divisions.
The reproachful apostrophes to 'thou
most perfidious ... void'st of honour ...

falsest cousin' seem to be tied to both
the preceding threat and the question
that follows. The exclamation point after
'kin', appropriate to the tone, should
not be thought of as separating the re-
proaches from the question that grows
out of them.
36–7 **gently looked, ... bore gentle token**
looked like a gentleman
40 **Void of appointment** without weapons
liest monosyllabic here, as shown by Q's
spelling, 'ly'st'
41 **chaffy** worthless
43 **house-clogs** prison fetters

133

PALAMON
  Cozener Arcite, give me language such
  As thou hast showed me feat.
ARCITE   Not finding in
  The circuit of my breast any gross stuff
  To form me like your blazon, holds me to
  This gentleness of answer: 'tis your passion
  That thus mistakes, the which, to you being enemy,
  Cannot to me be kind. Honour and honesty   50
  I cherish and depend on, howsoev'r
  You skip them in me, and with them, fair coz,
  I'll maintain my proceedings. Pray be pleased
  To show in generous terms your griefs, since that
  Your question's with your equal, who professes
  To clear his own way with the mind and sword
  Of a true gentleman.
PALAMON   That thou durst, Arcite!
ARCITE
  My coz, my coz, you have been well advertised
  How much I dare; you've seen me use my sword
  Against th'advice of fear. Sure of another   60
  You would not hear me doubted, but your silence
  Should break out, though i'th' sanctuary.
PALAMON   Sir,
  I have seen you move in such a place which well
  Might justify your manhood; you were called
  A good knight and a bold. But the whole week's not
      fair
  If any day it rain; their valiant temper
  Men lose when they incline to treachery,

44 **Cozener** deceiver. This play on words was
    familiar; compare 'Call me cousin but
    cozen me not' (Dent C739).
44–5 **such . . . feat** corresponding to your
    actions
47 **blazon** description (of me)
52 **skip** overlook
54 **generous terms** courteous language
55 **question** dispute
    professes claims
56 **clear . . . way** i.e. justify his conduct

57 **That thou durst** would that you dared to
58 **advertised** informed or warned
60 **advice** warning
    of another by someone else
61–2 **your . . . sanctuary** you would break
    silence to defend me even if you were
    hiding in a place of sanctuary
63 **such a place** i.e. a battlefield or tourna-
    ment
64 **manhood** courage
66 **temper** frame of mind

And then they fight like compelled bears—would fly
Were they not tied.

ARCITE   Kinsman, you might as well
Speak this and act it in your glass as to   70
His ear which now disdains you.

PALAMON   Come up to me,
Quit me of these cold gyves, give me a sword,
Though it be rusty, and the charity
Of one meal lend me. Come before me then,
A good sword in thy hand, and do but say
That Emily is thine, I will forgive
The trespass thou hast done me—yea, my life,
If then thou carry't; and brave souls in shades
That have died manly, which will seek of me
Some news from earth, they shall get none but this, 80
That thou art brave and noble.

ARCITE   Be content;
Again betake you to your hawthorn house.
With counsel of the night I will be here
With wholesome viands; these impediments
Will I file off; you shall have garments and
Perfumes to kill the smell o'th' prison; after,
When you shall stretch yourself and say but 'Arcite,
I am in plight', there shall be at your choice
Both sword and armour.

PALAMON   O you heavens, dares any
So noble bear a guilty business? None   90
But only Arcite; therefore none but Arcite
In this kind is so bold.

ARCITE   Sweet Palamon—

PALAMON
I do embrace you and your offer; for

---

68 **compelled** (accented on the first syllable)
fastened to a post, as bears were in bear-
baiting. Compare 'They have tied me to
a stake. I cannot fly, | But bear-like
I must fight the course' (*Macbeth* 5.7.
1–2).
70 **glass** mirror
72 **Quit** free
 gyves shackles
77 **trespass** wrong

78 **carry't** win the fight
 shades Hades, the underworld
82 **betake you** go into
83 **With . . . night** confiding only in the
 night; under cover of darkness
84 **viands** food
88 **in plight** ready
90 **bear . . . business** engage in a wrongful
 enterprise

Your offer do't I only; sir, your person
Without hypocrisy I may not wish
More than my sword's edge on't.
    Wind horns off. Cornetts sounded
ARCITE   You hear the horns.
Enter your muset, lest this match between's
Be crossed ere met. Give me your hand; farewell.
I'll bring you every needful thing; I pray you,
Take comfort and be strong.

PALAMON   Pray hold your promise,   100
And do the deed with a bent brow. Most certain
You love me not; be rough with me, and pour
This oil out of your language. By this air,
I could for each word give a cuff, my stomach
Not reconciled by reason.

ARCITE   Plainly spoken,
Yet pardon me hard language; when I spur
My horse, I chide him not; content and anger
In me have but one face.
    Wind horns
             Hark, sir, they call
The scattered to the banquet; you must guess
I have an office there.

PALAMON   Sir, your attendance   110
Cannot please heaven, and I know your office
Unjustly is achieved.

ARCITE   'Tis a good title.

96 *Wind . . . sounded*] *after l.* 95 *in* Q   *off*] LEECH (*conj.* Bertram); *of* Q   *sounded*] BAWCUTT;
not in Q   97 muset] DAVENANT (Muise); Musicke Q; musit KNIGHT   108 *Wind horns*] *after*
l. 106 *in* Q   112 'Tis] PROUDFOOT 2; If Q; I've SEWARD

96 *Wind* sound
  off off-stage
  Cornetts Some editors have thought that
  the direction for both cornetts and horns
  was a mistake, and that in the manuscript one instrument was supposed to
  be substituted for the other, but this is not
  necessarily the case. Horns traditionally
  accompany the hunt, which we are to
  imagine off-stage, and the direction at
  the opening of the act calls for cornetts
  associated with the off-stage maying.
97 muset 'gap in a hedge or fence through
  which hares habitually pass, or run,

when hunted, for relief' (Onions)
98 **crossed ere met** thwarted before (it is)
  begun
101 **bent brow** frown
104 **stomach** anger. The stomach was
  thought to be the seat of various emotions.
106 **pardon me** excuse me from using
  hard harsh, rude
108 **but one face** the same outward appearance
110 **office** duty (waiting on Emilia)
112 **'Tis . . . title** I earned my position;
  Proudfoot's emendation (see collations)

I am persuaded this question, sick between's,
By bleeding must be cured. I am a suitor
That to your sword you will bequeath this plea,
And talk of it no more.
PALAMON   But this one word:
You are going now to gaze upon my mistress—
For note you, mine she is—
ARCITE   Nay then—
PALAMON   Nay, pray you—
You talk of feeding me to breed me strength;
You are going now to look upon a sun   120
That strengthens what it looks on; there you have
A vantage o'er me, but enjoy't till
I may enforce my remedy. Farewell.   *Exeunt*

3.2   *Enter Jailer's Daughter alone with a file*
JAILER'S DAUGHTER
He has mistook the brake I meant, is gone
After his fancy. 'Tis now well-nigh morning.
No matter; would it were perpetual night,
And darkness lord o'th' world. Hark, 'tis a wolf!
In me hath grief slain fear, and but for one thing,
I care for nothing, and that's Palamon.
I reck not if the wolves would jaw me, so
He had this file. What if I hallowed for him?
I cannot hallow; if I whooped, what then?

3.2] Q (Scaena 2.)   0.1 *with a file*] *not in* Q   1 mistook‸] DAVENANT; ~ ; Q   brake] WEBER
(*conj.* Theobald); Beake Q; beach DAVENANT; Beck SEWARD; Brook SYMPSON (*conj.*)   7 reck]
Q (wreake)

makes good sense and may well have
been the manuscript reading, since maj-
uscule 'T' and 'I' and minuscule 's' and
'f' were easily confused in the secretary
hand.

113 **persuaded** convinced
    between's between us
114 **bleeding** Arcite's metaphor (and play on
    words) depends on the medical practice of
    bloodletting.
    am a suitor beg
115 **plea** lawsuit—the 'question' of l. 113
3.2 The location is the forest.
  1 **He . . . meant** The dismay of the Jailer's
    Daughter when she does not find Pala-

mon where she sent him (see 2.6.3–4)
again recalls Viola's predicament in *The
Coxcomb*: 'This is the place . . . he is not
here' (1.6.1–2).
brake thicket. 'Brake' makes the best
sense of the emendations proposed for
Q's 'Beake' (see collations).
  2 **After his fancy** as his fancy has directed
    him
  4 **Hark . . . wolf** The sounds of a wolf here,
    and of crickets and an owl at l. 35,
    were probably provided off-stage. Habicht
    notes that animal noises are referred to
    in many wood scenes (p. 80).
  7 **reck** care
    jaw gnaw

If he not answered, I should call a wolf,   10
And do him but that service. I have heard
Strange howls this livelong night; why may't not be
They have made prey of him? He has no weapons;
He cannot run; the jingling of his gyves
Might call fell things to listen, who have in them
A sense to know a man unarmed, and can
Smell where resistance is. I'll set it down
He's torn to pieces; they howled many together,
And then they fed on him; so much for that.
Be bold to ring the bell. How stand I then?   20
All's chared when he is gone. No, no, I lie;
My father's to be hanged for his escape,
Myself to beg, if I prized life so much
As to deny my act, but that I would not,
Should I try death by dozens. I am moped;
Food took I none these two days,
Sipped some water. I have not closed mine eyes
Save when my lids scoured off their brine. Alas,
Dissolve, my life; let not my sense unsettle,
Lest I should drown, or stab, or hang myself.   30
O state of nature, fail together in me,
Since thy best props are warped! So which way now?
The best way is the next way to a grave;
Each errant step beside is torment. Lo,
The moon is down, the crickets chirp, the screech owl
Calls in the dawn. All offices are done
Save what I fail in; but the point is this—
An end, and that is all.   *Exit*

19 fed] F; feed Q   28 brine] TONSON; bine Q

11 **do . . . service** i.e. summon a wolf to
    attack him
15 **fell things** fierce beasts
17 **set it down** record it (as a fact). Compare
    'meet it is I set it down' (*Hamlet* 1.5.108).
20 **ring the bell** i.e. the 'passing bell' to
    announce his death
    How stand I what is my situation (com-
    pare *Hamlet*, Add. Pass. J. 47)
21 **chared** done (chare = chore)
25 **try . . . dozens** experience death many
    times, or in many ways
    moped bewildered
28 **scoured . . . brine** i.e. wiped off their tears

29 **sense** reason
31 **state of nature** physical and mental
    health
    together all at once (not bit by bit)
33 **next** nearest
34 **errant** wandering
    beside in any other direction
36 **Calls in** summons
    offices tasks
37 **Save . . . in** except the one I have not
    succeeded in doing; i.e. giving the file to
    Palamon
38 **An end** i.e. death

138

3.3   *Enter Arcite with meat, wine, and files*

ARCITE

I should be near the place. Ho! Cousin Palamon!

Enter Palamon

PALAMON

Arcite.

ARCITE   The same. I have brought you food and files.

Come forth and fear not. Here's no Theseus.

PALAMON

Nor none so honest, Arcite.

ARCITE   That's no matter;

We'll argue that hereafter. Come, take courage;

You shall not die thus beastly. Here, sir, drink;

I know you are faint; then I'll talk further with you.

PALAMON

Arcite, thou mightst now poison me.

ARCITE   I might;

But I must fear you first. Sit down, and good now,

No more of these vain parleys; let us not,   10

Having our ancient reputation with us,

Make talk for fools and cowards. To your health, sir!

He drinks

PALAMON

Do.

ARCITE Pray sit down, then, and let me entreat you

By all the honesty and honour in you,

No mention of this woman; 'twill disturb us.

We shall have time enough.

PALAMON   Well, sir, I'll pledge you.

He drinks

3.3] Q (Scaena 3.)   12 sir!] PROUDFOOT; &c. Q   12.1, 16.1 *He drinks*] *not in* Q

3.3 The location is the forest. This scene and the remainder of the act are by Fletcher.
6 **thus beastly** so like an animal as you now are
9 **must** should have to
   good often used in the sense of 'good friend'
11 **ancient** long-established or former (but restored since their escape)

12 **sir** Q's '&c.' (see collations) may be correct, referring to such standard toasts as 'health and happiness' or 'health and pleasure', but Proudfoot's emendation makes a more metrically regular line and fits with the kinsmen's repeated use of 'sir' in addressing each other in this scene.

ARCITE
Drink a good hearty draught, it breeds good blood, man.
Do not you feel it thaw you?
PALAMON
Stay, I'll tell you after a draught or two more.
ARCITE
Spare it not; the Duke has more, coz. Eat now.   20
PALAMON
Yes.
    He eats
ARCITE I am glad you have so good a stomach.
PALAMON
I am gladder I have so good meat to't.
ARCITE
Is't not mad lodging here in the wild woods, cousin?
PALAMON
Yes, for them that have wild consciences.
ARCITE How tastes your victuals?
Your hunger needs no sauce, I see.
PALAMON   Not much.
But if it did, yours is too tart, sweet cousin.
What is this?
ARCITE   Venison.
PALAMON   'Tis a lusty meat.
Give me more wine; here, Arcite, to the wenches

21 *He eats*] *not in* Q   24 them] F; then Q

17 **breeds good blood** Compare the proverbial 'Good wine (drink) makes good
blood' (Dent W461).
19–24 These lines, printed here as in Q, are
rearranged by most editors with the first
half of each line printed as the last half
of the preceding line. These changes
do not, however, produce much more
regular verse, and they partly obscure
the almost stichomythic balance of the
lines.
21 **stomach** appetite
23 **mad lodging** an outlandish place to live,
or, more literally, a place that induces
madness. Habicht remarks the literary
association of 'the wood motif' with
madness (p. 83).
24 **wild** uncivilized
25 **tastes** see note on 1.2.64.

26 **hunger . . . sauce** Proverbial: 'Hunger is
the best sauce' (Dent H819).
28 **lusty** fortifying, well-flavoured
29–30 **to . . . days** Commentators have
observed a striking discrepancy between
Palamon's reminiscences here, in this
scene of Fletcher's, and his professions of
purity in his prayer to Venus (5.1.98 ff),
in a scene of Shakespeare's. Collaborative
oversight may well be in part responsible
for the inconsistency, but Fletcher alone
was capable of sacrificing consistency in
order to create an effective scene. Here
the camaraderie of the kinsmen provides
a variation on their assertions of undying
friendship in 2.1 while again preparing
for the shock of a sudden outburst of
hostility (at l. 43).

We have known in our days! The Lord Steward's
    daughter—   30
Do you remember her?
ARCITE   After you, coz.
PALAMON
She loved a black-haired man.
ARCITE   She did so; well, sir?
PALAMON
And I have heard some call him Arcite, and—
ARCITE
Out with't, faith.
PALAMON   She met him in an arbour.
What did she there, coz? Play o'th' virginals?
ARCITE
Something she did, sir.
PALAMON   Made her groan a month for't—
Or two, or three, or ten.
ARCITE   The marshal's sister
Had her share, too, as I remember, cousin,
Else there be tales abroad. You'll pledge her?
PALAMON   Yes.
    He drinks
ARCITE
A pretty brown wench 'tis. There was a time   40
When young men went a-hunting—and a wood,
And a broad beech—and thereby hangs a tale—heigh ho!
PALAMON
For Emily, upon my life! Fool,
Away with this strained mirth. I say again,
That sigh was breathed for Emily. Base cousin,
Dar'st thou break first?
ARCITE   You are wide.
PALAMON   By heaven and earth,
There's nothing in thee honest.

39.1 *He drinks*] *not in* Q

31 **After you, coz** 'This seems to mean "I   42 **thereby . . . tale** A familiar proverbial
   will propose my toast after you have   expression (Dent T48).
   finished yours" ' (Bawcutt).   44 **strained** forced
35 **virginals** a small keyboard instrument.   46 **break** i.e. break the agreement not to
   The name lent itself to sexual word-play.   mention Emilia
39 **tales** false rumours   **wide** off the mark, wrong

ARCITE   Then I'll leave you;
　You are a beast now.
PALAMON   As thou mak'st me, traitor.
ARCITE
　There's all things needful: files, and shirts, and perfumes.
　I'll come again some two hours hence and bring   50
　That that shall quiet all.
PALAMON   A sword and armour.
ARCITE
　Fear me not. You are now too foul; farewell.
　Get off your trinkets; you shall want naught.
PALAMON   Sirrah—
ARCITE
　I'll hear no more.   *Exit*
PALAMON   If he keep touch, he dies for't.   *Exit*

3.4   *Enter Jailer's Daughter*
JAILER'S DAUGHTER
　I am very cold, and all the stars are out too,
　The little stars and all, that look like aglets.
　The sun has seen my folly. Palamon!
　Alas, no; he's in heaven. Where am I now?
　Yonder's the sea, and there's a ship; how't tumbles!
　And there's a rock lies watching under water.
　Now, now, it beats upon it; now, now, now,
　There's a leak sprung, a sound one; how they cry!
　Open her before the wind, you'll lose all else;
　Up with a course or two, and tack about, boys.   10

53 Sirrah] COLMAN; Sir ha Q
　3.4] Q (Scaena 4.)   9 Open] RIVERSIDE (*conj.* Freehafer); Vpon Q; Spoom WEBER; Run
SKEAT   10 tack] F; take Q

51 **quiet** end
52 **fear me not** do not doubt me
　　foul dirty
53 **trinkets** i.e. fetters
54 **keep touch** keeps his word
3.4 The location is the forest.
　1 **I . . . cold** In *The Coxcomb* (1.6.9–12)
　　Viola complains of the cold as the Jailer's
　　Daughter does here.
　2 **aglets** spangles
　8 **sound** large
　9 **Open her** i.e. open her sails. Freehafer's
　　conjecture (see collations) accords with

contemporary nautical usage of 'open':
compare ' . . . we were forced every glass
to open a little of our foresail . . . '
(*Hawkins' Voyages*, Hakluyt Society, First
Series, 57 (1878), 206). I am indebted
to Robert K. Turner, who shared with
me the nautical information about this
passage, and one in 4.1, given to him by
P. T. van der Merwe of the National
Maritime Museum, who quoted Hawkins.
10 **course** sail attached to the lower yards
　　of a ship

Good night, good night, you're gone. I am very hungry;
Would I could find a fine frog; he would tell me
News from all parts o'th' world; then would I make
A carrack of a cockleshell, and sail
By east and north-east to the king of pygmies,
For he tells fortunes rarely. Now my father,
Twenty to one, is trussed up in a trice
Tomorrow morning. I'll say never a word.

(*Sings*)

  For I'll cut my green coat a foot above my knee,
  And I'll clip my yellow locks an inch below mine e'e;   20
    Hey, nonny, nonny, nonny.
  He s'buy me a white cut, forth for to ride,
  And I'll go seek him through the world that is so wide;
    Hey, nonny, nonny, nonny.
O for a prick now, like a nightingale,
To put my breast against; I shall sleep like a top else.

                       Exit

3.5   *Enter a Schoolmaster (Gerald), six Countrymen,*

19 Sings] Sing. Q (*in left margin*)   a foot] TONSON; *afoote* Q   20 e'e] WEBER; eie Q   22 He
s'] LITTLEDALE (*conj.* Skeat); *He's* Q
   3.5] Scaena 6. Q   0.1 Gerald] *not in* Q   six] BAWCUTT; 4 Q

14 **carrack** large cargo ship
16 **rarely** admirably
17 **is . . . trice** will be hanged quickly
19–20 **For . . . e'e** These lines are related to
the ballad of 'Child Waters':
  Then you must cut your gown of green
    An inch above your knee.
  So must you do your yellow locks
    Another inch above your eye.
  (Child, ii. 86, no. 63 A.)
20 **e'e** eye. Weber's emendation has the
advantage of making clear the pronunciation required for the rhyme; the north-
ern dialect form, 'ee', is frequently found
in ballads.
22–3 **He . . . wide** These lines are more
distantly related to some version of 'Lord
Thomas and Fair Annet' (Child, ii. 182–
98, no. 73). Fair Annet insists on riding
to the wedding of her faithless lover.
22 **s'buy** shall buy
  cut horse (with a cut tail, or possibly a
gelding)
25 **prick** thorn. The nightingale was supposed to press its breast against a thorn

to keep itself from falling asleep; compare
'To sit (sing) like a nightingale with a
thorn against one's breast' (Dent N183).
26 **sleep . . . top** sleep soundly. A proverbial
phrase that is still current (Dent T440).
3.5 The location is the forest. Stage directions are sometimes vague, sometimes
inaccurate. In order to understand how
the morris dance is to be performed it is
necessary to turn to *The Masque of the
Inner Temple and Gray's Inn*, from which
it is borrowed; see Appendix A. For the
misnumbering of the scene in Q see
collations and Introduction, p. 26.
0.1 **six Countrymen** When Gerald forms
couples of the men and the five named
wenches, he finds that one woman is
missing (ll. 29–35). Hence, there must
be six men, and he names six when he
lists the dancers for Theseus (ll. 123–30).
If the taborer takes one of the listed parts
in the dance, there need only be five
other Countrymen. Douce (p. 518) repro-
duces a fifteenth-century illustration of a
morris dancer costumed as a fool with

one of whom is dressed as a Babion, five Wenches,
and a taborer (Timothy)

SCHOOLMASTER Fie, fie, what tediosity and disinsanity is
here among ye! Have my rudiments been laboured so
long with ye, milked unto ye, and, by a figure, even the
very plum broth and marrow of my understanding laid
upon ye? And do you still cry 'Where?' and 'How?'
and 'Wherefore?' You most coarse frieze capacities, ye
jean judgements, have I said 'Thus let be', and 'There
let be', and 'Then let be' and no man understand me?
Proh deum, medius fidius, ye are all dunces! For why,
here stand I; here the Duke comes; there are you, close   10
in the thicket. The Duke appears; I meet him, and unto
him I utter learned things and many figures; he hears,
and nods, and hums, and then cries 'Rare!' and I go
forward. At length I fling my cap up; mark there! Then
do you as once did Meleager and the boar—break

0.2 one . . . Babion] OXFORD; *and Baum.* Q *(corr.); and Baum*ᴧ Q *(uncorr.); and the Bavian*
SEWARD   five] WEBER; *2 or* 3 Q   0.3 *and*] OXFORD; *with* Q   Timothy] *not in* Q   6 jean] DYCE
(jane); jave Q

pipe and tabor (see Fig. 6), but here the
Second Countryman probably takes the
part of the fool (see note on l. 87 and
Appendix A). I am assuming that the
taborer in this instance merely provides
the music for the other dancers, as was
often the case; six Countrymen are then
needed. The four called for in Q (see
collations) are obviously insufficient (and
'iv' is an easy error for 'vi'). In 2.3, when
four Countrymen are present, the Second
and Third Countrymen name three more
whom they expect to join them for the
dance (ll. 39–40), and one of these,
Arcas, is spoken to by name at l. 43 of
this scene.

0.2 *Babion* baboon. Q's '*Baum*' is evidently
a misprint for '*Bavian*', which appears in
Q at l. 29, an obsolete form of 'babion'.
five Five wenches are named in ll. 22–
4; the vagueness of Q's '2 or 3' is
surprising in prompt copy.

0.3 *taborer* one who plays the tabor, 'a
small drum, slung at the player's belt'
(Manifold, p. 64). Since pipe and tabor
provided the traditional music for the
morris dance, which is to be performed
for Theseus (see l. 106), it is probable
that the taborer also has a pipe, 'held

endways to the lips and fingered with
one hand, while the other beats the
tabor' (Manifold, p. 64).

1 **tediosity** the Schoolmaster's pedantic
variant of 'tediousness'
disinsanity utter folly. Another schoolmasterly coinage, based on the occasional use of 'dis' as an intensive in Latin.

2 **rudiments** basic principles; i.e. instruc-
tions for the entertainment they are to
put on

3 **figure** figure of speech, as also in l. 12,
'figures'

4 **plum-broth and marrow** i.e. essence.
Plum broth, like plum porridge (2.3.81),
was a hearty concoction of stewed fruits.

6 **frieze capacities** (people with) homespun
minds. Frieze is a rough woollen cloth.
jean cheap cotton cloth (as in today's
'jeans')

9 *Proh deum* O god (Latin)
medius fidius Elliptical for 'so help me
the god of truth' (Latin). Fidius was a
surname of Jupiter as god of truth or
faith (*fides*).

10 **close** hidden
13 **hums** murmurs approval
13–14 **go forward** continue
15 **Meleager** Greek warrior who slew the
Calydonian boar (see note on 1.1.78–9).

comely out before him. Like true lovers, cast yourselves
in a body decently, and sweetly, by a figure, trace and
turn, boys.

FIRST COUNTRYMAN
And sweetly we will do it, Master Gerald.

SECOND COUNTRYMAN
Draw up the company. Where's the taborer?   20

THIRD COUNTRYMAN
Why, Timothy!

TABORER   Here, my mad boys; have at ye!

SCHOOLMASTER
But I say, where's their women?

FOURTH COUNTRYMAN   Here's Friz and Maudline.

SECOND COUNTRYMAN
And little Luce with the white legs, and bouncing
    Barbery.

FIRST COUNTRYMAN
And freckled Nell, that never failed her master.

SCHOOLMASTER
Where be your ribbons, maids? Swim with your bodies,
And carry it sweetly and deliverly,
And now and then a favour and a frisk.

NELL
Let us alone, sir.

SCHOOLMASTER   Where's the rest o'th' music?

THIRD COUNTRYMAN
Dispersed, as you commanded.

SCHOOLMASTER   Couple then,
And see what's wanting. Where's the babion?   30
My friend, carry your tail without offence

---

30 babion] Q (*Bavian*)

15-16 **break comely out** come out gracefully
16 **lovers** loving subjects (of Theseus)
   cast . . . decently group yourselves properly
17 **figure** dance-figure
   trace step
21 **have at ye** come along; I'm ready for
   you
23 **bouncing** plump
24 **never failed** always did what was re-
   quested by

25 **ribbons** probably the streamers carried
   by morris dancers
   Swim move gracefully
26 **carry it** perform the dance
   deliverly nimbly
27 **favour** bow? or kiss?
   frisk caper
28 **Let us alone** leave it to us
   music i.e. musicians
29 **Couple** line up in twos

Or scandal to the ladies; and be sure
You tumble with audacity and manhood,
And when you bark, do it with judgement.

BABION   Yes, sir.

SCHOOLMASTER
Quousque tandem? Here is a woman wanting.

FOURTH COUNTRYMAN
We may go whistle; all the fat's i'th' fire.

SCHOOLMASTER   We have,
As learnèd authors utter, washed a tile;
We have been *fatuus* and laboured vainly.

SECOND COUNTRYMAN
This is that scornful piece, that scurvy hilding
That gave her promise faithfully she would be here—   40
Cicely, the seamstress' daughter.
The next gloves that I give her shall be dogskin;
Nay, an she fail me once—you can tell, Arcas,
She swore by wine and bread she would not break.

SCHOOLMASTER An eel and woman,
A learnèd poet says, unless by th' tail
And with thy teeth thou hold, will either fail.
In manners this was false position.

FIRST COUNTRYMAN
A fire ill take her! Does she flinch now?

---

41 seamstress'] Q (Sempsters)

33 **tumble** perform gymnastic feats. Tumbling was a characteristic feature of morris dancing.
manhood courage
35 *Quousque tandem* how long then (Latin, from the opening of Cicero's first oration against Catiline: 'How long then, Catiline, will you abuse our patience?')
wanting missing
36 **We . . . whistle** we may as well give up. Compare the proverbial 'You may (To) whistle (go whistle) for it' (Dent W313).
the fat's i'th' fire our work has come to nothing. Proverbial (Dent F79); the modern meaning is slightly different.
37 **washed a tile** laboured in vain. 'To wash a tile' was proverbial in both Latin (*laterem lavare*) and English (Dent T289).
38 *fatuus* foolish (Latin)
39 **piece . . . hilding** abusive terms for a woman

41 **seamstress'** The ending '-ster' in Q's 'Sempsters' was originally used for a feminine agent-noun; when it came to be considered masculine, '-stress' was substituted for the feminine form. Here the reference is presumably to a woman.
42 **dogskin** cheap leather
44 **wine and bread** i.e. the Eucharist or communion
break (her promise)
45-7 **An eel . . . fail** The Schoolmaster ascribes to 'A learnèd poet' what is in fact a proverbial saying: 'Who has a woman has an eel by the tail' (Dent W640).
47 **either** both
48 **In manners . . . position** (a schoolmasterly comparison of Cicely's bad manners to a false assertion in logic)
49 **fire ill** possibly venereal disease. Whether 'ill' is part of a compound subject or

THIRD COUNTRYMAN   What
  Shall we determine, sir?
SCHOOLMASTER   Nothing;   50
  Our business is become a nullity,
  Yea, and a woeful and a piteous nullity.
FOURTH COUNTRYMAN
  Now, when the credit of our town lay on it,
  Now to be frampold, now to piss o'th' nettle!
  Go thy ways, I'll remember thee, I'll fit thee!
    Enter Jailer's Daughter
JAILER'S DAUGHTER (*sings*)
  The *George Alow* came from the south,
    From the coast of Barbary-a;
  And there he met with brave gallants of war,
    By one, by two, by three-a.

  'Well hailed, well hailed, you jolly gallants,   60
    And whither now are you bound-a?
  O let me have your company
    Till I come to the sound-a.'

There was three fools fell out about an owlet—

(*Sings*)   The one he said it was an owl,
               The other he said nay,
               The third he said it was a hawk,
               And her bells were cut away.

THIRD COUNTRYMAN There's a dainty madwoman, master,

56 JAILER'S DAUGHTER] Q *prints marginal direction: Daughter. opposite l. 57   sings*] not in Q
61–2] Q *prints marginal direction: Chaire and | stooles out.*   63 I] TONSON; *not in* Q   65
Sings] not in Q   he] BAWCUTT; *not in* Q

functions adverbially the meaning is the
same.
take infect

50 **determine** decide to do
54 **frampold** peevish
   piss o'th' nettle be in a bad temper.
   Proverbial: 'He has pissed (To piss) on a
   nettle' (Dent N132).
55 **fit thee** get even with you
56–63 This fragment of a ballad is similar
   to parts of 'The George Aloe and the
   Sweepstake' (Child, v. 133, no. 285). A
   version of that ballad was entered in the

Stationers' Register on 19 March 1611.
56 *George Alow* The name of a ship.
58 **gallants of war** warships
61–2 Q's marginal direction, 'Chaire and
   stooles out' (see collations), is an advance
   warning for the furniture to be set out
   when Theseus arrives.
64–8 The earliest known version of a nursery rhyme included in *The Oxford Dictionary of Nursery Rhymes*, ed. I. and P. Opie
   (1952), p. 422.
68 **bells** attached to a hawk's legs in falconry
69 **dainty** fine

comes i'th' nick, as mad as a March hare. If we can get   70
her dance, we are made again. I warrant her, she'll do
the rarest gambols.

FIRST COUNTRYMAN A madwoman? We are made, boys.

SCHOOLMASTER
And are you mad, good woman?

JAILER'S DAUGHTER   I would be sorry else.
Give me your hand.

SCHOOLMASTER   Why?

JAILER'S DAUGHTER   I can tell your fortune.
You are a fool. Tell ten; I have posed him. Buzz!
Friend, you must eat no white bread; if you do,
Your teeth will bleed extremely. Shall we dance, ho?
I know you, you're a tinker. Sirrah tinker,
Stop no more holes but what you should.   80

SCHOOLMASTER *Dii boni!* A tinker, damsel?

JAILER'S DAUGHTER Or a conjurer. Raise me a devil now,
and let him play *Chi passa* o'th' bells and bones.

SCHOOLMASTER Go take her, and fluently persuade her to
a peace. *Et opus exegi, quod nec Iovis ira, nec ignis*—Strike
up, and lead her in.

SECOND COUNTRYMAN Come, lass, let's trip it.

JAILER'S DAUGHTER I'll lead.

THIRD COUNTRYMAN Do, do.

SCHOOLMASTER Persuasively and cunningly.   90
          Wind horns

83 *Chi*] Q (*Qui*)   90.1 *Wind horns*] *placed as in* LEECH; *after l. 88 in* Q

70 **i'th' nick** in the nick of time
   mad . . . hare Proverbial (Dent H148).
71 **dance** i.e. to dance
72 **rarest gambols** fanciest capers
76 **Tell count.** To count up to ten was a folk-
   ways test of sanity.
   posed stumped
   Buzz an exclamation of impatience or
   contempt
79 **tinker** mender of kettles, etc.
80 **Stop . . . should** Compare the proverbial
   'A tinker stops one hole and makes two
   (three)' (Dent T347); here there is an
   obvious sexual double meaning.
81 *Dii boni* good gods (Latin)
83 *Chi passa* The first words of a dance
   tune, *Chi passa per questa strada* ('Who
   passes through this street').

bones Used as percussion instruments,
along with the bells, to accompany the
dance.
84–5 **to a peace** to calm down and agree to
   dance with us
85 *Et . . . ignis* 'And I have completed a
   work which neither the anger of Jove nor
   fire [shall undo]' (Latin), a quotation,
   with one word altered, from Ovid's vale-
   dictory comment in *Metamorphoses*, xv.
   871.
85–6 **Strike up** begin the music
87 **Come . . . it** Since the mad Jailer's
   Daughter is clearly intended to dance as
   the 'She Fool', the Second Countryman,
   who takes her here as his partner, must
   be the 'He Fool'.

Away, boys; I hear the horns. Give me some meditation,
and mark your cue.   *Exeunt all but the Schoolmaster*
Pallas, inspire me.
> *Enter Theseus, Pirithous, Hippolyta, Emilia,*
> *Arcite, and train*

THESEUS
This way the stag took.
SCHOOLMASTER   Stay and edify.
THESEUS
What have we here?
PIRITHOUS   Some country sport, upon my life, sir.
THESEUS
Well, sir, go forward; we will edify.
> *A chair is brought out for Theseus, and stools for*
> *the ladies*

Ladies, sit down; we'll stay it.
> *They sit*

SCHOOLMASTER
Thou doughty Duke, all hail! All hail, sweet ladies!
THESEUS (*to Pirithous and the ladies*) This is a cold beginning.
SCHOOLMASTER
If you but favour, our country pastime made is.   100
We are a few of those collected here
That ruder tongues distinguish 'villager';
And to say verity, and not to fable,
We are a merry rout, or else a rabble,
Or company, or, by a figure, chorus,
That fore thy dignity will dance a morris.
And I that am the rectifier of all,
By title *pedagogus*, that let fall

---

92 *Exeunt . . . Schoolmaster*] placed as in DYCE; *after* boyes *in* Q   96 THESEUS] F (*Thes.*); *Per.* Q
96.1–2 *A chair . . . ladies*] *not in* Q   97.1 *They sit*] *not in* Q

91 **meditation** time for thought
94 **edify** be instructed
96.1–2 *A chair . . . ladies* This direction is
    based on the earlier marginal direction
    in Q; see note on ll. 61–2.
97 **stay** wait for
99 **cold beginning** Theseus pretends to take
    'hail' in its meteorological sense.
100–32 The Schoolmaster's presentation
    of the entertainment to Theseus recalls
    that of Quince to Theseus in *Dream*

(5.1.126–50).
102 **ruder** less civilized, less mannerly
    distinguish describe as
104 **rout** company
105 **figure** (of speech)
    chorus The Schoolmaster is probably
    alluding to the chorus of a classical play.
106 **morris** See Appendix A.
107 **rectifier** director
108 *pedagogus* schoolmaster (Latin)

The birch upon the breeches of the small ones,
And humble with a ferula the tall ones,   110
Do here present this machine, or this frame;
And, dainty Duke, whose doughty dismal fame
From Dis to Daedalus, from post to pillar,
Is blown abroad, help me, thy poor well-willer,
And with thy twinkling cyes, look right and straight
Upon this mighty 'Morr' (of mickle weight)—
'Is' now comes in, which being glued together,
Makes 'Morris', and the cause that we came hither.
The body of our sport, of no small study,
I first appear, though rude, and raw, and muddy,   120
To speak before thy noble grace this tenor,
At whose great feet I offer up my penner;
The next, the Lord of May and Lady bright;
The Chambermaid and Servingman, by night
That seek out silent hanging; then mine Host
And his fat Spouse, that welcomes to their cost
The gallèd traveller, and with a beck'ning
Informs the tapster to inflame the reck'ning;
Then the beest-eating Clown; and next the Fool;
The Babion with long tail and eke long tool,   130

---

129 beest-eating] Q (beast‸ eating)　　130 Babion] Q (*Bavian*)

110 **ferula** cane for punishment
111 **machine** (accented here on the first syllable). Synonymous with 'frame', both words meaning 'structure', i.e. the contrivance of the entertainment.
112 **dismal** calamitous (to the enemies of Theseus)
113 **Dis** god of the underworld
Daedalus Legendary inventor of the Labyrinth and of wings for human flight, but alliteration is obviously responsible for his appearance here.
116–18 **Morr . . . Is . . . Morris** The Schoolmaster apparently presents a little charade in which the two syllables of 'Morris' are represented, possibly by two of his dancers carrying placards; 'Morr' might be the depiction of a Moor.
116 **mickle** much
119 **body of our sport** main part of our entertainment
of . . . study devised with great care

121 **tenor** purport, argument
122 **penner** pen-case
123–30 The Schoolmaster's list of the characters in the dance to follow corresponds closely to that given in a stage direction for the second antimasque in Beaumont's *Masque of the Inner Temple and Gray's Inn*; see Appendix A.
125 **silent hanging** curtain which will not betray them if they hide behind it
127 **gallèd** sore
128 **inflame** inflate
reck'ning bill
129 **beest** thick milk which a cow gives for the first few days after calving (now called 'beestings'). See H. Kokeritz, 'The Beast-Eating Clown, *The Two Noble Kinsmen*, 3.5.151', *MLN*, 61 (1964), 532–5.
Clown countryman
130 **tool** penis

Cum multis aliis that make a dance;
Say 'ay', and all shall presently advance.
THESEUS
Ay, ay, by any means, dear dominie.
PIRITHOUS   Produce!
SCHOOLMASTER ⌈*knocks for the dance*⌉
Intrate, filii; come forth and foot it.
⌈*He flings up his cap.*⌉ *Music.*
⌈*Enter the Countrymen and the Taborer at one
door, and the Wenches and the Jailer's Daughter at
another. They dance a morris*⌉
Ladies, if we have been merry,
And have pleased ye with a derry,
And a derry and a down,
Say the schoolmaster's no clown.
Duke, if we have pleased thee too,
And have done as good boys should do,   140
Give us but a tree or twain
For a maypole, and again,
Ere another year run out,
We'll make thee laugh, and all this rout.
THESEUS
Take twenty, dominie. (*To Hippolyta*) How does my
   sweetheart?

---

134 SCHOOLMASTER . . . *dance*] OXFORD; Knocke for | Schoole. Enter | The Dance. *in margin at
ll. 134–6 in Q, which prints no speech-prefix here*   134.1 *He . . . cap*] OXFORD; *not in* Q. *See
l. 14.   Music*] *after l. 133 in* Q   134.2–4 *Enter . . . another*] This edition; *not in* Q   134.4
They dance a morris] This edition; *Dance* Q, *after l. 133*   136 ye] SEWARD; *thee* Q   139 thee]
F; *three* Q

---

131 *Cum multis aliis* with many others
(Latin). Although the Schoolmaster has
named only nine characters, there are
twelve dancers (and the Taborer?); see
Appendix A.
132 **presently** at once
133 **Produce** bring on (the 'country pastime')
134 SCHOOLMASTER . . . *dance* Q's marginal
direction (see collations) has puzzled all
editors. The Oxford editor's emendation
is based on the supposition that in the
margin of the manuscript, on one line,
was 'Knocke for Schoole' (or 'Sch'), and
below it 'The Dance', where 'Schoole' or
'Sch' was the speech-prefix and 'Knocke
for The Dance' the direction. The com-

positor, misunderstanding, might then
have interpolated 'Enter.'
Intrate, filii Come in, boys (literally, 'my
sons'; Latin). Within the fiction of the
play 'filii' refers, somewhat inappropri-
ately, to both the Countrymen and the
Wenches, as does 'boys' in l. 140, but
for spectators aware that the women's
parts were being played by boys, the
terms may have seemed particularly suitable.
134.2–4 *Enter . . . another* This direction is
adapted from Beaumont's masque, where
the dancers enter, 'the men issuing out
of one side of the boscage, and the women
from the other' (Bowers, i. 133).

HIPPOLYTA
  Never so pleased, sir.
EMILIA   'Twas an excellent dance,
  And for a preface, I never heard a better.
THESEUS
  Schoolmaster, I thank you.—One see 'em all rewarded.
PIRITHOUS
  And here's something to paint your pole withal.
        He gives the Schoolmaster money
THESEUS Now to our sports again.   150
SCHOOLMASTER
    May the stag thou hunt'st stand long,
    And thy dogs be swift and strong;
    May they kill him without lets,
    And the ladies eat his dowsets.
              Wind horns within. Exeunt Theseus and train
  Come, we are all made. *Dii deaeque omnes,*
  Ye have danced rarely, wenches.   *Exeunt*

3.6   *Enter Palamon from the bush*
PALAMON
  About this hour my cousin gave his faith
  To visit me again, and with him bring
  Two swords and two good armours; if he fail,
  He's neither man nor soldier. When he left me,
  I did not think a week could have restored
  My lost strength to me, I was grown so low
  And crest-fall'n with my wants. I thank thee, Arcite,
  Thou art yet a fair foe; and I feel myself,
  With this refreshing, able once again
  To outdure danger. To delay it longer   10

149.1 *He . . . money*] not in Q   154.1 *Wind horns*] *after* made (l. 155) *in* Q   *within . . . train*]
not in Q   155 deaeque] Q (*Deaeq;*)
3.6] Scaena 7. Q

151 **stand** resist the dogs; hence give you
  good sport
153 **lets** hindrances
154 **dowsets** testicles; considered a delicacy.
  George Turberville lists them among the
  'dainty morsels' to be presented 'to the
  prince or chief' at the conclusion of
  the hunt (*The Noble Art of Venery or*

Hunting (1575), p. 134).
155 *Dii deaeque omnes* all you gods and
  goddesses (Latin)
3.6 The location is the forest. For the misnumbering of the scene in Q see collations
  and Introduction, p. 26.
3 **armours** suits of armour
10 **outdure** outlast, endure

Would make the world think, when it comes to hearing,
That I lay fatting like a swine to fight,
And not a soldier. Therefore this blest morning
Shall be the last; and that sword he refuses,
If it but hold, I kill him with; 'tis justice.
So, love and fortune for me!
  Enter Arcite with suits of armour and swords
         O, good morrow.

ARCITE
Good morrow, noble kinsman.

PALAMON   I have put you
To too much pains, sir.

ARCITE   That too much, fair cousin,
Is but a debt to honour and my duty.

PALAMON
Would you were so in all, sir; I could wish ye   20
As kind a kinsman as you force me find
A beneficial foe, that my embraces
Might thank ye, not my blows.

ARCITE   I shall think either
Well done, a noble recompense.

PALAMON   Then I shall quit you.

ARCITE
Defy me in these fair terms, and you show
More than a mistress to me; no more anger,
As you love anything that's honourable!
We were not bred to talk, man; when we are armed,
And both upon our guards, then let our fury,
Like meeting of two tides, fly strongly from us,   30
And then to whom the birthright of this beauty
Truly pertains—without upbraidings, scorns,
Despisings of our persons, and such poutings,
Fitter for girls and schoolboys—will be seen,
And quickly, yours or mine. Will't please you arm, sir?
Or if you feel yourself not fitting yet

---

16 *Enter . . . swords*] *after* morrow *in* Q *suits of armour*] This edition; *Armors* Q

12 **fatting . . . fight** preparing myself for the fight like a swine being fattened for market
15 **If . . . hold** if only it does not break
24 **quit** repay, requite
25 **show** i.e. show yourself to be
31 **birthright** the right to which one of us was born
36 **fitting** ready, fit

And furnished with your old strength, I'll stay, cousin,
And ev'ry day discourse you into health,
As I am spared. Your person I am friends with,
And I could wish I had not said I loved her,   40
Though I had died; but loving such a lady,
And justifying my love, I must not fly from't.

PALAMON
Arcite, thou art so brave an enemy
That no man but thy cousin's fit to kill thee.
I am well and lusty; choose your arms.

ARCITE   Choose you, sir.

PALAMON
Wilt thou exceed in all, or dost thou do it
To make me spare thee?

ARCITE   If you think so, cousin,
You are deceivèd, for as I am a soldier,
I will not spare you.

PALAMON   That's well said.

ARCITE   You'll find it.

PALAMON
Then, as I am an honest man, and love   50
With all the justice of affection,
I'll pay thee soundly.

         He chooses one suit of armour
                        This I'll take.

ARCITE (*indicating the other suit*)   That's mine, then.
I'll arm you first.

PALAMON   Do. Pray thee tell me, cousin,
Where gott'st thou this good armour?

ARCITE (*arming Palamon*)   'Tis the Duke's,
And to say true, I stole it. Do I pinch you?

---

39 spared.] TONSON (*subs.*); ~, Q   52 *He . . . armour*] *not in* Q   *indicating . . . suit*] *not in* Q
54 *arming Palamon*] *not in* Q

39 **As . . . spared** in my spare time
40 **I could . . . her** The first intimation of the
   regret he expresses in his dying speech
   (5.4.92–3).
41 **Though . . . died** even if I had died with
   the effort of keeping still
43 **thou** A curious mixture of affection and
   irritation seems to inform Palamon's use

of the second person singular here and in
his next speeches (see note on 2.2.171).
45 **lusty** vigorous, eager to fight
46 **exceed in all** outdo me in every respect
49 **find it** i.e. find it so
52 **pay thee soundly** give you the full punishment you deserve
54, 70 **armour** See note on l. 3.

PALAMON
　No.
ARCITE Is't not too heavy?
PALAMON　　　　　　　　　I have worn a lighter,
　But I shall make it serve.
ARCITE　　　　　　　　　I'll buckle't close.
PALAMON
　By any means.
ARCITE　　　　　You care not for a grand guard?
PALAMON
　No, no, we'll use no horses. I perceive
　You would fain be at that fight.
ARCITE　　　　　　　　　I am indifferent.　　　　60
PALAMON
　Faith, so am I. Good cousin, thrust the buckle
　Through far enough.
ARCITE　　　　　I warrant you.
PALAMON　　　　　　　　My casque now.
ARCITE
　Will you fight bare-armed?
PALAMON　　　　　　We shall be the nimbler.
ARCITE
　But use your gauntlets, though. Those are o'th' least.
　Prithee take mine, good cousin.
PALAMON　　　　　　　Thank you, Arcite.
　How do I look? Am I fall'n much away?
ARCITE
　Faith, very little; love has used you kindly.
PALAMON
　I'll warrant thee, I'll strike home.
ARCITE　　　　　　　　Do, and spare not.
　I'll give you cause, sweet cousin.
PALAMON　　　　　　　Now to you, sir.
　(*Arming Arcite*) Methinks this armour's very like that,
　　Arcite,　　　　　　　　　　　　　　　　　　70
　Thou wor'st that day the three kings fell, but lighter.

70 *Arming Arcite*] *not in* Q

58 **grand guard** extra piece of armour worn
　in jousting to protect the chest and left
　shoulder
60 **would . . . fight** wish we could fight on
horseback
62 **casque** helmet
64 **o'th' least** i.e. too small? no good?
66 **Am . . . away** Have I lost much weight?

ARCITE

That was a very good one, and that day,
I well remember, you outdid me, cousin;
I never saw such valour. When you charged
Upon the left wing of the enemy,
I spurred hard to come up, and under me
I had a right good horse.

PALAMON   You had indeed;
A bright bay, I remember.

ARCITE   Yes, but all
Was vainly laboured in me; you outwent me,
Nor could my wishes reach you; yet a little   80
I did by imitation.

PALAMON   More by virtue;
You are modest, cousin.

ARCITE   When I saw you charge first,
Methought I heard a dreadful clap of thunder
Break from the troop.

PALAMON   But still before that flew
The lightning of your valour. Stay a little;
Is not this piece too strait?

ARCITE   No, no, 'tis well.

PALAMON

I would have nothing hurt thee but my sword;
A bruise would be dishonour.

ARCITE   Now I am perfect.

PALAMON

Stand off then.

ARCITE   Take my sword; I hold it better.

PALAMON

I thank ye. No, keep it; your life lies on it.   90
Here's one; if it but hold, I ask no more
For all my hopes. My cause and honour guard me!

ARCITE

And me my love!

76 **come up** move forward (to join you)
80 **wishes reach you** wish to equal your
  performance enable me to do so
81 **virtue** courage
86 **strait** tight

88 **perfect** completely armed, ready to
  fight
89 **hold** consider
90 **lies** depends

> *They bow several ways, then advance and stand*
> Is there aught else to say?

PALAMON

This only, and no more: thou art mine aunt's son,
And that blood we desire to shed is mutual—
In me, thine, and in thee, mine. My sword
Is in my hand, and if thou kill'st me,
The gods and I forgive thee. If there be
A place prepared for those that sleep in honour,
I wish his weary soul that falls may win it.   100
Fight bravely, cousin; give me thy noble hand.

ARCITE

Here, Palamon. This hand shall never more
Come near thee with such friendship.

PALAMON   I commend thee.

ARCITE

If I fall, curse me, and say I was a coward,
For none but such dare die in these just trials.
Once more farewell, my cousin.

PALAMON   Farewell, Arcite.

> *They fight.*
> *Horns within. They stand*

ARCITE

Lo, cousin, lo, our folly has undone us.

PALAMON   Why?

ARCITE

This is the Duke, a-hunting, as I told you;
If we be found, we are wretched. O, retire
For honour's sake, and safely, presently   110
Into your bush again. Sir, we shall find
Too many hours to die in; gentle cousin,
If you be seen, you perish instantly
For breaking prison, and I, if you reveal me,

---

93 *They . . . stand] in margin in* Q *at ll. 93–6, with an asterisk after* love: *in the text*   106.1
They] not in Q   110 safely] Q; safety SEWARD   112 die in; gentle cousin,] SEWARD (*subs.*);
dye in, gentle Cosen: Q; die. In, gentle cousin— OXFORD

93 ***They . . . stand*** An asterisk following
'love' in Q shows when the business
indicated in this marginal direction (see
collations) is to be performed.
several ways in different directions (as if

to the spectators at a tournament)
103 **commend thee** (to God)
105 **none . . . trials** Trial by combat was
supposed to establish moral worth.

For my contempt; then all the world will scorn us,
And say we had a noble difference,
But base disposers of it.
PALAMON   No, no, cousin,
I will no more be hidden, nor put off
This great adventure to a second trial.
I know your cunning, and I know your cause;   120
He that faints now, shame take him! Put thyself
Upon thy present guard.
ARCITE   You are not mad?
PALAMON
Or I will make th'advantage of this hour
Mine own, and what to come shall threaten me
I fear less than my fortune. Know, weak cousin,
I love Emilia, and in that I'll bury
Thee and all crosses else.
ARCITE   Then come what can come,
Thou shalt know, Palamon, I dare as well
Die as discourse or sleep; only this fears me:
The law will have the honour of our ends.   130
Have at thy life!
PALAMON   Look to thine own well, Arcite.
        They fight again.
        Horns. Enter Theseus, Hippolyta, Emilia, Pirithous,
        and train. ⌈Theseus separates Palamon and Arcite⌉
THESEUS
What ignorant and mad malicious traitors
Are you, that 'gainst the tenor of my laws

131.1 *They*] *not in* Q   131.3 *Theseus . . . Arcite*] OXFORD; *not in* Q

---

115 **contempt** disregard (of the order for his banishment)
116 **difference** quarrel
117 **base . . . it** were dishonourable in the way we settled it
119 **adventure** venture
121 **faints** is faint-hearted
122 **Upon . . . guard** on guard immediately
125 **my fortune** (in this combat)
127 **crosses else** other impediments
129 **fears** frightens
130 **of our ends** of killing us; i.e. they will be executed, and neither of them will have the honour of killing the other
131.3 **Theseus . . . Arcite** 'It is reasonably

certain that someone in Theseus' party separates the two combatants: in Chaucer this is clearly done by Theseus himself, and Theseus' comment near the end of the play, "e'en very here | I sundered you" (5.4.99–100) strongly suggests that he does so here as well' (Oxford editors). See *The Knight's Tale*, ll. A 1704–6.
132–5 **What . . . arms?** Compare 'But telleth me what mister men ye been, | That been so hardie for to fighten here | Without iudge or other officere | As though it were in listes rially?' (*The Knight's Tale*, ll. A 1710–13).

Are making battle, thus like knights appointed,
Without my leave and officers of arms?
By Castor, both shall die.
PALAMON   Hold thy word, Theseus;
We are certainly both traitors, both despisers
Of thee and of thy goodness. I am Palamon,
That cannot love thee, he that broke thy prison—
Think well what that deserves—and this is Arcite: 140
A bolder traitor never trod thy ground,
A falser nev'r seemed friend. This is the man
Was begged and banished, this is he contemns thee
And what thou dar'st do, and in this disguise,
Against thy own edict, follows thy sister,
That fortunate bright star, the fair Emilia,
Whose servant—if there be a right in seeing,
And first bequeathing of the soul to—justly
I am; and, which is more, dares think her his.
This treachery, like a most trusty lover,   150
I called him now to answer. If thou be'st
As thou art spoken, great and virtuous,
The true decider of all injuries,
Say 'Fight again', and thou shalt see me, Theseus,
Do such a justice thou thyself wilt envy.
Then take my life; I'll woo thee to't.
PIRITHOUS   O heaven,
What more than man is this!
THESEUS   I have sworn.
ARCITE   We seek not
Thy breath of mercy, Theseus. 'Tis to me
A thing as soon to die as thee to say it,
And no more moved. Where this man calls me traitor,   160
Let me say thus much: if in love be treason,

145 thy own] DYCE; this owne Q; thine own SKEAT

134 **appointed** armed
135 **officers of arms** officials to supervise the
combat
136 **By Castor** A familiar Roman oath; Castor and his twin brother Pollux were sons of Jupiter.
Hold keep
143 **begged** petitioned for (by Pirithous; see 2.2.246–7).

146 **fortunate . . . star** star that brings good luck
147 **servant** In the chivalric scheme of things the lover serves his lady.
152 **spoken** said to be
158–60 **'Tis . . . moved** I'm as ready to face death as you are to decree it, and will be no more moved by it than you

In service of so excellent a beauty,
As I love most, and in that faith will perish,
As I have brought my life here to confirm it,
As I have served her truest, worthiest,
As I dare kill this cousin that denies it,
So let me be most traitor, and ye please me.
For scorning thy edict, Duke, ask that lady
Why she is fair, and why her eyes command me
Stay here to love her; and if she say 'traitor',   170
I am a villain fit to lie unburied.

PALAMON
Thou shalt have pity of us both, O Theseus,
If unto neither thou show mercy. Stop,
As thou art just, thy noble ear against us;
As thou art valiant, for thy cousin's soul,
Whose twelve strong labours crown his memory,
Let's die together at one instant, Duke;
Only a little let him fall before me,
That I may tell my soul he shall not have her.

THESEUS
I grant your wish, for to say true, your cousin   180
Has ten times more offended, for I gave him
More mercy than you found, sir, your offences
Being no more than his. None here speak for 'em,
For ere the sun set both shall sleep for ever.

HIPPOLYTA (*to Emilia*)
Alas, the pity! Now or never, sister,
Speak not to be denied. That face of yours
Will bear the curses else of after ages
For these lost cousins.

EMILIA   In my face, dear sister,
I find no anger to 'em, nor no ruin;
The misadventure of their own eyes kill 'em.   190

174–5 us; . . . valiant,] COLMAN; us, . . . valiant; Q

163–6 These four lines beginning with 'As'
provide a striking example of anaphora,
one of the rhetorical figures of repetition
characteristic of Fletcher's style.
168 For as for
175 cousin Hercules

190 kill The plural is used here, as commonly in Elizabethan English, because of
the proximity of a plural noun ('eyes'),
although the singular subject ('misadventure') would require 'kills' in modern
English.

Yet that I will be woman and have pity,
⌜*She kneels*⌝
My knees shall grow to th' ground but I'll get mercy.
Help me, dear sister; in a deed so virtuous,
The powers of all women will be with us.
⌜*Hippolyta kneels*⌝
Most royal brother—
HIPPOLYTA   Sir, by our tie of marriage—
EMILIA
By your own spotless honour—
HIPPOLYTA   By that faith,
That fair hand, and that honest heart you gave me—
EMILIA
By that you would have pity in another,
By your own virtues infinite—
HIPPOLYTA   By valour,
By all the chaste nights I have ever pleased you—   200
THESEUS
These are strange conjurings.
PIRITHOUS (*kneeling*)   Nay then, I'll in too.
By all our friendship, sir, by all our dangers,
By all you love most, wars and this sweet lady—
EMILIA
By that you would have trembled to deny
A blushing maid—
HIPPOLYTA   By your own eyes, by strength,
In which you swore I went beyond all women,
Almost all men, and yet I yielded, Theseus—
PIRITHOUS
To crown all this, by your most noble soul,
Which cannot want due mercy, I beg first—

191.1 *She kneels*] not in Q   194.1 *Hippolyta kneels*] not in Q   201 *kneeling*] not in Q

191 **that** to show that
191.1, 194.1 Though it is clear that the
    ladies kneel, the absence of directions in
    Q leaves the exact moment when each
    should do so uncertain.
192 **but I'll** unless I
196–208 The thirteen repetitions of 'by' in
    these lines are characteristic of Fletcher's
    rhetorical style.
198 **that** your hope that
    have . . . another be pitied by someone

else
200 **chaste** 'pure from unlawful sexual inter-
    course' (*OED*); i.e. the nights they have
    spent together as man and wife
201 **conjurings** solemn appeals
204–5 **that . . . maid** i.e. the aid that chivalry
    requires you to give to damsels in distress.
    Note also that Theseus has promised
    Emilia special consideration (ll. 230–5).
206 **went beyond** excelled
209 **want** be lacking in

HIPPOLYTA
  Next hear my prayers—
EMILIA   Last let me entreat, sir—   210
PIRITHOUS
  For mercy.
HIPPOLYTA   Mercy.
EMILIA   Mercy on these princes.
THESEUS
  Ye make my faith reel. (*To Emilia*) Say I felt
  Compassion to 'em both, how would you place it?
      ⌜*They rise*⌝
EMILIA
  Upon their lives—but with their banishments.
THESEUS
  You are a right woman, sister; you have pity,
  But want the understanding where to use it.
  If you desire their lives, invent a way
  Safer than banishment. Can these two live,
  And have the agony of love about 'em,
  And not kill one another? Every day   220
  They'd fight about you, hourly bring your honour
  In public question with their swords. Be wise, then,
  And here forget 'em; it concerns your credit
  And my oath equally. I have said they die;
  Better they fall by th' law than one another.
  Bow not my honour.
EMILIA   O, my noble brother,
  That oath was rashly made, and in your anger;
  Your reason will not hold it. If such vows
  Stand for express will, all the world must perish.
  Beside, I have another oath 'gainst yours,   230
  Of more authority, I am sure more love,
  Not made in passion neither, but good heed.

213.1 *They rise*] *not in* Q   228 it.] TONSON (*subs.*); ~, Q

212 **faith reel** constancy to my oath waver
213.1 **They rise** This seems an appropriate
  moment for them to rise, though, once
  again, Q leaves it uncertain when they
  were to do so.
215 **right** true, typical
221–2 **bring . . . question** quarrel about you

  in public
226 **Bow . . . honour** don't force my honour
  to bend or yield
228 **hold** sustain
229 **express will** deliberate intention
232 **good heed** careful attention or thought

THESEUS
  What is it, sister?
PIRITHOUS   Urge it home, brave lady.
EMILIA
  That you would nev'r deny me anything
  Fit for my modest suit and your free granting.
  I tie you to your word now; if ye fail in't,
  Think how you maim your honour—
  For now I am set a-begging, sir, I am deaf
  To all but your compassion—how their lives
  Might breed the ruin of my name, opinion.   240
  Shall anything that loves me perish for me?
  That were a cruel wisdom; do men prune
  The straight young boughs that blush with
        thousand blossoms
  Because they may be rotten? O, Duke Theseus,
  The goodly mothers that have groaned for these,
  And all the longing maids that ever loved,
  If your vow stand, shall curse me and my beauty,
  And in their funeral songs for these two cousins
  Despise my cruelty, and cry woe worth me,
  Till I am nothing but the scorn of women.   250
  For heaven's sake, save their lives and banish 'em.
THESEUS
  On what conditions?
EMILIA   Swear 'em never more
  To make me their contention, or to know me,
  To tread upon thy dukedom, and to be,
  Wherever they shall travel, ever strangers
  To one another.
PALAMON   I'll be cut a-pieces
  Before I take this oath. Forget I love her?
  O all ye gods, despise me then. Thy banishment

236 fail] Q (fall)   240 name, opinion.] COLMAN (*subs.*); name; Opinion, Q

236 **fail** The word was sometimes spelt 'fall'   me
    in the 17th century, possibly by con-   244 **be** become
    fusion with a moral 'fall'. This may   245 **groaned** (in childbirth)
    account for the Q reading (see colla-   249 **worth** befall
    tions).   252 **Swear 'em** make them swear
240 **name** reputation   253 **know** i.e. acknowledge that they know
    opinion i.e. the opinion people have of

I not mislike, so we may fairly carry
Our swords and cause along; else never trifle,   260
But take our lives, Duke. I must love and will,
And for that love must and dare kill this cousin
On any piece the earth has.
THESEUS   Will you, Arcite,
   Take these conditions?
PALAMON   He's a villain, then.
PIRITHOUS   These are men!
ARCITE
   No, never, Duke. 'Tis worse to me than begging
   To take my life so basely; though I think
   I never shall enjoy her, yet I'll preserve
   The honour of affection, and die for her,
   Make death a devil.
THESEUS
   What may be done? For now I feel compassion.   270
PIRITHOUS
   Let it not fall again, sir.
THESEUS   Say, Emilia,
   If one of them were dead, as one must, are you
   Content to take th'other to your husband?
   They cannot both enjoy you. They are princes
   As goodly as your own eyes, and as noble
   As ever fame yet spoke of. Look upon 'em,
   And, if you can love, end this difference.
   I give consent; are you content too, princes?
PALAMON *and* ARCITE
   With all our souls.
THESEUS   He that she refuses
   Must die then.
PALAMON *and* ARCITE Any death thou canst invent, Duke.   280
PALAMON
   If I fall from that mouth, I fall with favour,
   And lovers yet unborn shall bless my ashes.

279, 280 PALAMON *and* ARCITE] *Both* Q

263 **piece** (of ground)   271 **fall** diminish; or fail (see note on l. 236)
269 **Make . . . devil** though death were a   281 **from that mouth** because of her decision
   devil (to torture me)

ARCITE
    If she refuse me, yet my grave will wed me,
    And soldiers sing my epitaph.
THESEUS (*to Emilia*)   Make choice then.
EMILIA
    I cannot, sir; they are both too excellent;
    For me, a hair shall never fall of these men.
HIPPOLYTA
    What will become of 'em?
THESEUS   Thus I ordain it,
    And by mine honour, once again, it stands,
    Or both shall die. (*To Palamon and Arcite*) You shall both
        to your country,
    And each, within this month, accompanied   290
    With three fair knights, appear again in this place,
    In which I'll plant a pyramid; and whether,
    Before us that are here, can force his cousin
    By fair and knightly strength to touch the pillar,
    He shall enjoy her; the other lose his head,
    And all his friends; nor shall he grudge to fall,
    Nor think he dies with interest in this lady.
    Will this content ye?
PALAMON   Yes. Here, cousin Arcite,
    I am friends again till that hour.
ARCITE   I embrace ye.
THESEUS
    Are you content, sister?
EMILIA   Yes, I must, sir,   300
    Else both miscarry.
THESEUS (*to Palamon and Arcite*)
                    Come, shake hands again, then,
    And take heed, as you are gentlemen, this quarrel
    Sleep till the hour prefixed, and hold your course.
PALAMON
    We dare not fail thee, Theseus.

---

285 excellent;] TONSON; ~∧ Q

286 **For** on account of
292 **plant** fix in the ground
    pyramid obelisk
    whether whichever of the two
296 **And . . . friends** (shall lose their heads)

grudge to fall feel that his execution is unjust
297 **interest in** a legitimate claim to
301 **miscarry** perish
303 **hold your course** keep to your resolve

THESEUS   Come, I'll give ye
Now usage like to princes and to friends.
When ye return, who wins I'll settle here;
Who loses yet I'll weep upon his bier.   *Exeunt*

4.1   *Enter Jailer and his Friend*
JAILER
Heard you no more? Was nothing said of me
Concerning the escape of Palamon?
Good sir, remember.
FRIEND   Nothing that I heard,
For I came home before the business
Was fully ended. Yet I might perceive,
Ere I departed, a great likelihood
Of both their pardons; for Hippolyta
And fair-eyed Emily, upon their knees,
Begged with such handsome pity that the Duke,
Methought, stood staggering whether he should follow   10
His rash oath, or the sweet compassion
Of those two ladies; and to second them
That truly noble prince, Pirithous—
Half his own heart—set in too, that I hope
All shall be well; neither heard I one question
Of your name or his scape.
          Enter Second Friend
JAILER   Pray heaven it hold so.
SECOND FRIEND
Be of good comfort, man; I bring you news,
Good news.
JAILER   They are welcome.
SECOND FRIEND   Palamon has cleared you,

4.1] Q (*Actus Quartus*. Scaena 1.)   1 Heard] BAWCUTT; Heare Q   3 FRIEND] 1. *Fr.* Q   11 oath] F; o'th Q

306 **settle here** establish in Athens
307 *Exeunt* If a property tree has been used
    it is presumably removed at this time.
4.1 The location is the prison. This scene
    and 4.2 are by Fletcher.
  1 **Heard** Q's 'Heare' (see collations) makes
    acceptable sense, but the Friend's reply,
    'Nothing that I heard', makes Bawcutt's
    emendation more probable.

  4 **business** trisyllabic here
 10 **staggering** hesitating
 14 **Half . . . heart** i.e. who shares Theseus'
    heart with Hippolyta. See 1.3.44–7.
    that so that
 16, 31 For the stage directions in these lines
    see note on 2.2.218.1, 244.1.
 16 **hold** continue
 18 **They** As often, 'news' is taken as plural.

And got your pardon, and discovered how
And by whose means he escaped, which was your
   daughter's,   20
Whose pardon is procured too, and the prisoner,
Not to be held ungrateful to her goodness,
Has given a sum of money to her marriage—
A large one, I'll assure you.
JAILER   Ye are a good man
And ever bring good news.
FIRST FRIEND   How was it ended?
SECOND FRIEND
Why, as it should be; they that nev'r begged
But they prevailed had their suits fairly granted;
The prisoners have their lives.
FIRST FRIEND   I knew 'twould be so.
SECOND FRIEND
But there be new conditions, which you'll hear of
At better time.
JAILER   I hope they are good.
SECOND FRIEND   They are honourable;   30
How good they'll prove I know not.
    Enter Wooer
FIRST FRIEND   'Twill be known.
WOOER
Alas, sir, where's your daughter?
JAILER   Why do you ask?
WOOER
O sir, when did you see her?
SECOND FRIEND (*aside*)   How he looks!
JAILER
This morning.
WOOER   Was she well? Was she in health?
Sir, when did she sleep?
FIRST FRIEND   These are strange questions.
JAILER
I do not think she was very well, for now
You make me mind her, but this very day

---

19 **discovered** revealed
23 **given . . . marriage** It may be because
  of an oversight in the collaboration that
  in Shakespeare's 5.4 we see Palamon

making such a gift, apparently for the
first time (ll. 31 ff.).
37 **mind** think of

I asked her questions, and she answered me
So far from what she was, so childishly,
So sillily, as if she were a fool,　　　　　　　　　　　40
An innocent, and I was very angry.
But what of her, sir?
WOOER　　　　　　　　　　Nothing but my pity;
But you must know it, and as good by me
As by another that less loves her.
JAILER
Well, sir?
FIRST FRIEND Not right?
SECOND FRIEND　　　　　Not well?
WOOER　　　　　　　　　　No, sir, not well.
'Tis too true, she is mad.
FIRST FRIEND　　　　　　It cannot be.
WOOER
Believe you'll find it so.
JAILER　　　　　　　　　I half suspected
What you told me; the gods comfort her!
Either this was her love to Palamon,
Or fear of my miscarrying on his scape,　　　　　　50
Or both.
WOOER　　'Tis likely.
JAILER　　　　　　　　But why all this haste, sir?
WOOER
I'll tell you quickly. As I late was angling
In the great lake that lies behind the palace,
From the far shore, thick set with reeds and sedges,
As patiently I was attending sport,
I heard a voice—a shrill one; and attentive,
I gave my ear, when I might well perceive
'Twas one that sung, and by the smallness of it
A boy or woman. I then left my angle

46 'Tis] Q (*Woo.* Tis)

39 So . . . was in a manner so unlike her
40 sillily feeble-mindedly
41 innocent simpleton
42 Nothing . . . pity I'm only sorry (about
　what I have to tell you)
45 right in her right mind

50 miscarrying on coming to harm because
　of
52 angling fishing
55 attending sport waiting for a bite
58 smallness softness
59 angle fishing rod

To his own skill, came near, but yet perceived not   60
Who made the sound, the rushes and the reeds
Had so encompassed it. I laid me down
And listened to the words she sung, for then,
Through a small glade cut by the fishermen,
I saw it was your daughter.

JAILER   Pray go on, sir.

WOOER

She sung much, but no sense, only I heard her
Repeat this often: 'Palamon is gone,
Is gone to th' wood to gather mulberries;
I'll find him out tomorrow.'

FIRST FRIEND   Pretty soul!

WOOER

'His shackles will betray him; he'll be taken,   70
And what shall I do then? I'll bring a bevy,
A hundred black-eyed maids that love as I do,
With chaplets on their heads of daffadillies,
With cherry lips and cheeks of damask roses,
And all we'll dance an antic fore the Duke,
And beg his pardon.' Then she talked of you, sir—
That you must lose your head tomorrow morning,
And she must gather flowers to bury you,
And see the house made handsome; then she sung
Nothing but 'Willow, willow, willow', and between   80
Ever was 'Palamon, fair Palamon',
And 'Palamon was a tall young man.' The place
Was knee-deep where she sat; her careless tresses
A wreath of bulrush rounded; about her stuck
Thousand freshwater flowers of several colours,
That methought she appeared like the fair nymph

---

63 sung] F; song Q   84 wreath] SEWARD; wreake Q

60 **his** its
62 **encompassed it** grown up around the place
64 **glade** passage
73 **chaplets** wreaths
74 **damask** a variety of red rose originally from Damascus
75 **antic** grotesque dance
76 **beg his pardon** beg the Duke to pardon Palamon

79 **handsome** tidy
80 **'Willow . . . willow'** The refrain of a popular song, one version of which Desdemona sings (*Othello* 4.3.38–55); see William Chappell, *Popular Music of the Olden Time* (London, 1859), p. 206.
82 **tall** brave
83 **knee-deep** (with rushes)
84 **rounded** encircled
86–7 **nymph . . . waters** See note on 3.1.8.

That feeds the lake with waters, or as Iris,
Newly dropped down from heaven. Rings she made
Of rushes that grew by, and to 'em spoke
The prettiest posies: 'Thus our true love's tied',   90
'This you may lose, not me', and many a one;
And then she wept, and sung again, and sighed,
And with the same breath smiled and kissed her hand.

SECOND FRIEND
    Alas, what pity it is!

WOOER   I made in to her.
    She saw me, and straight sought the flood; I saved her
    And set her safe to land; when presently
    She slipped away, and to the city made
    With such a cry and swiftness that, believe me,
    She left me far behind her. Three or four
    I saw from far off cross her—one of 'em   100
    I knew to be your brother—where she stayed
    And fell, scarce to be got away. I left them with her

        Enter Jailer's Brother, Jailer's Daughter, and others

    And hither came to tell you. Here they are.

JAILER'S DAUGHTER (*sings*)
        May you never more enjoy the light . . . (etc.)
    Is not this a fine song?

JAILER'S BROTHER   O, a very fine one.

JAILER'S DAUGHTER
    I can sing twenty more.

JAILER'S BROTHER   I think you can.

JAILER'S DAUGHTER
    Yes, truly can I; I can sing 'The Broom'
    And 'Bonny Robin'. Are not you a tailor?

102.1 *Enter Jailer's Brother, Jailer's Daughter and others*] *Enter Brother, Daughter, and others.*
Q   104 *sings*] *not in* Q

87 **Iris** Goddess of the rainbow and Juno's
    messenger.
88–9 **Rings . . . rushes** Rush rings were
    sometimes used as wedding rings in the
    country.
90 **posies** From 'poesies'; mottoes such as
    were often inscribed on rings.
94 **made in to** went towards
95 **straight . . . flood** at once went into the
    water
100 **cross** intercept

101 **stayed** stopped
104 **May . . . light** A song unknown today;
    'etc.' normally takes the place of the
    remainder of a familiar quotation—here
    the rest of the song.
107 **'The Broom'** A popular song (Chappell,
    p. 458).
108 **'Bonny Robin'** Another popular song—
    probably a Robin Hood ballad—of which
    almost all the words are lost (Chappell,
    p. 233). Ophelia sings one line, 'For

JAILER'S BROTHER
Yes.

JAILER'S DAUGHTER Where's my wedding gown?

JAILER'S BROTHER   I'll bring it tomorrow.

JAILER'S DAUGHTER

Do, very rarely; I must be abroad else   110
To call the maids and pay the minstrels,
For I must lose my maidenhead by cocklight;
'Twill never thrive else.
(*Sings*)   O fair, O sweet . . . (etc.)

JAILER'S BROTHER
You must ev'n take it patiently.

JAILER   'Tis true.

JAILER'S DAUGHTER
Good ev'n, good men; pray, did you ever hear
Of one, young Palamon?

JAILER   Yes, wench, we know him.

JAILER'S DAUGHTER
Is't not a fine young gentleman?

JAILER   'Tis, love.

JAILER'S BROTHER
By no mean cross her; she is then distempered
Far worse than now she shows.

FIRST FRIEND (*to the Jailer's Daughter*)

                          Yes, he's a fine man.   120

---

110 rarely] Q; early SEWARD; rearly SYMPSON   114 *Sings*] *at end of line,* Q   119 mean] Q;
means COLMAN   120 Far] TONSON; For Q

bonny sweet Robin is all my joy' (*Hamlet* 4.5.185). Harry Morris has shown that Robin was probably 'one of the cant terms' for penis (*PMLA*, 73 (1958), 601–3); Peter Seng summarizes the evidence in *The Vocal Songs in the Plays of Shakespeare* (Cambridge, Mass., 1967), pp. 151–3.

110 **rarely** early. In Elizabethan English one meaning of 'rare' was 'early' (*OED*, rare, a.³); hence, emendation (see collations) is unnecessary.
I . . . else otherwise I shall be away from home
112 **by cocklight** at cockcrow, before dawn. A sexual double meaning is appropriate to her obsession.

114 **O . . . sweet** The first words of the seventh poem in Sir Philip Sidney's *Certain Sonnets*, first printed with the 1598 edition of the *Arcadia*. The four stanzas of the poem begin identically:
O fair, O sweet, when I do look on thee,
In whom all joys so well agree,
Heart and soul do sing in me.
(*Poems*, ed. W. A. Ringler (Oxford, 1962), pp. 139–40.)

119 **mean** means. Since 'mean' is a legitimate but seldom used alternative for *means* in phrases such as this (*OED*, II. 5b) there is no need to emend (see collations).
cross contradict
is then distempered will become deranged

171

JAILER'S DAUGHTER
    O, is he so? You have a sister.
FIRST FRIEND   Yes.
JAILER'S DAUGHTER
    But she shall never have him, tell her so,
    For a trick that I know; you'd best look to her,
    For if she see him once, she's gone—she's done
    And undone in an hour. All the young maids
    Of our town are in love with him, but I laugh at 'em
    And let 'em all alone. Is't not a wise course?
FIRST FRIEND   Yes.
JAILER'S DAUGHTER
    There is at least two hundred now with child by him—
    There must be four; yet I keep close for all this,
    Close as a cockle; and all these must be boys—   130
    He has the trick on't—and at ten years old
    They must be all gelt for musicians,
    And sing the wars of Theseus.
SECOND FRIEND   This is strange.
⌈JAILER'S BROTHER⌉
    As ever you heard, but say nothing.
FIRST FRIEND   No.
JAILER'S DAUGHTER
    They come from all parts of the dukedom to him;
    I'll warrant ye, he had not so few last night
    As twenty to dispatch. He'll tickle't up
    In two hours, if his hand be in.
JAILER   She's lost
    Past all cure.
JAILER'S BROTHER Heaven forbid, man!
JAILER'S DAUGHTER (*to the Jailer*)
    Come hither; you are a wise man.
FIRST FRIEND   Does she know him?   140

134 JAILER'S BROTHER] PROUDFOOT; *Daugh.* Q

123 **For because** of. The Jailer's Daughter
    hints that she can keep Palamon for
    herself.
129 **keep close** keep to myself, or keep quiet;
    literally, closed up
130 **Close as a cockle** Proverbial (Dent
    C499).
    cockle clam

131 **trick on't** i.e. of begetting boys
132 **gelt for musicians** castrated in order to
    be male sopranos
137 **tickle't up** finish the task (but with an
    obvious sexual double meaning)
138 **his ... in** he's in good form; proverbial
    (Dent H67)
140 **know** recognize

SECOND FRIEND
　No, would she did.

JAILER'S DAUGHTER　You are master of a ship?

JAILER
　Yes.

JAILER'S DAUGHTER　Where's your compass?

JAILER　　　　　　　　　　　Here.

JAILER'S DAUGHTER　　　　　　　Set it to th' north;
　And now direct your course to th' wood, where Palamon
　lies longing for me. For the tackling, let me alone. Come,
　weigh, my hearts, cheerly all. Owgh, owgh, owgh! 'Tis
　up; the wind's fair; top the bowline; out with the
　mainsail! Where's your whistle, master?

JAILER'S BROTHER　Let's get her in.

JAILER　Up to the top, boy!

JAILER'S BROTHER　Where's the pilot?　　　　　　　　　150

FIRST FRIEND　Here.

JAILER'S DAUGHTER　What kenn'st thou?

SECOND FRIEND　A fair wood.

JAILER'S DAUGHTER　Bear for it, master. Tack about.
　(*Sings*)
　　When Cynthia with her borrowed light ... (etc.)
　　　　　　　　　　　　　　　　　　Exeunt

4.2　*Enter Emilia alone with two pictures*

EMILIA
　Yet I may bind those wounds up, that must open

141 SECOND FRIEND] F; 1. *Fr.* Q　145 cheerly∧ all.] LEECH; cheerely. | *All.* (*as speech-prefix*) Q　146 bowline] Q (Bowling)　154 Tack] Q (take)　155 *Sings*] Q *prints at end of l. 154*　4.2 Q (*Scaena 2.*)

142 **Set . . . north** i.e. find the north by setting up the compass
144 **tackling** rigging
　let me alone i.e. I'll handle it
145 **weigh** (anchor)
　Owgh The Jailer's Daughter imitates the imaginary exertions of the crew hauling up the anchor.
146 **top the bowline** tighten the rope that keeps the sail steady in a wind
148 **Let's . . . in** Presumably an aside to the Jailer, though in his next speech the Brother joins the Jailer in pretending, for the Daughter's benefit, to be on shipboard.

in into her room?
149 **top** small look-out platform near the top of the mast
152 **kenn'st** see'st
155 **When . . . light** The song is unknown. Proudfoot points to the line, 'And pale Cynthia with her borrowed light' (l. 43), in Thomas Sackville's Induction to the 'Complaint of Henry Duke of Buckingham' in *The Mirror for Magistrates* (1563).
4.2 The location is the ducal palace in Athens.
1–54 Emilia's debate with herself resembles many a soliloquy in romance literature.

And bleed to death for my sake else; I'll choose,
And end their strife. Two such young handsome men
Shall never fall for me; their weeping mothers,
Following the dead cold ashes of their sons,
Shall never curse my cruelty. Good heaven,
What a sweet face has Arcite! If wise nature,
With all her best endowments, all those beauties
She sows into the births of noble bodies,
Were here a mortal woman, and had in her   10
The coy denials of young maids, yet doubtless
She would run mad for this man. What an eye,
Of what a fiery sparkle and quick sweetness,
Has this young prince! Here love himself sits smiling;
Just such another wanton Ganymede
Set Jove afire with, and enforced the god
Snatch up the goodly boy, and set him by him,
A shining constellation. What a brow,
Of what a spacious majesty, he carries,
Arched like the great-eyed Juno's, but far sweeter,   20
Smoother than Pelops' shoulder! Fame and honour,
Methinks, from hence, as from a promontory
Pointed in heaven, should clap their wings and sing
To all the under world the loves and fights
Of gods and such men near 'em. Palamon

16 Jove] SEWARD; Love Q   25 such] Q (sueh)

The soliloquy of Eumenides in Lyly's
Endymion (3.4.90–121), referred to in
the Introduction (p. 54), is a striking
dramatic example.

4 **for** because of
11 **coy** modest
13 **quick** lively
14 **Here** i.e. in his eye
15 **Ganymede** A beautiful youth whom Jove,
in the form of an eagle, carried off to be
his cupbearer.
16 **with** As the lines stand, the word is
superfluous. Perhaps Fletcher intended
to add 'as he' after 'Ganymede', making
love the subject of 'set . . . afire' and
'enforced'. The objection to making such
an emendation is the extra foot this
would add to l. 15.
18 **constellation** Eventually, Ganymede was

changed into Aquarius.
21 **Pelops' shoulder** When Tantalus killed
his son Pelops and offered him as food to
the gods, they restored the youth to life,
but only after a part of his shoulder had
been eaten by Demeter. The gods replaced
this piece with ivory.
21–5 Skeat notes a striking parallel between
these lines and Beaumont and Fletcher's
Philaster (4.6.90–4): 'Place me, some
god, upon a pyramid | Higher than hills
of earth, and lend a voice | Loud as your
thunder to me, that from thence, | I may
discourse to all the under world, | The
worth that dwells in him.'
22 **hence** his brow
23 **Pointed** coming to a point
24 **under world** i.e. the earth as seen from
above
25 **near 'em** approaching them in character

Is but his foil, to him a mere dull shadow;
He's swart and meagre, of an eye as heavy
As if he had lost his mother, a still temper,
No stirring in him, no alacrity,
Of all this sprightly sharpness not a smile.—   30
Yet these that we count errors may become him:
Narcissus was a sad boy but a heavenly.
O, who can find the bent of woman's fancy?
I am a fool, my reason is lost in me,
I have no choice, and I have lied so lewdly
That women ought to beat me. On my knees
I ask thy pardon; Palamon, thou art alone
And only beautiful, and these the eyes,
These the bright lamps of beauty, that command
And threaten love, and what young maid dare
      cross 'em?   40
What a bold gravity, and yet inviting,
Has this brown manly face! O love, this only
From this hour is complexion. Lie there, Arcite;
Thou art a changeling to him, a mere gypsy,
And this the noble body. I am sotted,
Utterly lost; my virgin's faith has fled me.
For if my brother but even now had asked me
Whether I loved, I had run mad for Arcite;
Now if my sister, more for Palamon.
Stand both together: now come ask me, brother—   50
Alas, I know not; ask me now, sweet sister—
I may go look. What a mere child is fancy,

27 swart] Q (swarth)   40 cross 'em?] SEWARD; ~∧ Q   49 Palamon.] F; ~, Q

27 **swart** swarthy
  meagre thin
  heavy sad
28 **still temper** lethargic temperament
30 **this** i.e. Arcite's
32 **sad** serious
33 **O . . . fancy** Bawcutt notes the close
  resemblance to Spenser's 'O who does
  know the bent of women's fantasy?'
  (*Faerie Queene*, I. iv. 24).
  bent . . . fancy direction in which a
  woman's affections will lead her
35 **choice** capacity for choosing
  lewdly ignorantly

37–8 **alone | And only** solely, uniquely
40 **cross** oppose
42–3 **this only . . . complexion** this (dark)
  colouring is now the only one (for me)
44 **changeling** ugly or deformed child supposedly left by fairies in exchange for one
  they have stolen
45 **sotted** besotted, stupified
46 **faith** faithfulness in love
48 **Whether** which one
50 **Stand both together** She addresses the
  pictures.
52 **I . . . look** i.e. I may look in vain for an
  answer

That having two fair gauds of equal sweetness,
Cannot distinguish, but must cry for both!
          Enter a Gentleman
How now, sir?

GENTLEMAN   From the noble Duke, your brother,
Madam, I bring you news: the knights are come.

EMILIA
To end the quarrel?

GENTLEMAN   Yes.

EMILIA   Would I might end first!
What sins have I committed, chaste Diana,
That my unspotted youth must now be soiled
With blood of princes, and my chastity   60
Be made the altar where the lives of lovers—
Two greater and two better never yet
Made mothers joy—must be the sacrifice
To my unhappy beauty?
          Enter Theseus, Hippolyta, Pirithous and attendants

THESEUS   Bring 'em in
Quickly, by any means; I long to see 'em.
Your two contending lovers are returned,
And with them their fair knights. Now, my fair sister,
You must love one of them.

EMILIA   I had rather both,
So neither for my sake should fall untimely.

THESEUS
Who saw 'em?

PIRITHOUS   I awhile.

GENTLEMAN   And I.   70
          Enter a Messenger

54.1 *Enter a Gentleman*] TONSON; *Enter Emil. and Gent:* Q   55 How] COLMAN; *Emil.* How Q
70.1 *Enter a Messenger*] TONSON (*subs.*); *Enter Messengers. Curtis.* Q (*after l.* 69)

53 **gauds** toys, trinkets
54 **distinguish** choose between them
54.1 *Enter a Gentleman* Q's second entrance
   for Emilia, who is already on stage (see
   collations), may point to second
   thoughts. Perhaps Fletcher originally
   began the scene here, and later wrote
   the preceding soliloquy.
63 **joy** rejoice
70.1 The direction in Q (see collations) includes an actor's name, 'Curtis'; see

Introduction, p. 3. Since Curtis Greville
was with the King's Men only in 1625–
6, this part of the direction is clearly an
addition. It is possible that, as Gary Taylor
suggests, the text was altered in other
ways for performance at this time, and
originally two or more messengers entered and took part in the following
descriptions of the knights (Oxford *Textual
Companion*, p. 633). This would explain
Q's '*Messengers*'.

THESEUS
  From whence come you, sir?
MESSENGER   From the knights.
THESEUS   Pray speak,
  You that have seen them, what they are.
MESSENGER   I will, sir,
  And truly what I think. Six braver spirits
  Than these they have brought, if we judge by
      the outside,
  I never saw nor read of. He that stands
  In the first place with Arcite, by his seeming
  Should be a stout man, by his face a prince;
  His very looks so say him, his complexion
  Nearer a brown than black—stern and yet noble—
  Which shows him hardy, fearless, proud of dangers.   80
  The circles of his eyes show fire within him,
  And as a heated lion, so he looks;
  His hair hangs long behind him, black and shining
  Like ravens' wings; his shoulders broad and strong,
  Armed long and round; and on his thigh a sword
  Hung by a curious baldric, when he frowns
  To seal his will with—better, o' my conscience,
  Was never soldier's friend.
THESEUS
  Thou hast well described him.
PIRITHOUS   Yet a great deal short,
  Methinks, of him that's first with Palamon.   90
THESEUS
  Pray speak him, friend.
PIRITHOUS   I guess he is a prince too,

---

76 first] Q (fitst)   81 fire] DYCE (*conj.* Heath); faire Q

75–88 He . . . friend Many details of this
  portrait are taken from Chaucer's description of King Lygurge (*The Knight's Tale*,
  ll. A 2129–54), who, however, accom-
  panies Palamon. The comparison to a
  lion is taken from the following description of Arcite's supporter, King Emetrius.
76 seeming appearance
77 stout brave
78 say proclaim
82 heated angry

84 Like ravens' wings A standard comparison, still familiar today, like several in
  5.1, all of which could be called proverbial, but for which it seems unnecessary to refer to Dent.
85 Armed . . . round with long round arms
86 curious baldric artfully made belt
86–7 when . . . with with which to carry
  out his will when he is angry
87 better i.e. a better sword
91 speak describe

And, if it may be, greater; for his show
Has all the ornament of honour in't.
He's somewhat bigger than the knight he spoke of,
But of a face far sweeter; his complexion
Is, as a ripe grape, ruddy; he has felt
Without doubt what he fights for, and so apter
To make this cause his own. In's face appears
All the fair hopes of what he undertakes,
And when he's angry, then a settled valour,   100
Not tainted with extremes, runs through his body,
And guides his arm to brave things. Fear he cannot—
He shows no such soft temper. His head's yellow,
Hard-haired and curled, thick-twined like ivy tods,
Not to undo with thunder. In his face
The livery of the warlike maid appears,
Pure red and white, for yet no beard has blessed him;
And in his rolling eyes sits victory,
As if she ever meant to court his valour.
His nose stands high, a character of honour;   110
His red lips, after fights, are fit for ladies.

EMILIA
Must these men die too?

104 ivy tods] LITTLEDALE (*subs.*); Ivy tops Q   109 court] LITTLEDALE (*conj.* Dyce); corect Q;
crown SEWARD

92 **show** appearance
94–116 **He's ... twenty** Many details of this portrait come from Chaucer's description of King Emetrius (ll. A 2155–78), but the curious fact that his 'pure red and white' face is marred by no beard (l. 107), although he is 'some five-and-twenty' (l. 116), while the beard of King Emetrius 'was well begun' (l. A 2173), recalls Boccaccio's description of King Peleus, to which Chaucer was indebted. This king is specifically said to be young and to have a countenance '*bianco e vermiglio*' like a May rose (*Teseida*, ed. S. Battaglia (Florence, 1938), vi. 15). Like Arcite's knight in the play, but unlike Chaucer's King Emetrius, he is said to be very attractive to the ladies and carries an axe (17–18). It is tempting to suppose that Fletcher had read this description.
94 **he** (the messenger)
97 **what ... for** i.e. love
100 **settled** steady

101 **extremes** excessive emotions
104 **Hard-haired** The meaning is uncertain. The curly yellow hair of Chaucer's King Emetrius is 'glittering as ye son' (l. A 2166); 'hard-haired' may suggest that it was shiny, or may be due to a mistake in the previous line of Speght's 1602 edition of Chaucer, where, as R. K. Turner has noted, 'was yronne' becomes 'was of yron' (see Introduction, p. 26). **tods** bushes
105 **undo** be undone, destroyed
106 **warlike maid** Probably Athena, who was especially revered in Athens, and as a goddess of war was called *area*, 'warlike'.
109 **court** Although Seward's emendation, 'crown' (see collations), makes better sense, it is easier to see, as Dyce pointed out, how 'court' might have been misread as 'corect' by the Q printer.
110 **character of** feature indicating

PIRITHOUS   When he speaks, his tongue
  Sounds like a trumpet. All his lineaments
  Are as a man would wish 'em—strong and clean.
  He wears a well-steeled axe, the staff of gold;
  His age some five-and-twenty.
MESSENGER   There's another—
  A little man, but of a tough soul, seeming
  As great as any; fairer promises
  In such a body yet I never looked on.
PIRITHOUS
  O, he that's freckle-faced?
MESSENGER   The same, my lord.   120
  Are they not sweet ones?
PIRITHOUS   Yes, they are well.
MESSENGER   Methinks,
  Being so few, and well disposed, they show
  Great and fine art in nature. He's white-haired—
  Not wanton white, but such a manly colour
  Next to an auburn; tough and nimble-set,
  Which shows an active soul. His arms are brawny,
  Lined with strong sinews—to the shoulder-piece
  Gently they swell, like women new-conceived,
  Which speaks him prone to labour, never fainting
  Under the weight of arms; stout-hearted still,   130
  But when he stirs, a tiger. He's grey-eyed,
  Which yields compassion where he conquers; sharp
  To spy advantages, and where he finds 'em,
  He's swift to make 'em his. He does no wrongs,
  Nor takes none. He's round-faced, and when he smiles

---

115 **staff** handle
118 **great** both large and noble
120 **freckle-faced** This detail is taken from
    Chaucer's King Emetrius (l. A 2169).
    Chaucer describes only two knights.
121 **they** the freckles
122 **disposed** arranged
123 **white-haired** blond
124 **wanton white** effeminate
125 **nimble-set** agile
128 **new-conceived** recently pregnant
129 **labour** hard work (with a pun on child-
    bearing)
130 **still** i.e. when standing still

131 **grey-eyed** The term was used for what
    we should call blue or blue-grey eyes. In
    *A Dictionary of English–Latin and Latin–
    English* (2nd edn., London, 1679) Elisha
    Coles gives for 'Gray-eyed' '*glaucopsis*',
    an epithet applied to Athena. For 'Glau-
    cus' he gives 'Gray, or Blewish-bay'.
    Today 'glaucous' is defined as bluish-
    grey or grey (*OED*). 'Grey' eyes were
    apparently thought to indicate a com-
    passionate disposition, and to be marks
    of beauty in a woman.
135 **Nor takes none** i.e. he stands up for his
    rights

He shows a lover, when he frowns, a soldier.
About his head he wears the winner's oak,
And in it stuck the favour of his lady;
His age some six-and-thirty. In his hand
He bears a charging-staff embossed with silver.   140
THESEUS
Are they all thus?
PIRITHOUS   They are all the sons of honour.
THESEUS
Now, as I have a soul, I long to see 'em.
(*To Hippolyta*) Lady, you shall see men fight, now.
HIPPOLYTA   I wish it,
But not the cause, my lord. They would show
Bravely about the titles of two kingdoms;
'Tis pity love should be so tyrannous.
O, my soft-hearted sister, what think you?
Weep not till they weep blood; wench, it must be.
THESEUS (*to Emilia*)
You have steeled 'em with your beauty. (*To Pirithous*)
          Honoured friend,
To you I give the field; pray order it   150
Fitting the persons that must use it.
PIRITHOUS   Yes, sir.
THESEUS
Come, I'll go visit 'em; I cannot stay—
Their fame has fired me so—till they appear.
Good friend, be royal.
PIRITHOUS   There shall want no bravery.
EMILIA
Poor wench, go weep, for whosoever wins
Loses a noble cousin for thy sins.   *Exeunt*

153 so— ... appear.] TONSON (*subs.*); so; ... appeare, Q

136 **shows** looks like
137 **winner's oak** wreath of oak leaves awarded for valour
140 **charging-staff** lance for tilting
141 **They ... honour** The portraits of the three knights are further evidence of the romance tradition, where, as here, ideal traits of character are often suggested by description. The portraits serve to magnify Emilia's misgivings about the contest for which she feels guiltily responsible (see ll. 155–6).
144–5 **show ... about** look splendid if they were fighting about
149 **steeled** hardened
150 **the field** management of the tournament
152 **stay** wait
153 **fame** i.e. what has been said of them
154 **be royal** make the arrangements regally lavish
   bravery splendour

4.3   *Enter Jailer, Wooer, Doctor*

DOCTOR Her distraction is more at some time of the moon
than at other some, is it not?

JAILER She is continually in a harmless distemper, sleeps
little; altogether without appetite, save often drinking;
dreaming of another world, and a better; and what
broken piece of matter soe'er she's about, the name
Palamon lards it, that she farces ev'ry business withal,
fits it to every question.

Enter Jailer's Daughter

Look where she comes; you shall perceive her behaviour.

They stand apart

JAILER'S DAUGHTER I have forgot it quite; the burden on't   10
was 'Down-a, down-a', and penned by no worse man
than Geraldo, Emilia's schoolmaster. He's as fantastical,
too, as ever he may go upon's legs; for in the next
world will Dido see Palamon, and then will she be out
of love with Aeneas.

DOCTOR What stuff's here! Poor soul.

JAILER Ev'n thus all day long.

JAILER'S DAUGHTER Now for this charm that I told you of,
you must bring a piece of silver on the tip of your
tongue, or no ferry; then if it be your chance to come   20
where the blessed spirits are—there's a sight now! We
maids that have our livers perished, cracked to pieces
with love, we shall come there, and do nothing all day
long but pick flowers with Proserpine. Then will I make
Palamon a nosegay, then let him mark me, then—

4.3] Q (Scaena 3.)   8.1 *Enter Jailer's Daughter*] *after* busines (l. 7) *in* Q   *Jailer's*] *not in* Q
9.1 *They stand apart*] *not in* Q   21 spirits‸ are—] WEBER (*subs., conj.* Mason); spirits, as‸ Q

4.3 The location is the prison. The scene
may be by Shakespeare.
2 **other some** i.e. other times
3 **distemper** derangement
5–6 **what . . . soe'er** whatever bit of business
7 **lards it** is inserted into it (like bacon into
lean meat)
  farces stuffs
10 **burden** refrain (of the song she has forgot-
ten)
12 **fantastical** fanciful
13 **ever . . . legs** any man that walks.
Compare the proverbial 'As good a man
as ever trod on shoe (neat's) leather (as

ever went on legs)' (Dent M66).
19–20 **piece . . . ferry** Charon, who ferried
the shades of the dead across the river
Styx to the underworld, required pay-
ment; it was a custom to place a small
coin on the tongue of a corpse before
burial.
22 **livers** The liver was thought to be the
seat of the passions.
  perished destroyed
24 **Proserpine** While picking flowers, she
was carried off by Pluto to be queen of
the underworld.
25 **mark** notice

DOCTOR How prettily she's amiss! Note her a little further.

JAILER'S DAUGHTER Faith, I'll tell you: sometime we go to
barley-break, we of the blessèd. Alas, 'tis a sore life they
have i'th' other place—such burning, frying, boiling,
hissing, howling, chatt'ring, cursing—O, they have   30
shrewd measure, take heed! If one be mad, or hang or
drown themselves, thither they go, Jupiter bless us, and
there shall we be put in a cauldron of lead and usurers'
grease, amongst a whole million of cutpurses, and there
boil like a gammon of bacon that will never be enough.

DOCTOR How her brain coins!

JAILER'S DAUGHTER Lords and courtiers that have got maids
with child, they are in this place; they shall stand in
fire up to the navel and in ice up to th' heart, and there
th'offending part burns and the deceiving part freezes—   40
in truth a very grievous punishment, as one would
think, for such a trifle. Believe me, one would marry a
leprous witch to be rid on't, I'll assure you.

DOCTOR How she continues this fancy! 'Tis not an engrafted madness, but a most thick and profound melancholy.

JAILER'S DAUGHTER To hear there a proud lady and a proud
city wife howl together—I were a beast an I'd call it

29 i'th' other] F (i' th' | Other); i'th' | Thother Q   35 enough.] enough. *Exit.* Q   41 truth]
Q (troth)   punishment] Q (*corr.*); punishuent Q (*uncorr.*)   44–5 engrafted] Q (engraffed)
48 were] Q (*corr.*); weare Q (*uncorr.*)

28 **barley-break** A game played by couples,
one couple in a central area called 'hell'
trying to catch the others.

29 **other place** i.e. hell. Compare 'seek him
i'th' other place yourself' (*Hamlet*
4.3.34).

31 **shrewd measure** harsh punishment

33–4 **cauldron . . . grease** The punishment
in hell for avarice was to be put in a
cauldron of boiling lead and oil.

34 **grease** the fat they sweat

35 **enough** i.e. cooked enough. Q's *Exit* for
the Jailer's Daughter at this point (see
collations) may indicate either that her
following two speeches were after-
thoughts or, as Bertram suggests (pp.
100–1), that they were censored because
of their satire on the nobility.

36 **coins** fabricates, spins fancies

44–5 **engrafted** implanted. Although there
is, as Lawrence Babb says, 'no discover-
able line of distinction in the old psy-

chiatry between melancholy and madness' (*The Elizabethan Malady* (East Lans-
ing, Mich., 1951), p. 36), the Doctor
here attempts to draw one rather similar
to that of the Doctor attending Lady
Macbeth: 'Not so sick . . . As she is
troubled with thick-coming fancies'
(*Macbeth* 5.3.39–40).

45–6 **most . . . melancholy** very deep de-
pression. The Jailer's Daughter is presumably suffering from 'love melancholy',
one cause of which was thwarted love;
its symptoms included loss of appetite
and inability to sleep (Babb, pp. 134–5).

45 **thick** suggesting, perhaps 'thick-coming
fancies' like Lady Macbeth's (see preceding note). Love melancholy was also
thought to thicken the blood.

47 **lady** (connoting superior social position
to that of the 'city wife')

48 **I were** I'd be

good sport. One cries, 'O, this smoke!', th'other 'This
fire!'; one cries, 'O, that ever I did it behind the arras!',   50
and then howls; th'other curses a suing fellow and her
garden house.
(*Sings*)
    I will be true, my stars, my fate . . . (etc.)
                                          Exit Jailer's Daughter
JAILER What think you of her, sir?
DOCTOR I think she has a perturbèd mind, which I cannot
    minister to.
JAILER Alas, what then?
DOCTOR Understand you she ever affected any man ere she
    beheld Palamon?
JAILER I was once, sir, in great hope she had fixed her   60
    liking on this gentleman, my friend.
WOOER I did think so too, and would account I had a great
    penn'orth on't to give half my state that both she and
    I, at this present, stood unfeignedly on the same terms.
DOCTOR That intemp'rate surfeit of her eye hath distem-
    pered the other senses; they may return and settle again
    to execute their preordained faculties, but they are now
    in a most extravagant vagary. This you must do: confine
    her to a place where the light may rather seem to steal
    in than be permitted. Take upon you, young sir, her   70
    friend, the name of Palamon; say you come to eat with
    her, and to commune of love. This will catch her
    attention, for this her mind beats upon; other objects
    that are inserted 'tween her mind and eye become the

---

49 th'other] DAVENANT; another Q   50 behind] Q (*corr.*); behold Q (*uncorr.*)   53.1 *Jailer's*]
not in Q   64 same] Q (*corr.*: Same); Sawe Q (*uncorr.*; *turned* m)

---

50 **arras** tapestry often used as a wall-
    hanging
51 **suing fellow** persistent wooer
52 **garden house** a small house in a garden.
    Such houses were notorious as places of
    assignation.
53 I . . . **fate** The song is unknown today.
55–6 I . . . **to** Reminiscent of 'Canst thou
    not minister to a mind diseased . . . ?'
    (*Macbeth* 5.3.42).
58 **affected** was attracted to
62–3 **account . . . on't** consider I had a good

bargain (pennyworth)
63 **state** estate
65–8 **That . . . vagary** The medical jargon
    of the Doctor's diagnosis is no doubt
    intended to provoke a smile.
65 **intemp'rate . . . eye** excessive gazing (at
    Palamon)
    distempered deranged, unbalanced
67 **faculties** functions
68 **extravagant vagary** capricious wander-
    ing (from their proper functions)
73 **beats upon** harps on

pranks and friskins of her madness. Sing to her such
green songs of love as she says Palamon hath sung in
prison; come to her stuck in as sweet flowers as the
season is mistress of, and thereto make an addition of
some other compounded odours which are grateful to
the sense. All this shall become Palamon, for Palamon   80
can sing, and Palamon is sweet and ev'ry good thing.
Desire to eat with her, carve her, drink to her, and
still among intermingle your petition of grace and
acceptance into her favour. Learn what maids have
been her companions and playferes, and let them repair
to her with Palamon in their mouths, and appear with
tokens, as if they suggested for him. It is a falsehood
she is in, which is with falsehoods to be combatted. This
may bring her to eat, to sleep, and reduce what's now
out of square in her into their former law and regiment.   90
I have seen it approved, how many times I know not,
but to make the number more, I have great hope in
this. I will between the passages of this project come in
with my appliance. Let us put it in execution, and
hasten the success, which doubt not will bring forth
comfort.   *Exeunt*

5.1   *Flourish. Enter Theseus, Pirithous, Hippolyta,*
         attendants

77 sweet‸ flowers] Q (*corr.*); sweet, flowers Q (*uncorr.*)   82 carve] F; crave Q   88 falsehoods]
Q (fasehoods)
  5.1] Q (*Actus Quintus. Scaena* I.)   0.1 *Flourish*] *at end of* 4.3 *in* Q

75 **friskins** frolics
76 **green** youthful
77 **stuck in** decked with
79 **compounded odours** mixed perfumes
   grateful pleasing
80 **sense** (of smell)
   become be appropriate to
82 **carve** carve for
83 **still among** continually amidst or along
   with (these other activities)
85 **playferes** playfellows
87 **suggested** pleaded, interceded
   falsehood delusion
87–8 **It . . . combatted** Compare the proverbial 'One deceit (falsehood) drives out
   another' (Dent D174).
89 **reduce** bring back

90 **out of square** disordered
   regiment rule
91 **it** i.e. this method of treatment
   approved demonstrated to be effective
93 **passages** proceedings
94 **appliance** remedy (presumably the plan
   put forward in 5.2 that the Wooer go to
   bed with her)
95 **success** outcome
5.1 The location is the forest, near where
   Theseus has arranged a field for the
   tournament on the site of the interrupted
   fight between Palamon and Arcite (see
   3.6.291–2). Temples have been built to
   Mars, Venus, and Diana. In this scene
   one large altar, placed in front of a
   trapdoor upstage centre, probably repre-

THESEUS

Now let 'em enter, and before the gods
Tender their holy prayers. Let the temples
Burn bright with sacred fires, and the altars
In hallowed clouds commend their swelling incense
To those above us. Let no due be wanting;
They have a noble work in hand, will honour
The very powers that love 'em.

  Flourish of cornetts. Enter Palamon and his
  three knights ⌜at one door⌝, Arcite and his three
  knights ⌜at the opposite door⌝

PIRITHOUS   Sir, they enter.

THESEUS

You valiant and strong-hearted enemies,
You royal german foes, that this day come
To blow that nearness out that flames between ye,   10
Lay by your anger for an hour, and dove-like,
Before the holy altars of your helpers,
The all-feared gods, bow down your stubborn bodies.
Your ire is more than mortal; so your help be,
And as the gods regard ye, fight with justice.
I'll leave you to your prayers, and betwixt ye
I part my wishes.

PIRITHOUS   Honour crown the worthiest!

        Exeunt Theseus and his train

PALAMON

The glass is running now that cannot finish
Till one of us expire. Think you but thus,
That were there aught in me which strove to show   20

---

7 *Flourish of cornetts*] *after l. 5 in* Q   *Enter . . . door*] OXFORD (*subs.*); *Enter Palamon and Arcite, and their Knights.* Q   17.1 *Exeunt*] TONSON; *Exit* Q

sents successively the altar to each of these deities (see Introduction, p. 62). Possibly, as Professor R. A. Foakes has suggested to me, the altar is ornamented in each case with some sign or symbol of the deity to whom it is dedicated. The scene is mainly the work of Shakespeare, though Fletcher may have written or revised the first thirty-three lines.

3 **fires** disyllabic here
5 **due** appropriate ceremony
6 **will** that will

7 *Enter . . . other* Although the Q direction does not specify the use of both doors (see collations), the Oxford editor's direction is plausible. It would produce a suitably spectacular effect.
9 **german** closely related
10 **nearness** intimacy of friendship and blood relationship
15 **regard** watch over
16 **prayers** disyllabic here
18 **glass** hourglass
20 **show** appear as

Mine enemy in this business, were't one eye
Against another, arm oppressed by arm,
I would destroy th'offender, coz—I would,
Though parcel of myself. Then from this gather
How I should tender you.

ARCITE   I am in labour
To push your name, your ancient love, our kindred,
Out of my memory, and i'th' selfsame place
To seat something I would confound. So hoist we
The sails that must these vessels port even where
The heavenly limiter pleases.

PALAMON   You speak well.   30
Before I turn, let me embrace thee, cousin.
          They embrace
This I shall never do again.

ARCITE   One farewell.

PALAMON

Why, let it be so; farewell, coz.

ARCITE   Farewell, sir.
          Exeunt Palamon and his knights
Knights, kinsmen, lovers, yea, my sacrifices,
True worshippers of Mars, whose spirit in you
Expels the seeds of fear, and th'apprehension
Which still is father of it, go with me
Before the god of our profession; there
Require of him the hearts of lions and
The breath of tigers, yea the fierceness too,   40
Yea, the speed also—to go on, I mean;
Else wish we to be snails. You know my prize
Must be dragged out of blood; force and great feat

31.1 *They embrace*] not in Q   33.1 *Exeunt . . . knights*] *after* coz. *in* Q   37 father of] WEBER
(*conj.* Theobald); farther off Q

24 **parcel** part
25 **tender** regard
28 **confound** ruin
29 **port** carry, or bring to port
30 **limiter** arbiter, controller of the limits of
   our lives
31 **turn** turn away
36 **apprehension** idea or anticipation
37 **father of it** Since the idea or anticipation
   of danger may well beget fear, Theobald's
   emendation (see collations) makes good

sense. Q's 'farther off it' is harder to
explain, but might mean that the idea of
fear precedes its first beginnings.
38 **of our profession** whom we profess to
   worship, or of our calling as knights
39 **Require** ask
   hearts of lions See note on 4.2.84.
40 **breath** endurance (rarely being 'out of
   breath')
41 **go on** advance (as opposed to giving
   ground or retreating, as in l. 42)

Must put my garland on, where she sticks,
The queen of flowers. Our intercession, then,
Must be to him that makes the camp a cistern
Brimmed with the blood of men; give me your aid,
And bend your spirits towards him.

    They advance to the altar, fall on their faces, then kneel
Thou mighty one, that with thy power hast turned
Green Neptune into purple, whose approach   50
Comets prewarn, whose havoc in vast field
Unearthèd skulls proclaim, whose breath blows down
The teeming Ceres' foison, who dost pluck
With hand armipotent from forth blue clouds
The masoned turrets, that both mak'st and break'st
The stony girths of cities; me thy pupil,
Youngest follower of thy drum, instruct this day
With military skill, that to thy laud
I may advance my streamer, and by thee
Be styled the lord o'th' day. Give me, great Mars,   60
Some token of thy pleasure.

---

44 on] Q; on me PROUDFOOT (*conj.* Littledale)   48.1 *They . . . kneel*] DYCE (*subs., following*
Weber); *They kneele.* Q   50 whose approach] SEWARD; *not in* Q   54 armipotent] 1750;
armenypotent Q

44 **garland** i.e. the victor's wreath
  on Littledale's conjectural addition of
  'me' (see collations) makes the metre
  more regular but is not essential to the
  sense.
44–5 **she . . . flowers** Emily, the queen of
  flowers, is fastened (since she is the
  reward for winning)
48.1 **They . . . kneel** Here, as in 3.5,
  Q's stage directions are disappointingly
  meagre (see collations). Weber and succeeding editors have tried to reconstruct
  the stage business by combining the
  direction to kneel with the actions implied
  by Arcite's 'go with me' (l. 37) and
  the later direction: '*fall on their faces as
  formerly*' (l. 61.1).
49–50 **turned . . . purple** Compare 'Making
  the green one red' (*Macbeth* 2.2.61) and
  the immediately preceding lines.
50 **Neptune** The god of the sea, symbolizing
  the sea.
  whose approach Q's half-line here (see
  collations) clearly leaves a gap in sense.
  Seward's emendation fits with the common belief that comets foreshadow wars.

Chaucer devotes several lines of his description of the temple of Mars to predic-
tions of death in the stars (*The Knight's
Tale*, ll. A 2031–40).
52 **Unearthèd** OED's first recorded use of the
  word as ppl. a.[1]
53 **teeming . . . foison** plentiful crop furnished
  by the fertile goddess of agriculture
53–6 **who . . . cities** In *The Knight's Tale*
  Saturn boasts of similar powers: 'Mine is
  the ruin of the high hals, | The falling of
  the toures and of the wals' (ll. A 2463–
  4).
53 **pluck** pull down
54 **armipotent** powerful in arms. Accented
  here armìpotènt; Chaucer applies this
  term to Mars in l. A 1982 of the description of his temple, and again in l. A
  2441, shortly before Saturn's speech.
  from . . . clouds i.e. Mars strikes from
  high in the sky
55 **masoned** built of stone (the first recorded
  use in OED)
56 **girths** walls
59 **streamer** banner
60 **styled** named

Here they fall on their faces as formerly, and there
is heard clanging of armour, with a short thunder,
as the burst of a battle, whereupon they all rise
and bow to the altar

O great corrector of enormous times,
Shaker of o'er-rank states, thou grand decider
Of dusty and old titles, that heal'st with blood
The earth when it is sick, and cur'st the world
O'th' plurisy of people; I do take
Thy signs auspiciously, and in thy name
To my design march boldly. (*To his knights*) Let us go.

                                                        Exeunt

Enter Palamon and his knights with the former
observance

PALAMON

Our stars must glister with new fire, or be
Today extinct. Our argument is love,   70
Which, if the goddess of it grant, she gives
Victory too. Then bend your spirits with mine,
You whose free nobleness do make my cause
Your personal hazard. To the goddess Venus
Commend we our proceeding, and implore
Her power unto our party.

Here they advance to the altar, fall on their faces,
then kneel as formerly

68 design∧] TONSON; ~; Q   boldly.] TONSON (*subs.*); ~, Q (*corr.*); ~∧ Q (*uncorr.*)   72
bend] This edition; blend Q   76 Her] Q (*corr.*); His Q (*uncorr.*)   76.1–2 *Here . . . formerly*]
DYCE (*subs.*); *Here they kneele as formerly.* Q

61.3 **burst** violent outbreak
62 **enormous** disordered
63 **o'er-rank** over-ripe, rotten
64 **with blood** i.e. by bleeding (a common
   Elizabethan cure; see 3.1.114)
66 **plurisy** In Elizabethan times the disease
   pleurisy was attributed to excess of humours; the word (often spelt 'plu-') was
   derived by false etymology from Latin
   plus, 'more', hence its figurative use to
   mean 'excess'.
68.1–2 **with ... observance** Weber took this
   to mean that Palamon and his knights
   fall on their faces and kneel here, but
   it is more likely that they do so at
   l. 76.1–2 where Q has '*Here they kneele*
   as formerly', just before Palamon begins
   his prayer. In this case the direction at

l. 68.1–2 means that Palamon and his
knights will perform the same ceremonies
as Arcite and his knights.
69 **stars** fortunes
70 **extinct** extinguished
   argument is quarrel concerns
71 **Which . . . grant** i.e. if Venus grants
   success in love
72 **bend** Although Q's 'blend' (see collations)
   makes good sense, it is reasonable to
   suppose that it should be 'bend', match-
   ing Arcite's injunction, 'give me your
   aid, | And bend your spirits towards him'
   just before his prayer (ll. 47–8).
73 **free** generous
   do The plural form seems to result from
   thinking of the possessors of 'nobleness'.
76.1–2 **Here . . . formerly** It seems reason-

Hail, sovereign queen of secrets, who hast power
To call the fiercest tyrant from his rage
And weep unto a girl; that hast the might
Even with an eye-glance to choke Mars's drum   80
And turn th'alarm to whispers; that canst make
A cripple flourish with his crutch, and cure him
Before Apollo; that mayst force the king
To be his subject's vassal, and induce
Stale gravity to dance; the polled bachelor—
Whose youth, like wanton boys through bonfires,
Have skipped thy flame—at seventy thou canst catch,
And make him, to the scorn of his hoarse throat,
Abuse young lays of love. What godlike power
Hast thou not power upon? To Phoebus thou   90
Add'st flames hotter than his; the heavenly fires
Did scorch his mortal son, thine him; the huntress,
All moist and cold, some say, began to throw
Her bow away and sigh. Take to thy grace
Me, thy vowed soldier, who do bear thy yoke
As 'twere a wreath of roses, yet is heavier
Than lead itself, stings more than nettles.
I have never been foul-mouthed against thy law;
Nev'r revealed secret, for I knew none; would not,
Had I kenned all that were. I never practised   100
Upon man's wife, nor would the libels read

86 wanton] Q (*corr.*); wonton Q (*uncorr.*)   91 his;] SEWARD; ~₍ₐ₎ Q

ably certain that the prostration and kneeling should occur here, as Dyce thought (see collations). There is no reason for Palamon and his knights to be on their knees when he addresses them in ll. 69–76.

77 **queen of secrets** (because secrecy was an essential feature of the code of love to which the knights of romance were supposed to subscribe)
79 **weep** make him weep
80 **choke** silence
81 **alarm** call to arms
82 **flourish with** brandish
83 **Before Apollo** sooner than the god of healing
85 **polled** bald
87 **Have** Here the plural form results from the comparison to 'boys'.

skipped jumped over; hence, avoided
88 **scorn** (on the part of his listeners)
89 **Abuse** i.e. sing badly
    young . . . love love-songs suitable for youth
92 **his mortal son** Phaethon. See note on 1.2.85.
    the huntress Diana, goddess of chastity, who fell in love with Endymion.
93 **moist** (possibly because, as huntress, she frequented mountain streams)
    cold i.e. chaste. See l. 137.
96 **yet is** i.e. yet it (the yoke) is
98–126 With regard to Palamon's claims in these lines, see note on 3.3.29–30.
99 **secret** See note on l. 77.
100 **kenned** known
100–1 **practised | Upon** sought to seduce

Of liberal wits. I never at great feasts
Sought to betray a beauty, but have blushed
At simp'ring sirs that did. I have been harsh
To large confessors, and have hotly asked them
If they had mothers—I had one, a woman,
And women 'twere they wronged. I knew a man
Of eighty winters—this I told them—who
A lass of fourteen brided; 'twas thy power
To put life into dust. The agèd cramp   110
Had screwed his square foot round;
The gout had knit his fingers into knots;
Torturing convulsions from his globy eyes
Had almost drawn their spheres, that what was life
In him seemed torture. This anatomy
Had by his young fair fere a boy, and I
Believed it was his, for she swore it was,
And who would not believe her? Brief, I am
To those that prate and have done, no companion;
To those that boast and have not, a defier;   120
To those that would and cannot, a rejoicer.
Yea, him I do not love that tells close offices
The foulest way, nor names concealments in
The boldest language; such a one I am,
And vow that lover never yet made sigh
Truer than I. O then, most soft sweet goddess,
Give me the victory of this question, which

118 Brief,] SEWARD (*subs.*); ~ ‸ Q   119 done, no companion;] F; done; no Companion ‸ Q
120 not, a defier;] F; not; a defyer ‸ Q   121 cannot, a rejoicer.] F; cannot; a Rejoycer, Q

102 **liberal** licentious
103 **betray** reveal the love-life of
105 **large confessors** men who boast of many
sexual conquests
hotly angrily
106 **had mothers** Proverbial (Dent
M1201.1).
107–18 It has been noted that Palamon's
grotesque example of the power of Venus
gives a singularly unfavourable view of
love. In emphasizing its negative effects
Shakespeare is following in the footsteps
of Chaucer in his description of the
Temple of Venus (*The Knight's Tale*, ll. A
1918–66).
109 **brided** married
111 **screwed** twisted

square sturdy; but when twisted 'round'
it becomes 'out of square', or contorted
113 **globy** swollen
114 **drawn their spheres** forced the eyeballs
out
115 **anatomy** skeleton
116 **fere** mate
118 **Brief** in short
119 **have done** (what they say they have)
120 **defier** one who challenges their boasts
or disdains them
122 **close offices** secret affairs
123 **nor** or
concealments what should be concealed
124 **boldest** crudest
127 **question** subject of our conflict

Is true love's merit, and bless me with a sign
Of thy great pleasure.
> *Here music is heard; doves are seen to flutter;*
> *they fall again upon their faces, then on their*
> *knees*

O thou that from eleven to ninety reign'st   130
In mortal bosoms, whose chase is this world
And we in herds thy game, I give thee thanks
For this fair token, which being laid unto
Mine innocent true heart, arms in assurance
My body to this business. (*To his knights*) Let us rise
And bow before the goddess.
> *They rise and bow*

                              Time comes on.   *Exeunt*
> *Still music of recorders. Enter Emilia in white,*
> *her hair about her shoulders, and wearing a*
> *wheaten wreath; one in white holding up her train,*
> *her hair stuck with flowers; one before her*
> *carrying a silver hind, in which is conveyed incense*
> *and sweet odours; which being set upon the altar,*
> *her maids standing aloof, she sets fire to it. Then*
> *they curtsy and kneel.*

EMILIA
O sacred, shadowy, cold, and constant queen,
Abandoner of revels, mute contemplative,
Sweet, solitary, white as chaste, and pure
As wind-fanned snow, who to thy female knights   140
Allow'st no more blood than will make a blush,
Which is their order's robe, I here, thy priest,
Am humbled fore thine altar. O, vouchsafe

---

130 O] COLMAN (Oh,); *Pal.* O Q (*speech-prefix repeated*)   136 *They rise and bow*] *They bow.* Q
(*after l. 134*)   136.1 *recorders*] Q (*Records*)   136.2 *and wearing*] DYCE; *not in* Q

128 **true love's merit** the reward of true
love; i.e. the determination of which is
the truest lover
129.1 *doves* (sacred to Venus). Presumably
doves, brought from under the stage
through the trapdoor, were released from
behind the altar (see Louis Wright, 'Animal Actors on the English Stage', *PMLA*,
42 (1927), 656–69; p. 666).
131 **chase** hunting ground
136.1 *Still* soft
136.5 **hind** (sacred to Diana). Shakespeare
may have had the story of the sacrifice

of Iphigenia at the back of his mind (he
gratuitously inserted a reference to Aulis
at 1.1.212); according to one legend,
Artemis (Diana) substituted a hind for
Iphigenia, sparing her, just as Agamemnon was about to kill her. When Emilia
sees the hind disappear (l. 162.1), she at
first thinks Diana has spared her the
painful choice between the kinsmen.
136.7 *aloof* at a slight distance
137 **shadowy** Diana, also goddess of the
moon, is associated with night.
141 **blood** (as a symbol of sexual desire)

With that thy rare green eye, which never yet
Beheld thing maculate, look on thy virgin;
And, sacred silver mistress, lend thine ear—
Which nev'r heard scurril term, into whose port
Ne'er entered wanton sound—to my petition,
Seasoned with holy fear. This is my last
Of vestal office; I am bride-habited,   150
But maiden-hearted. A husband I have 'pointed,
But do not know him; out of two I should
Choose one, and pray for his success, but I
Am guiltless of election; of mine eyes
Were I to lose one—they are equal precious—
I could doom neither; that which perished should
Go to't unsentenced. Therefore, most modest queen,
He of the two pretenders that best loves me
And has the truest title in't, let him
Take off my wheaten garland, or else grant   160
The file and quality I hold I may
Continue in thy band.

> *Here the hind vanishes under the altar, and in the*
> *place ascends a rose tree, having one rose upon it*

See what our general of ebbs and flows
Out from the bowels of her holy altar

151 maiden-hearted.] mayden harted, Q; Maiden-hearted: F   154 election;] DYCE (~ :);
~∧ Q

145 **maculate** spotted, dirty
147 **scurril** scurrilous
  port portal
149 **holy fear** religious awe
149–57 The section of Emilia's prayer from
  'This is my last . . . ' to 'Go to't unsentenced' is punctuated in Q only with
  commas, leaving some doubt about the
  relationship between the component
  clauses. I follow F in making a major
  division after 'maiden-hearted' (see collations, l. 151), where she begins speaking about a husband. I follow Dyce in
  making another major division after
  'election' (see collations, l. 154), assuming that Emilia then compares choosing
  between her suitors to choosing between
  her eyes.
154 **guiltless** suggesting that choice of a
  husband might be a crime against Diana
  election having chosen
156 **doom** condemn

158 **pretenders** suitors
159 **truest title** most genuine claim
160 **wheaten garland** the wreath worn by
  the bride. See 1.1.0.4, 1.1.64–5, and
  5.1.136.3.
161–2 **The . . . Continue** I may retain my
  present rank and condition (of a virgin)
162.1–2 **Here . . . it** The staging of Emilia's
  prayer, more elaborate than that of the
  other two prayers, provides a spectacular
  climax for the scene. Using the trapdoor
  behind the altar, a stage-hand removes
  the hind and then lifts up a 'tree' to
  which a single rose is fastened in such a
  way that it can later (at ll. 168.1–2) be
  easily released, perhaps by pulling a
  thread.
162.2 **rose** symbol of virginity. See 2.2.
  136–7.
163 **general . . . flows** Diana was also the
  goddess of the moon.

With sacred act advances—but one rose!
If well inspired, this battle shall confound
Both these brave knights, and I, a virgin flower,
Must grow alone, unplucked.
> *Here is heard a sudden twang of instruments,*
> *and the rose falls from the tree*
The flower is fall'n, the tree descends. O mistress,
Thou here dischargest me; I shall be gathered—   170
I think so, but I know not thine own will.
Unclasp thy mystery. (*Aside*) I hope she's pleased;
Her signs were gracious.   *They curtsy and exeunt*

5.2   *Enter Doctor, Jailer, and Wooer in the habit*
          of Palamon

DOCTOR Has this advice I told you done any good upon
her?

WOOER O, very much. The maids that kept her company
have half persuaded her that I am Palamon. Within this
half-hour she came smiling to me, and asked me what
I would eat, and when I would kiss her. I told her
presently, and kissed her twice.

DOCTOR
'Twas well done; twenty times had been far better,
For there the cure lies mainly.

WOOER   Then she told me
She would watch with me tonight, for well she knew   10
What hour my fit would take me.

DOCTOR   Let her do so,
And when your fit comes, fit her home,
And presently.

WOOER   She would have me sing.

5.2] Q (Scaena 2.) 0.1 *the*] *not in* Q   3 kept] F; hept Q   12-13 home, | And presently]
Q; home, and presently SEWARD

166 **If well inspired** if this is a genuine omen,
    or if I am prophetically inspired
    confound destroy
172 **Unclasp** reveal the meaning of
5.2 The location is the prison. The scene is
    probably by Fletcher.
0.1–2 *in . . . of* dressed as
  7 **presently** immediately
 10 **watch** sit up

11 **fit** sudden inclination
12 **fit her home** give her all she needs
12–13 Many editors follow Seward in print-
    ing 'and presently' in l. 12 to fill out
    what is otherwise a four-foot line (see
    collations); l. 13 then becomes a half-
    line (in most texts). Since this is not a
    great improvement, I follow Q.

DOCTOR
  You did so?
WOOER   No.
DOCTOR   'Twas very ill done, then;
  You should observe her ev'ry way.
WOOER   Alas,
  I have no voice, sir, to confirm her that way.
DOCTOR
  That's all one, if ye make a noise.
  If she entreat again, do anything—
  Lie with her if she ask you.
JAILER   Ho there, doctor!
DOCTOR
  Yes, in the way of cure.
JAILER   But first, by your leave,   20
  I'th' way of honesty.
DOCTOR   That's but a niceness.
  Nev'r cast your child away for honesty.
  Cure her first this way, then if she will be honest,
  She has the path before her.
JAILER
  Thank ye, doctor.
DOCTOR   Pray bring her in,
  And let's see how she is.
JAILER   I will, and tell her
  Her Palamon stays for her. But, doctor,
  Methinks you are i'th' wrong still.   *Exit Jailer*
DOCTOR   Go, go;
  You fathers are fine fools! Her honesty?
  An we should give her physic till we find that—   30
WOOER
  Why, do you think she is not honest, sir?
DOCTOR
  How old is she?

---

15 **observe** humour, gratify
16 **confirm** strengthen
17 **That's all one** that makes no difference
21 **I'th' way of honesty** morally, chastely
     (i.e. after marriage)
     niceness fastidious scruple
22 **Nev'r . . . away** don't abandon your

daughter (to her madness)
23 **will be** wants to be
27 **stays** waits
30 **An . . . that** if we continued to treat her
     until we were convinced that she was a
     virgin

WOOER   She's eighteen.
DOCTOR   She may be,
But that's all one; 'tis nothing to our purpose.
Whate'er her father says, if you perceive
Her mood inclining that way that I spoke of,
Videlicet, the way of flesh—you have me?
WOOER
Yes, very well, sir.
DOCTOR   Please her appetite,
And do it home; it cures her, *ipso facto*,
The melancholy humour that infects her.
WOOER
I am of your mind, doctor.   40
    Enter Jailer and his Daughter, ⌈mad⌉
DOCTOR
You'll find it so. She comes; pray humour her.
    Doctor and Wooer stand aside
JAILER
Come, your love Palamon stays for you, child,
And has done this long hour, to visit you.
JAILER'S DAUGHTER
I thank him for his gentle patience.
He's a kind gentleman, and I am much bound to him.
Did you nev'r see the horse he gave me?
JAILER   Yes.
JAILER'S DAUGHTER
How do you like him?

37 Yes] F; Yet Q   40.1 *and his*] *not in* Q   *mad*] OXFORD; *Maide.* Q   41 humour] 1750;
honour Q   41.1 *Doctor . . . aside*] *not in* Q

33 **nothing . . . purpose** not at all relevant
to our design
36 *Videlicet* namely (Latin)
way of flesh Proverbial (Dent W166).
38 **her** for her
ipso facto by the very act (Latin)
39 **melancholy humour** Melancholy was one
of the four humours thought to constitute
the fluid content of the body. An excess
of the melancholy humour led to such
disorders as the love-melancholy or madness from which the Jailer's Daughter
suffers; see notes on 4.3.44–5 and
45–6.
40.1 *mad* The Oxford editor's emendation

(see collations) is plausible, since the
maid specified in Q never speaks, and
since, as the Oxford editor says, it is
improbable that the Jailer's Daughter
would have a maid. If the reading of the
MS were '*Madde*', it could easily have
been misread as '*Maide*'. In an Elizabethan or Jacobean play the direction for
a woman to enter 'mad' would imply
dishevelled clothes and 'her hair about
her ears'; see Alan Dessen, *Elizabethan
Stage Conventions and Modern Interpreters*
(Cambridge, 1984), p. 36.
45 **bound** obliged

JAILER   He's a very fair one.

JAILER'S DAUGHTER
  You never saw him dance?

JAILER   No.

JAILER'S DAUGHTER   I have, often.
  He dances very finely, very comely,
  And for a jig, come cut and long tail to him,   50
  He turns ye like a top.

JAILER   That's fine indeed.

JAILER'S DAUGHTER
  He'll dance the morris twenty mile an hour,
  And that will founder the best hobby-horse,
  If I have any skill, in all the parish;
  And gallops to the tune of 'Light o' love'.
  What think you of this horse?

JAILER   Having these virtues,
  I think he might be brought to play at tennis.

JAILER'S DAUGHTER
  Alas, that's nothing.

JAILER   Can he write and read too?

JAILER'S DAUGHTER
  A very fair hand, and casts himself th'accounts
  Of all his hay and provender. That ostler   60
  Must rise betime that cozens him. You know
  The chestnut mare the Duke has?

55 tune] THEOBALD *and* SEWARD; turne Q

47 **fair** handsome
48 **You . . . dance** The ensuing account of
  the horse probably alludes, as Littledale
  suggested, to 'a celebrated dancing horse
  named Marocco', belonging to a certain
  Banks, who exhibited it in London in the
  1590s.
50 **come . . . him** Proverbial (Dent C398);
  no matter what sort of horse competes
  with him.
  cut horse with a docked tail (hence 'cut
  and long tail' = all sorts of horses)
51 **ye** for you
52 **dance . . . hour** In *Kemp's Nine Days'
  Wonder* (1600) the comedian, Will Kemp,
  described his dancing a morris at great
  speed all the way from London to Nor-
  wich.
53 **founder** lame

hobby-horse A man dressed as a hobby-
  horse was a traditional figure in the
  morris dance, but one frequently left out
  in Elizabethan times. 'The hobby-horse
  is forgot' became a standard phrase.
54 **skill** judgement
55 **Light o' love** inconstant lover; 'a ballet
  (ballad) to be sung and danced' (Chappell, p. 221). The music is known but
  not the words, though the song is often
  referred to.
59 **fair hand** beautiful handwriting
  casts . . . accounts keeps track for himself
  of the expense
60–1 **That . . . him** Compare the proverbial
  'He must rise early (betimes) that will go
  beyond (etc.) me' (Varied) (Dent R133.1).
61 **betime** early
  cozens cheats

JAILER   Very well.

JAILER'S DAUGHTER
She is horribly in love with him, poor beast,
But he is like his master, coy and scornful.

JAILER
What dowry has she?

JAILER'S DAUGHTER   Some two hundred bottles,
And twenty strike of oats, but he'll ne'er have her.
He lisps in's neighing able to entice
A miller's mare. He'll be the death of her.

DOCTOR What stuff she utters!
       Wooer approaches her

JAILER
Make curtsy; here your love comes.

WOOER   Pretty soul,   70
How do ye? (*She curtsies*) That's a fine maid; there's a
       curtsy!

JAILER'S DAUGHTER
Yours to command i'th' way of honesty.
How far is't now to th'end o'th' world, my masters?

DOCTOR
Why, a day's journey, wench.

JAILER'S DAUGHTER (*to Wooer*)   Will you go with me?

WOOER
What shall we do there, wench?

JAILER'S DAUGHTER   Why, play at stool-ball.
What is there else to do?

WOOER   I am content,
If we shall keep our wedding there.

69.1 *Wooer approaches her*] *not in* Q   71 *She curtsies*] *not in* Q

64 coy aloof
65 **bottles** bundles
66 **strike** a measure of grain—usually a
    bushel
68 **miller's mare** 'As sober as a miller's mare'
    was proverbial: M. P. Tilley, *A Dictionary
    of the Proverbs in England in the Sixteenth
    and Seventeenth Centuries* (Ann Arbor,
    1950) M960.
72 **Yours to command** a standard expression
    of courteous deference

75 **stool-ball** 'An old country game some-
    what resembling cricket, played chiefly
    by young women, or, as an Easter game,
    between men and women . . . The "stool"
    was the wicket' (*OED*).
76 **content** (with this plan)
77 **keep** celebrate
77–81 Ann Thompson points to the similar
    situation of Mopsa in Book 4 of the
    Arcadia (see Introduction, p. 29).

JAILER'S DAUGHTER   'Tis true,
For there, I will assure you, we shall find
Some blind priest for the purpose, that will venture
To marry us; for here they are nice, and foolish.   80
Besides, my father must be hanged tomorrow,
And that would be a blot i'th' business.
Are not you Palamon?
WOOER   Do not you know me?
JAILER'S DAUGHTER
Yes, but you care not for me; I have nothing
But this poor petticoat and two coarse smocks.
WOOER
That's all one; I will have you.
JAILER'S DAUGHTER   Will you surely?
WOOER
Yes, by this fair hand, will I.
JAILER'S DAUGHTER   We'll to bed then.
WOOER
Ev'n when you will.
        He kisses her
JAILER'S DAUGHTER (*wiping her mouth*)
                        O sir, you would fain be nibbling.
WOOER
Why do you rub my kiss off?
JAILER'S DAUGHTER   'Tis a sweet one,
And will perfume me finely against the wedding.   90
(*Pointing to the Doctor*) Is not this your cousin Arcite?
DOCTOR   Yes, sweetheart,
And I am glad my cousin Palamon
Has made so fair a choice.
JAILER'S DAUGHTER   Do you think he'll have me?
DOCTOR
Yes, without doubt.
JAILER'S DAUGHTER (*to the Jailer*) Do you think so too?
JAILER   Yes.

---

85 two] F; too Q   88 *He kisses her*] *not in* Q   *wiping her mouth*] *not in* Q   91 *Pointing . . . Doctor*]
not in Q

---

80 **nice** over-scrupulous   90 **against** in preparation for
85 **smocks** undergarments

JAILER'S DAUGHTER
We shall have many children. (*To the Doctor*) Lord, how
    you're grown!
My Palamon, I hope, will grow too, finely,
Now he's at liberty. Alas, poor chicken,
He was kept down with hard meat and ill lodging,
But I'll kiss him up again.
    Enter a Messenger
MESSENGER
What do you here? You'll lose the noblest sight   100
That ev'r was seen.
JAILER   Are they i'th' field?
MESSENGER   They are.
You bear a charge there too.
JAILER   I'll away straight.
(*To the others*) I must ev'n leave you here.
DOCTOR   Nay, we'll go with you.
I will not lose the fight.
JAILER   How did you like her?
DOCTOR
I'll warrant you, within these three or four days
I'll make her right again. (*To the Wooer*) You must not
    from her,
But still preserve her in this way.
WOOER   I will.
DOCTOR
Let's get her in.
WOOER (*to the Jailer's Daughter*)
                    Come, sweet, we'll go to dinner,
And then we'll play at cards.

104 fight] Q; sight DYCE

95 **how you're grown** The Jailer's Daughter
called Arcite 'the lower of the twain'
(2.1.49–50).
96 **grow** That there is a double meaning—
'have an erection'—is confirmed by the
immediately following lines.
98 **kept down** kept from growing (and from
sexual excitation)
  hard meat coarse food
99 **up** See note on l. 96
102 **bear a charge** have official duties

104 **fight** Because of the references by the
Messenger to 'the noblest sight' (l. 100)
and by Pirithous to 'this sight' (5.3.1)
many editors follow Dyce in emending
here to 'sight' (see collations), but it is
perfectly logical for the Doctor to say he
does not want to miss the 'fight'.
  How . . . her What did you think about
her condition?
107 **still preserve her** continue to treat her

JAILER'S DAUGHTER   And shall we kiss too?
WOOER
  A hundred times.
JAILER'S DAUGHTER And twenty.
WOOER   Ay, and twenty.   110
JAILER'S DAUGHTER
  And then we'll sleep together.
DOCTOR (*to the Wooer*)   Take her offer.
WOOER (*to the Jailer's Daughter*)
  Yes, marry, will we.
JAILER'S DAUGHTER   But you shall not hurt me.
WOOER
  I will not, sweet.
JAILER'S DAUGHTER If you do, love, I'll cry.   *Exeunt*

5.3   *Flourish. Enter Theseus, Hippolyta, Emilia,*
       Pirithous, and some attendants
EMILIA
  I'll no step further.
PIRITHOUS   Will you lose this sight?
EMILIA
  I had rather see a wren hawk at a fly
  Than this decision; ev'ry blow that falls
  Threats a brave life; each stroke laments
  The place whereon it falls, and sounds more like
  A bell than blade. I will stay here.
  It is enough my hearing shall be punished
  With what shall happen, 'gainst the which there is
  No deafing, but to hear; not taint mine eye
  With dread sights it may shun.

5.3] Q (Scaena 3.)   0.1 *Flourish*] *at end of* 5.2 *in* Q   0.2 *attendants*ʌ] SEWARD; *Attendants,*
T. Tucke: Curtis. Q   3 decision; ev'ry] F; decision ev'ry; Q

5.3 The location is the forest, near the field of combat. This scene and the following one are by Shakespeare.

0.2 **attendants** The direction in Q (see collations) includes the names of two actors who were with the King's Men only in 1625–6: 'T. Tucke' (Thomas Tuckfield) and 'Curtis' (Curtis Greville, also mentioned at 4.2.70.1); see Introduction, p. 3.

2 **hawk at** attack on the wing (as a hawk does; the destruction of a mere fly is compared to the potential losses in the approaching contest)

3 **decision** i.e. the outcome of the fight

6 **bell** (tolling for the dead)

9 **No . . . hear** no way of deafening oneself so as not to hear. See 'but' as used in Elizabethan English after verbs meaning 'prevent', 'hinder', etc. (*OED*, C. 22).

PIRITHOUS (*to Theseus*)   Sir, my good lord,   10
  Your sister will no further.
THESEUS   O, she must;
  She shall see deeds of honour in their kind,
  Which sometime show well, pencilled. Nature now
  Shall make and act the story, the belief
  Both sealed with eye and ear. (*To Emilia*) You must
      be present;
  You are the victor's meed—the prize and garland
  To crown the question's title.
EMILIA   Pardon me;
  If I were there, I'd wink.
THESEUS   You must be there;
  This trial is as 'twere i'th' night, and you
  The only star to shine.
EMILIA   I am extinct.   20
  There is but envy in that light which shows
  The one the other. Darkness, which ever was
  The dam of horror, who does stand accursed
  Of many mortal millions, may even now,
  By casting her black mantle over both,
  That neither could find other, get herself
  Some part of a good name, and many a murder
  Set off whereto she's guilty.
HIPPOLYTA   You must go.
EMILIA
  In faith, I will not.
THESEUS   Why, the knights must kindle
  Their valour at your eye. Know, of this war   30
  You are the treasure, and must needs be by
  To give the service pay.
EMILIA   Sir, pardon me;

16 prize] Q (price)

12 **kind** true nature, actuality
13 **pencilled** when drawn or painted
14 **make and act** create and perform
   belief (in the story)
15 **Both sealed with** confirmed by both
16 **meed** reward
17 **question's title** right of the dispute, i.e.
   winner
18 **wink** close my eyes

20 **extinct** See note on 5.1.70.
21 **envy** malice
23 **dam** mother
26 **That** so that
27 **name** reputation
28 **Set off** compensate for
   whereto of which
32 **give . . . pay** reward the service (to you
   of the winning knight)

The title of a kingdom may be tried
Out of itself.
THESEUS   Well, well, then—at your pleasure.
Those that remain with you could wish their office
To any of their enemies.
HIPPOLYTA   Farewell, sister.
I am like to know your husband fore yourself
By some small start of time. He whom the gods
Do of the two know best, I pray them he
Be made your lot.   *Exeunt all but Emilia*   40
⌜*Emilia takes out two pictures, which she holds,
one in each hand*⌝

EMILIA
Arcite is gently visaged, yet his eye
Is like an engine bent, or a sharp weapon
In a soft sheath; mercy and manly courage
Are bedfellows in his visage. Palamon
Has a most menacing aspect; his brow
Is graved, and seems to bury what it frowns on;
Yet sometime 'tis not so, but alters to
The quality of his thoughts. Long time his eye
Will dwell upon his object. Melancholy
Becomes him nobly; so does Arcite's mirth;   50
But Palamon's sadness is a kind of mirth,
So mingled, as if mirth did make him sad,
And sadness merry. Those darker humours that
Stick misbecomingly on others, on him

40 *all but Emilia*] OXFORD; *Theseus, Hipolita, Perithous, &c.* Q   40.1 *Emilia . . . pictures*] OXFORD;
not in Q   40.1–2 *which . . . hand*] This edition; *not in* Q   54 him] SEWARD; them Q

34 **Out of itself** outside its boundaries
39 **know** know to be
40.1–2 **Emilia . . . hand** It seems very likely,
as the Oxford editor suggests, that Emilia
holds pictures of Palamon and Arcite in
this scene as in 4.2. She refers (ll. 73–4)
to wearing them, one on her right side,
one on her left.
42 **engine** weapon such as a bow
45 **aspect** (accented here on the second
syllable) look
46 **graved** engraved, deeply lined (with a
pun on 'grave')
47 **to** in accordance with
48 **quality** nature
49 **his** its
49–53 **Melancholy . . . merry** Compare
Cleopatra on Antony: 'He was not
sad, . . . he was not merry, . . . but
between both. | O heavenly mingle! Be'st
thou sad or merry, | The violence of
either thee becomes' (*Antony* 1.5.54–9).
50 **Becomes** suits
53 **humours** moods
54 **Stick . . . on** seem out of place in (as if
just stuck on)
54–5 **on him . . . dwelling** are becoming to
him

Live in fair dwelling.
    Cornetts. Trumpets sound as to a charge
Hark how yon spurs to spirit do incite
The princes to their proof! Arcite may win me,
And yet may Palamon wound Arcite to
The spoiling of his figure. O, what pity
Enough for such a chance? If I were by,   60
I might do hurt, for they would glance their eyes
Toward my seat, and in that motion might
Omit a ward or forfeit an offence
Which craved that very time. It is much better
I am not there—O, better never born
Than minister to such harm!
    Cornetts. A great cry and noise within,
    crying 'A Palamon!'
    Enter Servant
                What is the chance?

SERVANT
The cry's 'A Palamon!'

EMILIA
Then he has won. 'Twas ever likely;
He looked all grace and success, and he is
Doubtless the prim'st of men. I prithee run   70
And tell me how it goes.
    Shout and cornetts, crying 'A Palamon!'

SERVANT   Still 'Palamon'.

EMILIA
Run and enquire.   *Exit Servant*
 ⌈*To the picture in her right hand*⌉
              Poor servant, thou hast lost.

---

66 *Cornetts . . . Palamon!*⌉ *placed as in* WEBER; *after l. 64 in* Q   *Enter Servant*] *placed as in*
KITTREDGE; *after l. 66 in* Q   72 *Exit Servant*] DYCE (subs.); *not in* Q

56 **spirit** courage
57 **proof** trial by combat
58–9 **to . . . figure** in such a way as to cripple
    his body
60 **Enough** would be enough
    chance misfortune
63 **ward** defensive action
    offence opportunity for offensive action
64 **craved . . . time** needed to be taken at
    that very moment

66 *A Palamon* A warcry shouted by fol-
    lowers of the combatant to whose name
    '*A*' is prefixed.
    What . . . chance whom is fortune
    favouring
70 **prim'st** best
72 **servant** i.e. Arcite. In the love-relation-
    ship the knight was the 'servant', his
    lady the 'mistress'.

Upon my right side still I wore thy picture,
Palamon's on the left—why so I know not;
I had no end in't else; chance would have it so.
On the sinister side the heart lies; Palamon
Had the best-boding chance.
      Another cry and shout within and cornetts
                        This burst of clamour
Is sure th'end o'th' combat.
      Enter Servant

SERVANT
They said that Palamon had Arcite's body
Within an inch o'th' pyramid, that the cry   80
Was general 'A Palamon!' But anon
Th'assistants made a brave redemption, and
The two bold titlers at this instant are
Hand to hand at it.
EMILIA   Were they metamorphosed
Both into one!—O why? There were no woman
Worth so composed a man; their single share,
Their nobleness peculiar to them, gives
The prejudice of disparity, value's shortness
To any lady breathing.
      Cornetts. Cry within, 'Arcite, Arcite!'
                   More exulting?
'Palamon' still?
SERVANT   Nay, now the sound is 'Arcite'.   90
EMILIA
I prithee lay attention to the cry;
Set both thine ears to th' business.
      Cornetts. A great shout and cry, 'Arcite,
      victory!'

---

75 in't‸ else;] WEBER (*conj.* Mason); in't; else‸ Q   77 *Another . . . cornetts*] *placed as in*
WEBER; *after l. 75 in* Q   89 *Cornetts . . . Arcite!*] *placed as in* DYCE; *after l. 88 in* Q   92
Cornetts . . . victory!] *placed as in* WEBER; *after l. 91 in* Q

73 **still** always
75 **end** purpose
76 **sinister** left
77 **best-boding** most auspicious
82 **assistants** i.e. Arcite's knights
    redemption rescue
84 **Were they** if only they were
85-6 **O . . . man** Having wished that the
    two knights, instead of fighting, could be

merged into one, Emilia checks herself
with the thought that no woman would
be worthy of a man so made.
86 **their single share** the virtue of each one
    singly
87 **peculiar to them** distinctively theirs
87-9 **gives . . . breathing** makes any living
    woman seem, in comparison, unequal in
    worth

SERVANT   The cry is
'Arcite' and 'Victory!' Hark, 'Arcite, victory!'
The combat's consummation is proclaimed
By the wind instruments.
EMILIA   Half-sights saw
That Arcite was no babe. God's lid, his richness
And costliness of spirit looked through him; it could
No more be hid in him than fire in flax—
Than humble banks can go to law with waters
That drift winds force to raging. I did think   100
Good Palamon would miscarry, yet I knew not
Why I did think so. Our reasons are not prophets
When oft our fancies are. They are coming off.
Alas, poor Palamon!
    Cornetts. Enter Theseus, Hippolyta, Pirithous,
    Arcite as victor, and attendants
THESEUS
Lo, where our sister is in expectation,
Yet quaking and unsettled! Fairest Emily,
The gods by their divine arbitrament
Have given you this knight; he is a good one
As ever struck at head. (*To Emilia and Arcite*) Give me
    your hands.
(*To Arcite*) Receive you her, (*to Emilia*) you him; be
    plighted with   110
A love that grows as you decay.
ARCITE   Emily,
To buy you I have lost what's dearest to me
Save what is bought, and yet I purchase cheaply,
As I do rate your value.
THESEUS   O lovèd sister,
He speaks now of as brave a knight as e'er

104.2 *attendants*ₐ] OXFORD; *attendants, &c.* Q

94 **consummation** end
95 **Half-sights saw** half a look showed
96 **God's lid** by God's eyelid (a common
    oath)
97 **looked through him** was transparent
98 **fire in flax** That 'Fire cannot be hidden
    in flax (straw)' was proverbial (Dent
    F255).

99 **humble** low
100 **drift** driving
103 **coming off** leaving the arena
104.2 **attendants** Q adds '&c.' to the direc-
    tion (see collations), which usually refers
    to others in a procession or train, but
    here 'attendants' already covers such
    supernumeraries.

Did spur a noble steed. Surely the gods
Would have him die a bachelor, lest his race
Should show i'th' world too godlike. His behaviour
So charmed me that methought Alcides was
To him a sow of lead. If I could praise   120
Each part of him to th'all I have spoke, your Arcite
Did not lose by't; for he that was thus good
Encountered yet his better. I have heard
Two emulous Philomels beat the ear o'th' night
With their contentious throats, now one the higher,
Anon the other, then again the first,
And by and by out-breasted, that the sense
Could not be judge between 'em. So it fared
Good space between these kinsmen, till heavens did
Make hardly one the winner. (*To Arcite*) Wear
    the garland   130
With joy that you have won.—For the subdued,
Give them our present justice, since I know
Their lives but pinch 'em. Let it here be done.
The scene's not for our seeing; go we hence
Right joyful, with some sorrow. (*To Arcite*) Arm
    your prize;
I know you will not lose her.
        ⌈*Arcite takes Emilia's arm in his. Flourish*⌉
                            Hippolyta,
I see one eye of yours conceives a tear,
The which it will deliver.

---

121 all͜] F; ~; Q   136 lose] Q (loose)   136 *Arcite . . . his*] BAWCUTT; *not in* Q   *Flourish*]
placed as in PROUDFOOT; *after* deliver (*l. 138*) *in* Q; *after l. 146 in* DYCE 1866

119 **Alcides** Hercules
120 **sow** mass of solidified metal taken from
    a furnace
121 **to . . . spoke** as much as I have praised
    him in general
122 **Did** would
124 **emulous Philomels** rival nightingales
127 **out-breasted** outsung (*OED*'s only re-
    corded occurrence of the word)
    sense (of hearing)
129 **Good space** for a considerable time
130 **hardly** with difficulty, or by a narrow
    margin
132 **present** immediate

133 **pinch** pain, embarrass
135 **Arm** give your arm to
136 **lose** The common Elizabethan spelling,
    'loose' (see collations), allows for a double
    meaning here: both 'be deprived of' and
    'release'
136 *Arcite . . . his* Bawcutt's stage direction
    seems to be needed here, and the flourish
    which Q calls for after Theseus' words to
    Hippolyta (see collations) would more
    properly accompany Arcite's gesture. It
    is possible, however, that it should come,
    as Dyce thought, at the end of the scene.

EMILIA   .   Is this winning?
O all you heavenly powers, where is your mercy?
But that your wills have said it must be so,   140
And charge me live to comfort this unfriended,
This miserable prince, that cuts away
A life more worthy from him than all women,
I should and would die too.
HIPPOLYTA   Infinite pity
That four such eyes should be so fixed on one
That two must needs be blind for't.
THESEUS   So it is.   *Exeunt*

5.4   *Enter, guarded, Palamon and his knights
           pinioned; Jailer and Executioner*

PALAMON
There's many a man alive that hath outlived
The love o'th' people; yea, i'th' selfsame state
Stands many a father with his child; some comfort
We have by so considering. We expire,
And not without men's pity; to live still,
Have their good wishes; we prevent
The loathsome misery of age, beguile
The gout and rheum that in lag hours attend
For grey approachers; we come towards the gods
Young and unwappered, not halting under crimes   10
Many and stale—that sure shall please the gods
Sooner than such, to give us nectar with 'em,
For we are more clear spirits. My dear kinsmen,

139 your] F; you Q
  5.4] Q (Scaena 4.)   0.1 *guarded*] OXFORD; *not in* Q   0.2 *and*] *not in* Q   *Executioner*ᴧ] This
edition; *Executioner &c. Gard.* Q   1 PALAMON] *not in* Q   10 unwappered, not,] TONSON;
unwapper'dᴧ not, Q

141 **unfriended** deprived of his (best) friend   8 **rheum** catarrh
5.4 The location is unchanged, but a scaffold   **lag** last
  has been set up for the execution of   9 **grey approachers** old men who approach
  Palamon and his knights.   them (and death)
0.2 *Executioner* Here, as at 5.3.104.2, Q's   10 **unwappered** unfatigued, fresh (*OED*'s
  added '*&c.*' (see collations) seems super-   earliest recorded occurrence of the word;
  fluous.   see *OED*, wappered)
5–6 **to . . . wishes** people want us to go on   **halting under** limping, burdened by
  living   11 **stale** i.e. committed long ago
6 **prevent** forestall   12 **such** i.e. the old and wicked
7 **beguile** cheat   13 **clear** unstained, innocent

Whose lives for this poor comfort are laid down,
You have sold 'em too too cheap.

FIRST KNIGHT   What ending could be
Of more content? O'er us the victors have
Fortune, whose title is as momentary
As to us death is certain; a grain of honour
They not o'erweigh us.

SECOND KNIGHT   Let us bid farewell,
And with our patience anger tott'ring fortune,   20
Who at her certain'st reels.

THIRD KNIGHT   Come, who begins?

PALAMON
Ev'n he that led you to this banquet shall
Taste to you all. (*To the Jailer*) Aha, my friend,
      my friend,
Your gentle daughter gave me freedom once;
You'll see't done now for ever. Pray, how does she?
I heard she was not well; her kind of ill
Gave me some sorrow.

JAILER   Sir, she's well restored,
And to be married shortly.

PALAMON   By my short life,
I am most glad on't; 'tis the latest thing
I shall be glad of—prithee tell her so.   30
Commend me to her, and to piece her portion
Tender her this.

      He gives the Jailer his purse

FIRST KNIGHT   Nay, let's be offerers all.

SECOND KNIGHT
Is it a maid?

PALAMON   Verily, I think so—
A right good creature, more to me deserving
Than I can quit or speak of.

32 *He . . . purse*] *not in* Q

17 **title** i.e. favour
18–19 **a grain . . . us** they do not in the
    slightest degree exceed us in honour
20–1 **tott'ring . . . reels** The instability of
    Fortune is a commonplace; compare
    1.2.67.
23 **Taste . . . you** you taste the food for you (like
    the taster at a state banquet, who tasted

the food to prove that it was not poisoned)
25 **see't done** see freedom given to me
26 **ill** sickness
29 **latest** last
31 **piece her portion** add to her dowry. See
    note on 4.1.23.
33 **maid** virgin
35 **quit** requite

ALL THE KNIGHTS   Commend us to her.
    They give their purses
JAILER
The gods requite you all, and make her thankful.
PALAMON
Adieu, and let my life be now as short
As my leave-taking.
    He mounts the scaffold and puts his head on
    the block
FIRST KNIGHT   Lead, courageous cousin.
SECOND *and* THIRD KNIGHTS
We'll follow cheerfully.
    A great noise within, crying 'Run! Save! Hold!'
    Enter in haste a Messenger
MESSENGER
Hold, hold! O hold, hold, hold!   40
    Enter Pirithous in haste
PIRITHOUS
Hold, ho! It is a cursèd haste you made
If you have done so quickly. Noble Palamon,
The gods will show their glory in a life
That thou art yet to lead.
PALAMON   Can that be,
When Venus, I have said, is false? How do things fare?
PIRITHOUS
Arise, great sir, and give the tidings ear
That are most dearly sweet and bitter.
PALAMON ⌈*rising and descending from the scaffold*⌉ What
Hath waked us from our dream?
PIRITHOUS   List then. Your cousin,
Mounted upon a steed that Emily
Did first bestow on him, a black one, owing   50

---

35 ALL THE KNIGHTS] Q (*All K.*)   38 *He . . . block*] This edition; *Lies on the Blocke.* Q   39
SECOND . . . KNIGHTS] LITTLEDALE (*subs.*); 1.2.K. Q   47 dearly] SEWARD; early Q; rarely
SYMPSON (*conj.*)   *rising . . . scaffold*] This edition; *not in* Q

42 **done** finished (executing Palamon)
47 **dearly** intensely. Seward justifies his
emendation (see collations) by pointing
to 'dearly sorry' (l. 129) in Theseus' last
speech.
    rising . . . scaffold The directions in Q
give very little idea of how this scene is

to be staged. It seems likely that Palamon
not only rises from the block here but
also descends from the scaffold, where he
stands with his knights until the entrance
of Arcite at l. 85.1.
50 **owing** owning

Not a hair-worth of white—which some will say
Weakens his price, and many will not buy
His goodness with this note; which superstition
Here finds allowance—on this horse is Arcite
Trotting the stones of Athens, which the calkins
Did rather tell than trample, for the horse
Would make his length a mile, if't pleased his rider
To put pride in him. As he thus went counting
The flinty pavement, dancing, as 'twere, to th' music
His own hooves made—for, as they say, from iron   60
Came music's origin—what envious flint,
Cold as old Saturn, and like him possessed
With fire malevolent, darted a spark,
Or what fierce sulphur else, to this end made,
I comment not—the hot horse, hot as fire,
Took toy at this, and fell to what disorder
His power could give his will—bounds, comes on end,
Forgets school-doing, being therein trained
And of kind manège; pig-like he whines
At the sharp rowel, which he frets at rather   70
Than any jot obeys; seeks all foul means
Of boist'rous and rough jadery to disseat
His lord, that kept it bravely. When naught served,

69 manège] Q (mannadge)

52 **Weakens his price** (since uniformly dark horses were popularly thought to be vicious)
53 **note** distinctive feature
54 **allowance** confirmation
55 **calkins** turned-down edges under a horseshoe
56 **tell** count; i.e. seemed to do so since they touched them so lightly
57 **make . . . mile** 'take mile-long paces' (Leech)
60–1 **from . . . origin** William Chappell records the popular story 'that Pythagoras discovered the law of musical consonances through passing a blacksmith's shop, and weighing the hammers that were striking fourths, fifths, and octaves upon an anvil' (*The History of Music* (London, 1874), p. 7); biblical commentators told similar stories about Tubalcain, the first metalworker (Genesis 4:

21–2).
62 **Saturn** In *The Knight's Tale* Saturn, who has promised Venus that Palamon will have Emelye, sends a fury to start up out of the ground and frighten Arcite's horse (ll. A 2684–5).
64 **sulphur** 'In popular belief . . . associated with the fires of hell, with devils' (*OED*).
to this end for this purpose
65 **comment not** will not speculate on
66 **toy at** a capricious aversion to
fell to began to indulge in
68 **school-doing** what he learned in riding-school
69 **of kind manège** having been taught the movements of a trained horse (here pronounced like *manage*)
72 **jadery** behaviour of a 'jade' (an inferior horse)
73 **it** his seat
bravely splendidly, excellently

When neither curb would crack, girth break,
   nor diff'ring plunges
Disroot his rider whence he grew, but that
He kept him 'tween his legs, on his hind hooves
On end he stands,
That Arcite's legs, being higher than his head,
Seemed with strange art to hang. His victor's wreath
Even then fell off his head; and presently   80
Backward the jade comes o'er, and his full poise
Becomes the rider's load. Yet is he living,
But such a vessel 'tis that floats but for
The surge that next approaches. He much desires
To have some speech with you. Lo, he appears.
> *Enter Theseus, Hippolyta, Emilia, followed by*
> *Arcite in a chair borne by attendants.* ⌈*Palamon*
> *moves to Arcite's side while his knights remain*
> *close to the scaffold*⌉

PALAMON
O miserable end of our alliance!
The gods are mighty, Arcite. If thy heart,
Thy worthy, manly heart, be yet unbroken,
Give me thy last words. I am Palamon,
One that yet loves thee dying.

ARCITE   Take Emilia,   90
And with her all the world's joy. Reach thy hand—
Farewell; I have told my last hour. I was false,
Yet never treacherous; forgive me, cousin.

---

79 victor's] Q (*corr.*: victors); victoros Q (*uncorr.*)   85.2 *borne by attendants*] *not in* Q   85.2–
4 *Palamon . . . scaffold*] This edition; *not in* Q   87 mighty, Arcite. If] BROOKE (*subs.*); mightie∧
Arcite, if Q; mighty! — Arcite, if DYCE

74 **diff'ring** various sorts of
75 **Disroot** (OED's first recorded occurrence of the word)
77 **On . . . stands** In Q these words appear half-way across the line and without an initial capital. Possibly the words were inserted between the lines of the manuscript, as F. O. Waller suggests, to replace 'on his hind hooves' in the line above ('Printer's Copy for *The Two Noble Kinsmen*', *Studies in Bibliography*, 11 (1958), 69).
81 **poise** weight
83–4 **but . . . approaches** only until the next wave comes

85.3–4 **moves . . . scaffold** Since Theseus tells Palamon to call his knights 'from the stage of death' at l. 123, he must by that time have moved away from them. It would be natural for him to do this at the moment that Arcite is carried in.
91 **Reach** give me
92 **told** counted out
92–3 **false . . . treacherous** While conceding Palamon's prior claim to Emilia, as Theseus notes (l. 116), Arcite denies that he has ever used dishonourable means in the contest with his friend and kinsman.

One kiss from fair Emilia— (*they kiss*) 'tis done;
Take her; I die.   *He dies*
PALAMON   Thy brave soul seek Elysium!
EMILIA
I'll close thine eyes, prince. Blessèd souls be with thee!
Thou art a right good man, and while I live,
This day I give to tears.
PALAMON   And I to honour.
THESEUS (*to Palamon*)
In this place first you fought—ev'n very here
I sundered you. Acknowledge to the gods   100
Our thanks that you are living.
His part is played, and though it were too short,
He did it well. Your day is lengthened, and
The blissful dew of heaven does arrouse you.
The powerful Venus well hath graced her altar,
And given you your love. Our master, Mars,
Hath vouched his oracle, and to Arcite gave
The grace of the contention. So the deities
Have showed due justice. (*To the attendants*) Bear
       this hence.   ⌈*Exeunt attendants with Arcite's body*⌉
PALAMON   O cousin,
That we should things desire which do cost us   110
The loss of our desire! That naught could buy
Dear love but loss of dear love!
THESEUS   Never Fortune
Did play a subtler game: the conquered triumphs,
The victor has the loss. Yet in the passage
The gods have been most equal. Palamon,
Your kinsman hath confessed the right o'th' lady
Did lie in you, for you first saw her and
Even then proclaimed your fancy. He restored her
As your stol'n jewel, and desired your spirit
To send him hence forgiven. The gods my justice   120
Take from my hand, and they themselves become

---

94 *they kiss*] *not in* Q   95 *He dies*] *not in* Q   101 Our] Q; Your DYCE   107 Hath] DYCE
1866; Hast Q; Has TONSON   109 *Exeunt . . . body*] OXFORD; *not in* Q

---

104 **arrouse** sprinkle (compare the French   108 **grace of** favour of victory in
   arroser)   114 **passage** (of arms), combat
107 **vouched** made good   115 **equal** impartial

The executioners. Lead your lady off,
And call your lovers from the stage of death,
Whom I adopt my friends.
⌈*The knights join Theseus and the others*⌉
                                    A day or two
Let us look sadly, and give grace unto
The funeral of Arcite, in whose end
The visages of bridegrooms we'll put on
And smile with Palamon, for whom an hour,
But one hour since, I was as dearly sorry
As glad of Arcite, and am now as glad   130
As for him sorry. O you heavenly charmers,
What things you make of us! For what we lack
We laugh, for what we have are sorry; still
Are children in some kind. Let us be thankful
For that which is, and with you leave dispute
That are above our question. Let's go off,
And bear us like the time.   *Flourish. Exeunt*

Epilogue   *Enter Epilogue*
EPILOGUE
I would now ask ye how ye like the play,
But, as it is with schoolboys, cannot say;
I am cruel fearful. Pray yet stay a while,
And let me look upon ye. No man smile?
Then it goes hard, I see. He that has
Loved a young handsome wench, then, show his face—
'Tis strange if none be here—and if he will,
Against his conscience, let him hiss, and kill

124 *The knights . . . others*] This edition; *not in* Q   133 sorry; still‸] WEBER (*conj.* Mason);
sorry‸ still, Q
    Epilogue 0.1 *Enter Epilogue*] *not in* Q   1 EPILOGUE] *not in* Q

123 **lovers** supporters
    stage of death i.e. the scaffold
126 **in whose end** at the end of which
131 **charmers** i.e. the gods (who charm, or
    enchant, us)
135 **with . . . dispute** cease to dispute with
    you
136 **That** i.e. you that
    above our question beyond our capacity
    to question
137 **bear . . . time** behave in a manner
    appropriate to both the sorrow and joy

of the occasion
Epilogue Probably written, like the Prologue,
    by Fletcher (see note on Prologue, ll. 7–
    8).
2 **schoolboys** The actor who spoke the
    epilogue was a boy—probably the in-
    terpreter of Emilia or of the Jailer's
    Daughter.
    say speak
3 **cruel fearful** terribly worried
8–9 **kill | Our market** ruin our chances of
    success

213

Our market. 'Tis in vain, I see, to stay ye.
Have at the worst can come, then! Now, what say ye?   10
And yet mistake me not—I am not bold—
We have no such cause. If the tale we have told—
For 'tis no other—any way content ye
(For to that honest purpose it was meant ye)
We have our end; and ye shall have ere long,
I dare say, many a better to prolong
Your old loves to us. We and all our might
Rest at your service. Gentlemen, good night.

                                   Flourish. Exit
                    FINIS

    18.1 *Exit*] *not in* Q

  9 **stay** restrain   **tale** (alluding to *The Knight's Tale*)
 10 **Have . . . come** we'll face the worst you   14 **meant ye** intended for you
    can do   15 **end** aim
 12 **cause** purpose (as to be contentious)

THE MORRIS DANCE IN 3.5

THE morris dance seems originally to have been a combination of an ancient native dance with the Spanish *morisco*, or 'Moor's dance', from which it got its name. It came to be closely associated with various festivities, and especially with the May games. Hence, Robin Hood, Maid Marian, and Friar Tuck, or the Lord and Lady of May were often among the dancers. A fool was usually included, and, in earlier times, a hobby-horse. Typical morris dancers wear bells attached to their arms or legs, and have streamers fastened to their sleeves, or handkerchiefs in their hands. The jingling of the bells is a characteristic feature of the dance (see Palamon's words to the Jailer at 2.2.274–5).

The dance performed in this play is borrowed from the second

6. A Fool with tabor and pipe (from Francis Douce, *Illustrations of Shakespeare, and of Ancient Manners*, new edn. (1839), p. 518).

7. The Betley window. This window depicting morris dancers, now in
the Victoria and Albert Museum, was originally in Betley Old Hall, an
early Tudor house in Staffordshire. The coloured glass cannot be dated
exactly, but is probably of the early sixteenth century, and may have
been painted by a Flemish artist working in England. It is thought to be
the earliest representation of English morris dancers. Godfrey Brown
identifies the panels (from the top left corner) as: the Fool; the Imper-
sonation of a Nobleman; a Fleming or Spaniard; a Gentleman of Fortune;
the Maypole; Tom the Piper; a Clown, Peasant, or Yeoman; the King
of the May on a Hobby Horse; Parish Clerk or Marian's Gentleman-
Usher; the Tumbler; Maid Marian or Queen of the May; the Friar.

antimasque of Beaumont's *The Masque of the Inner Temple and Gray's Inn*, where the dancers are listed as 'May Lord, May Lady. Servingman, Chambermaid. A Country Clown, or Shepherd, Country Wench. An Host, Hostess. A He Baboon, She Baboon. A He Fool, She Fool.' (Bowers, i. 133). The Schoolmaster, who replaces the 'Pedant' of Beaumont's masque, names nine of these characters, omitting only the Country Wench, She Baboon (or 'Babion'), and the She Fool, who presumably constitute the 'many others' to whom he refers (l. 131). The nine named characters are presumably to be danced by the six countrymen and three of the Wenches. It is clear that the Jailer's Daughter is pressed into service as the She Fool, and the Second Countryman, who dances with her, must be the He Fool. Two wenches remain to impersonate the Country Wench and the She Babion. Since the dancers in the masque are said to be 'apparelled to the life', we may assume that their opposite numbers in the play are similarly costumed. Most of them probably wear bells, and we know the Wenches have ribbons (l. 25). The Lord and Lady of May do not necessarily wear bells; the Lady of May has none in the fifteenth-century engraving reproduced by Douce (opposite p. 577), and in the stained-glass window at Betley, Staffordshire, the oldest known depiction of English morris dancers, neither the lady (in this case Maid Marian) nor the piper-taborer wears bells (see Fig. 7).

Of the dance as performed in the masque we are told: '. . . the music was extremely well fitted, having such a spirit of country jollity as can hardly be imagined, but the perpetual laughter and applause was above the music. The dance likewise was of the same strain, and the dancers, or rather actors, expressed every one their part so naturally and aptly, as when a man's eye was caught with the one, and then passed on to the other, he could not satisfy himself which did best. It pleased his Majesty to call for it again at the end . . .' (Bowers, i. 134). It is important to recall that antimasques on these occasions were normally performed by professional actors, and hence that the actors of the King's Men were presumably the successful performers of the morris dance.

ALTERATIONS TO LINEATION

As explained in the Editorial Procedures, all changes in lineation are recorded here and here only. The presentation differs from that in the textual collations in the following ways: both within the lemma and in the quotation of a rejected line-arrangement, punctuation at the end of the line is ignored, and spelling modernized; attribution of an emendation or variant reading indicates only that the text or editor cited *arranges* the lines in a certain way.

The lineation of certain scenes constitutes one of the few difficult problems with the Q text of *The Two Noble Kinsmen*. There has been a general consensus among editors since the time of Weber that two entire scenes (2.1 and 4.3), the first printed entirely as verse in Q, and the second mostly as verse, are, in fact, prose. Why so much prose was printed as verse is difficult to explain, even when it is recalled that in dramatic manuscripts the first word of a line of verse was not necessarily capitalized. The printer might be uncertain for a line or two whether his text was verse or prose, but could hardly mistake an entire scene of prose for verse. Since both compositors worked on one of these scenes, Werstine suggests that the mistake may have been made by the scribe who prepared the manuscript (see Introduction, p. 25).

Paul Bertram argues persuasively (pp. 22–30) that some lines printed as verse in several other scenes are also prose, but on this matter there is no general agreement. Both Shakespeare and Fletcher (but especially Fletcher) sometimes wrote irregular blank verse almost indistinguishable from conversational prose, and in some scenes of their plays verse and prose are mixed (as, for example, in plays written shortly before this one, in *The Winter's Tale*, 4.4, or *The Coxcomb*, 1.2). There is therefore no reason to be surprised if such mixtures occur in *The Two Noble Kinsmen*. Recent editors, however, have been reluctant to admit prose into any scenes other than 2.1 and 4.3. In distinguishing prose from verse I have been guided mainly by the extent of departure from the rhythmical norms of blank verse, and assisted by the useful criterion described by Fredson Bowers in 'Establishing Shakespeare's Text: Notes on Short Lines and the Problem of Verse Division' (*Studies in Bibliography*, 33 (1980), 74–130). It often happens, as Bowers shows, that a verse speech ends with a short line that is not completed by another short line beginning the next speech (as at 1.1.28–9), but 'unlinked short lines beginning a pentameter speech are much rarer' (p. 78). The short beginning line usually completes a preceding short line. Bowers's observation helps not only to divide lines of verse properly but also to distinguish verse from prose, since a short line beginning a speech strongly suggests that the author wrote it so with a metrical pattern in mind. In 2.1 and 4.3 as set in Q, for example, no speech begins with a short line. Although in scenes such as 2.3 it is hard to tell exactly where verse changes to prose and prose to verse, I think it is important to recognize that both are present.

Here and there in passages of verse the lines are wrongly divided in Q for reasons that are easy to understand. In the manuscript it was possible to get more words on a line than on the printed page, and authors sometimes ran together a half-line of verse with the full line preceding it. The printer might then divide this overlong line incorrectly, or, if he had room, print it as a single line. Most errors of this sort have been corrected by earlier editors.

1.1.95–6   As . . . knee] SEWARD; *as one line* Q
1.3.96–7   The . . . mine] SEWARD; Q divides after 'heart', 'faith', *and* 'mine'.
2.1]   *as prose* WEBER; *as verse* Q, *dividing after* 'I', 'I', 'seldom', 'number', 'lined', 'true', 'am', 'what', 'at', 'death', 'offer', 'I', 'promised', 'solemnity', 'her', 'consent', 'comes', 'name', 'that', 'will', 'tenderly', 'princes', 'they', 'I', 'adversity', 'and', 'chamber', 'men', 'they', 'report', 'doers', 'I', 'been', 'enforce', 'their', 'at', 'so', 'their', 'eat', 'things', 'disasters', ''twere', 'them', 'rebuke', 'chid', 'comforted', ''em', 'night', 'I', 'that's', 'out', 'the', 'part', 'him', 'not', 'sight', 'the', *and* 'men'.

2.3]   In this scene I follow Q's distinctions between prose and verse except at ll. 24–44 and 60–3, which I believe to be prose though set as verse. Whether Q's capitalization of 'Boys' in 'Away | Boys' ('Away, boys', This edition, l. 65) indicates verse is unclear, since the word is also capitalized earlier in the middle of a line. Even though there are two speeches beginning with short lines ('I am sure', l. 30, 'And Sennois', l. 40), no arrangement of the entire scene as verse results in regular pentameter lines, and the fact that the compositor twice switched to prose indicates clearly his belief that there was some mixture. Since only Arcite's opening soliloquy and the end of the scene after he has entered into conversation with the Countrymen are clearly blank verse, it seems logical to set the entire middle section as prose.

24–44   My . . . know] *as prose* This edition; *as verse* Q, *dividing after* 'certain', 'there', 'I', 'chiding', 'out', 'tomorrow', 'sure', 'turkey', 'mumble', 'her', 'again', 'her', 'wench', 'Maying', 'us', 'there', 'Sennois', 'tree', 'ha', 'touch', *and* 'know'.

60–3   We'll . . . on't] *as prose* This edition; *as verse* Q, *dividing after* 'and', 'before', 'what', *and* 'on't'.

3.1.121–2   That . . . till] COLMAN; Q *divides after* 'there' *and* 'till'.
3.3.16–53   We . . . for't] Although the lineation is problematic, I agree with previous editors that these lines are verse rather than prose, as Bertram believes (p. 30). It is verse so imitative of familiar conversation,

however, that it borders on prose, and the compositor, possibly following the lineation of the manuscript, has printed several very long lines. Most editors have rearranged the lines more drastically than I have, thereby concealing what seem to me some characteristically Fletcherian line-endings, such as 'two more' (l. 19), 'Eat now' (l. 20), and 'meat to't' (l. 22).

25–6   How . . . see] COLMAN; *as one line* Q

27–8   But . . . this] SEWARD; *as one line* Q

36–7   Made . . . ten] SEWARD; *as one line* Q

43   For . . . Fool] Many editors begin this line with 'Heigh-ho' from the preceding six-foot line, making 'Fool' an eleventh syllable. Retaining the lineation of Q has the advantage of putting more stress on 'Fool', following a brief pause, which takes the place of a missing light syllable. The stress is expressive of Palamon's renewed anger, aroused by Arcite's sign ('heigh-ho').

46–8   You . . . now] SEWARD; Q *divides after* 'wide', 'honest', *and* 'now'.

3.4.25–6   O . . . else] SEWARD; Q *divides after* 'breast' *and* 'else'.

3.5]   The printing of this scene in Q presents many problems. The first speech and one other (ll. 69–72) are printed as prose, and most of the rest as verse, though it is impossible to tell whether short lines such as ll. 73–4 are intended as prose or verse. Some of the verse is, in any case, so irregular that it is more like prose. Editors since Seward have attempted to make it all into verse; here it is presented as a mixture of prose and verse, largely, but not entirely, as in Q.

36   We have] These words are printed in Q as a short line beginning a speech, as if, metrically, they completed the previous line, although that line already has five feet. I follow Q rather than those editors who attach the words to the next line, thereby making it, rather than l. 36, a six-foot line.

56–7   The . . . Barbary-a] SEWARD; Q *divides after* 'south, from' *and* 'Barbary-a'.

62–3   O . . . sound-a] COLMAN; *as one line* Q

67–8   The . . . away] SEWARD; *as one line* Q

74–80]   The short lines beginning the Jailer's Daughter's speeches in ll. 74 and 75 suggest that this passage, following the prose of the Third Countryman, is again in verse. Q's lineation is accordingly accepted.

81–93   Dii . . . me] *as prose* This edition; *as verse* Q, *dividing after* 'damsel'. 'play', 'bones', 'peace', '*ignis*', 'in', 'it', 'lead', 'do', 'boys', 'some', 'cue', *and* 'me'. Neither the Schoolmaster's speeches, with their Latin quotations, nor the other speeches in this passage fit well into the pattern of blank verse.

146–7   Never . . . better] SEWARD; Q *divides after* 'sir', 'preface', *and* 'better'.

154–6   And . . . wenches] DYCE; Q *divides after* 'made' *and* 'wenches'.

3.6.201–2 Nay . . . dangers] SEWARD; *as one line* Q

255–6   Wherever . . . another] SEWARD; *as one line* Q

4.1.19   how] COLMAN; Q *places at beginning of l. 20.*

34–5   Was she well . . . sleep] COLMAN; *as one line* Q

42–3   Nothing . . . me] SEWARD; *as one line* Q

143–54 And . . . about] *as prose* This edition; *as verse* Q, *dividing after* 'Palamon', 'tackling', 'cheerly', 'top the', 'your', 'master', 'in', 'boy', 'pilot', 'Here', 'thou', 'wood', *and* 'about'. Here the dialogue seems to shift from irregular verse to prose, the better, perhaps, to express the mad ramblings of the Jailer's Daughter. The Q compositor continued to set the lines as verse, though they are as irregular as those in 2.1 and 4.3 which editors recognize as prose.

4.2.65 Quickly] COLMAN; Q *places at end of l. 64*

4.3] *as prose* SEWARD; *with the exception of two speeches* (*ll. 37–43, 47–52*), *as verse* Q, *dividing after* 'moon', 'not', 'sleeps', 'drinking', 'what', 'name', 'business', 'where', 'behaviour', 'was "Down"', 'then', 'as', 'legs', 'and', 'Aeneas', 'soul', 'long', 'must', 'tongue', 'where', 'maids', 'with', 'long', 'make', 'then', 'further', 'barley-break', 'i'th'', 'hissing', 'shrewd', 'or', 'bless', 'of', 'of', 'bacon', 'enough', 'coins', 'engrafted', 'melancholy', '*etc.*', 'sir', 'to', 'then', 'ere', 'Palamon', 'her', 'friend', 'great', 'both', 'the', 'terms', 'the', 'to', 'are', 'you', 'light', 'take', 'of', 'to', 'for', 'are', 'pranks', 'green', 'in', 'the', 'of', 'the', 'can', 'desire', 'still', 'acceptance', 'her', 'to', 'with', 'falsehood', 'combatted', 'what's', 'and', 'times', 'have', 'of', 'us', 'not', *and* 'comfort'.

5.2.1–7 Has . . . twice] *as prose* This edition; *as verse* Q, *dividing after* 'her', 'company', 'this', 'I', 'her', *and* 'twice'. These first two speeches, though set as verse, are much more like prose, and can be made into loose verse only by rearranging them, as most editors since Seward have done. The rest of the scene, containing many short lines at the beginnings of speeches, seems clearly to have been written as verse.

27 Go, go] *at the beginning of l. 28 in* Q

28–9 Methinks . . . honesty] DYCE 1866; Q *divides after* 'still' *and* 'honestly'.

68 A . . . her] SEWARD; Q *divides after* mare.

5.4.36 The . . . thankful] DYCE 1866; Q *divides after* all.

INDEX

THIS is a guide to words defined in the Commentary and to a selection of names and topics in the Introduction and Commentary. Proverbial allusions are grouped together. Comments on the text and on stage business are not listed, and references to Shakespeare and Fletcher are limited, with a few exceptions, to mention of specific plays. Plays believed to be collaborations are listed only under their joint authorship. An asterisk indicates that the note supplements information given in *OED*.

Index